THE GUGGENHEIM

THE GUGGENHEIM

FRANK LLOYD WRIGHT AND THE MAKING OF THE MODERN MUSEUM

Guggenheim MUSEUM

Published on the occasion of the 50th Anniversary of the
Solomon R. Guggenheim Museum, New York

**THE FIFTIETH
ANNIVERSARY
OF THE
GUGGENHEIM
MUSEUM**

For more information, please visit
www.guggenheim.org/50.

ISBN: 978–0–89207–385–6 (hardcover)
ISBN: 978–0–89207–381–8 (softcover)

Guggenheim Museum Publications
1071 Fifth Avenue
New York, New York 10128

Available through
D.A.P./Distributed Art Publishers
155 Sixth Avenue, 2nd Floor
New York, New York 10013
Tel.: 212 627 1999; fax: 212 627 9484

Distributed outside the United States and Canada by
Thames & Hudson, Ltd.
181a High Holborn Road
London WC1V 7QX
United Kingdom

Design: Abbott Miller, Susan Brzozowski, Pentagram
Editorial: Domenick Ammirati, Kamilah Foreman
Production: Minjee Cho, Melissa Secondino
Printed in Germany by GZD

Front cover: Frank Lloyd Wright, Solomon R. Guggenheim
Museum, New York, 1943–59

Back cover: Frank Lloyd Wright, Solomon R. Guggenheim
Museum, New York, 1943–59. Interior view, 1959

Endpapers: Archival materials from "Keeping Faith with an
Idea: A Time Line of the Guggenheim Museum, 1943–59,"
pages 143–219. Collage by Pentagram

Title page: Frank Lloyd Wright at the Solomon R.
Guggenheim Museum during construction, ca. 1957

CONTENTS

Ramps and walls of the Solomon R.
Guggenheim Museum's rotunda
under construction, ca. 1958

The Solomon R. Guggenheim Foundation

View of the museum from
Eighty-eighth Street, 1959

PREFACE AND ACKNOWLEDGMENTS

The Inverted Cupcake, the Hot-Cross Bun, and the Washing Machine: by the time
the Solomon R. Guggenheim Museum opened its doors in 1959, after a design and
construction period that spanned sixteen years, New Yorkers had made nicknam-
ing the spiraling building between Eighty-eighth and Eighty-ninth streets on Fifth
Avenue a favorite pastime. Designed by one of the country's most renowned yet
controversial architects, Frank Lloyd Wright, the building had elicited a plethora
both of public criticism and admiration, which must have prompted critic Ada
Louise Huxtable to title her *New York Times* review of the building "That Museum:
Wright or Wrong?" Voicing the city's anxiety, Huxtable wondered if Wright's new
building would ever really become a museum or whether it would remain a mere
monument to—or a mausoleum for—its architect, who had died some six months
before its October 21 opening.

"Was sich liebt das neckt sich" is what the Germans say: "To love is to tease."
Nothing is more true for our most adored and reviled buildings. Their creators
can pride themselves on puzzling both the establishment and the public, just as
Wright and his supporters did in the years leading up to the Guggenheim's opening. And as with much nicknamed architecture—the Flavian Amphitheater in Rome
(a building now known mainly as the Colosseum), Norman Foster's skyscraper in
London (the Gherkin), or the UN Studio–designed Erasmus Bridge in Rotterdam
(the Swan)—the monikers for the museum translated the Guggenheim's new and
unknown idiom into the vernacular tongue of the day. Cupcakes, buns, washing
machines: the everyday points of reference helped make the alien concrete structure more familiar until a suitable language had arisen to describe the building.
In the years to follow, we would come to realize that the unfamiliar shape contained
within it a world of spatial freedom greater than any nickname could possibly
suggest, and greater than anyone could imagine.

Throughout his seventy-year career, Wright sought to create buildings that
would open up richer possibilities for their programs. With the Guggenheim,
Wright designed a testament to his idea that all buildings should liberate the life
of the individual. He firmly believed that the architecture of the future could no longer be a mere shell or shelter, proposing an alternative architecture designed from
within outward, spacious and exuberant. Instead of being contained by the standard
expectations of what a museum should look like, Wright expanded these conceptions, hoping to stimulate the individual freedom of both visitor and staff. With its

View of central skylight during the
museum's expansion and restoration,
ca. 1990

continuous ramp and its impressive rotunda, the Guggenheim's flowing interior space would slowly render unnecessary the pseudonyms that were based solely on its powerful exterior image. What had been nothing more in the eyes of the public than an inverted cupcake would grow into itself as a new space in which to experience art, architecture, and the pleasures of being in a crowd.

Over the years, the building and its curved surfaces have provoked its directors, curators, and designers to rethink the typical ideas of museum practice, in particular the notion of exhibition presentation and interaction with the visitor. Sometimes reflective, sometimes emphatic exhibitions featuring the work of Matthew Barney, Joseph Beuys, Daniel Buren, Alexander Calder, Frank O. Gehry, Jenny Holzer, Claes Oldenberg, and the Russian and Soviet avant-gardes were all, to a certain extent, a direct result of the interaction with Wright's architecture. Wright's building has shown us the potential that good architecture can have not only to reflect its present but to shape that present and its future. After the Peggy Guggenheim Collection in Venice and the palazzo that houses it were bequeathed to the Solomon R. Guggenheim Foundation in 1976, the foundation became an international organization that continued to develop its unique relationship with architects and their ideas. Together the Guggenheim Museum SoHo (1992, designed by Arata Isozaki), the Guggenheim Museum Bilbao (1997, designed by Gehry), the Deutsche Guggenheim, Berlin (1997, with interiors designed by Richard Gluckman), the Guggenheim Hermitage Museum, Las Vegas (2001, designed by OMA/Rem Koolhaas), and the Guggenheim Abu Dhabi Museum (estimated completion date 2013, designed by Gehry) have set new examples for relationships between art, architecture, and the public.

In 2009, under the expert guidance of Deputy Director for External Affairs Eleanor Goldhar, the museum has adopted the theme "See It New" in celebration of the Wright building's golden anniversary. As the building has continuously challenged us to renew our practice and, indeed, our entire field, we now invite the public to reacquaint itself with the treasures the museum houses and the experience that the museum itself presents. In anticipation of the anniversary, the Solomon R. Guggenheim Museum undertook a four-year restoration, the results of which were unveiled in September 2008. At the outset of the process, a team of architects, structural engineers, and conservators undertook a comprehensive assessment and found that, while the building was in good structural condition overall, certain work needed to be executed to ensure its ongoing health, including the removal of ten to twelve coats of paint, the infilling of exterior cracks, the treatment of corroded steel structures, and the repair and reinforcement of the concrete. I would like to thank all of those who made this

complex renovation possible. I am most grateful to my predecessors Thomas Krens, former Director, Solomon R. Guggenheim Foundation, and Lisa Dennison, former Director, Solomon R. Guggenheim Museum, for their profound dedication to this project, and we are all deeply indebted to Peter B. Lewis, former Chairman of the Guggenheim Board of Trustees, who in 2003 pledged a significant gift that initiated and sustained the restoration, as well as to our other generous trustees who kindly followed his gesture. Marc Steglitz, the museum's Chief Operating Officer, expertly managed the restoration project, assembling an excellent team of architects, restorers, and engineers. We are also grateful to the Department of Cultural Affairs of the City of New York for its major funding, and in particular we would like to acknowledge the considerable efforts of Mayor Michael R. Bloomberg, the New York City Council, Manhattan Borough President Scott M. Stringer, and Commissioner of Cultural Affairs Kate D. Levin in support of this project. We are also most grateful to the State of New York and MAPEI Corporation for their generous grants, which helped make this restoration a reality.

As just one of the many elements in the See It New program for 2009 and 2010, this book shines a new light on the original Solomon R. Guggenheim Museum building, which so many have come to love. Our deep appreciation goes to the writers, editors, and curators who have contributed their prodigious talents to this book. Early in the process, Chief Curator Nancy Spector and former Assistant Curator of Architecture and Design Mónica Ramírez-Montagut conceived of the book's overall organization, with three major essays considering Wright's museum in smaller to larger contexts: the Guggenheim's relationship to New York City, its impact on national design, and how Wright's conception of a museum compared to the work of his contemporaries outside the United States. To that end, we are very fortunate to have the insightful work of professors Hilary Ballon of New York University, Joseph M. Siry of Wesleyan University, and Neil Levine of Harvard's Graduate School of Design. They have contributed outstanding essays that add significantly to the literature about Wright and how the reverberations of his Guggenheim have spread from New York to points around the globe. Dr. Ramírez-Montagut also decided that a suite of shorter essays should contemplate formal aspects of the building, and so Gillermo Zuaznabar of the School of Architecture Reus, Rovira i Virgili University, discusses Wright's ideas about color; Pat Kirkham, of the Bard Graduate Center for the Study of the Decorative Arts, Design, and Culture, and Scott W. Perkins, of the Price Tower Arts Center, investigate the use of recurring shapes in the museum; Luis E. Carranza of Roger Williams University's School of Architecture places the shape of the building into the context of Wright's earlier work and skyscraper architecture of the 1920s and '30s; and Bruce Brooks

Pfeiffer, Director of the Frank Lloyd Wright Foundation Archives, tackles the long-standing debate about Wright's intentions for exhibiting fine art in the museum. Their excellent texts contribute enormously to our understanding of the building and the ideas that quite literally shaped it.

The Frank Lloyd Wright Foundation has offered enormous support to the creation of this book by furnishing us with its entire staff's expertise on the architect's oeuvre as well as many beautiful drawings and photographs to illustrate the essays and time line. Particular thanks go to Margo Stipe, Curator and Registrar of Collections, and Oskar Muñoz, Assistant Director, both of the Frank Lloyd Wright Foundation Archives, who pored over hundreds of documents and images pertinent to the story of the Guggenheim building. In addition to writing an essay for this book, Bruce Brooks Pfeiffer proved invaluable to the writing of the time line thanks to his years of scholarship about Wright and the museum.

From the start of this project, Elizabeth Levy, Director of Publications, contributed greatly in formulating the book's organization and design. She and her colleagues Elizabeth Franzen, Associate Director of Publications, Editorial; Stephen Hoban, Managing Editor; Domenick Ammirati, Senior Editor; Kamilah Foreman, Associate Editor; and Kara Mason, Assistant Editor, painstakingly edited texts and layouts with an eye both to accuracy and aesthetics. The tireless efforts of Melissa Secondino, Associate Director of Publications, Production; Minjee Cho, Associate Production Manager; Jonathan Bowen, Associate Production Manager; and Suzana Greene, Production Associate, have assured that the letters, photos, and drawings that appear in the following pages have been reproduced as accurately as possible. Their work was greatly supported by the Photography Department: David Heald, Director of Photographic Services and Chief Photographer; Kristopher McKay, Assistant Photographer and Digital Imaging Specialist; Ryan Peters, former Photography Archive Coordinator; and Carin Johnson, Photography Archive Coordinator. Special thanks go to Sharon Dively, Photo Researcher/Rights and Reproduction Manager, for her exceptional efforts in securing permission to reprint photographs, newspaper articles, letters, and drawings. Many of the documents used to inform and illustrate the book came from the archives of the Solomon R. Guggenheim Museum. Our researchers had wonderful resources at their disposal because of the outstanding dedication of the library and archives staff: Francine Snyder, Manager of Library and Archives; Rachel Chatalbash, Processing Archivist; Rebecca Clark, Art Librarian; and Rachel Cartwright, intern. The story of the construction of the Guggenheim Museum was greatly enhanced by the work of Pentagram's Abbott Miller, partner, and Susan Brzozowski, graphic designer. Karole Vail, Assistant

Curator, and writer Don Quaintance graciously shared their exhaustive research on the Museum of Non-Objective Painting, greatly enriching the book's time line.

Though not directly tied to the exhibition *Frank Lloyd Wright: From Within Outward*, this book would not have been possible without the assistance provided by the exhibition team: Thomas Krens, curator and Senior Advisor for International Affairs at the Solomon R. Guggenheim Foundation; David van der Leer, Assistant Curator of Architecture and Design; Maria Nicanor, Curatorial Assistant; and Violeta Janeiro, intern. On countless occasions, they provided invaluable support to the book's editors, writers, and researchers. Profound thanks are also due to Angela Starita, lead researcher and project manager, who authored the detailed time line and handled the entire publication with the greatest care and enthusiasm. The book's intricate, layered structure has benefited enormously from her expert knowledge.

Finally, and above all, I am profoundly grateful to all the artists and curators who have worked within and interpreted Frank Lloyd Wright's exuberant building during the past fifty years, expanding our notions of what a museum can be and providing us with inspiration for many years to come.

Richard Armstrong
Director, Solomon R. Guggenheim Foundation and Museum

1

FIG. 1 1075 Fifth Avenue, at the southeast corner of Eighty-ninth Street, ca. 1910. Milstein Division of United States History, Local History and Genealogy, New York Public Library, Astor, Lenox and Tilden Foundations

THE GUGGENHEIM MUSEUM: THE NEW YORK CONTEXT

Hilary Ballon

FRANK LLOYD WRIGHT WAITED A LONG LIFETIME TO BUILD IN NEW YORK CITY, as Robert Moses remarked at the dedication of the Solomon R. Guggenheim Museum on October 21, 1959, some six months after Wright's death: "With all his pretended extravagant contempt for New York, Cousin Frank was convinced in his heart that the big city could not survive without at least one major building designed by him."[1]

Wright despised the architectural environment of New York: the overbuilt chaos and congestion, the absence of nature, the boxy buildings devoid of spatial expression. He associated the architectural regime of New York with the loss of individuality and a crowd mentality, and beginning with his early books, *Modern*

FIG. 2 Frank Lloyd Wright,
St. Mark's-in-the-Bouwerie Towers
(unbuilt), 1927–31. Perspective. Pencil
on tracing paper, 21.3 x 39.1 cm. Frank
Lloyd Wright Foundation, Scottsdale,
Arizona 2905.028

Architecture (1931) and *The Disappearing City* (1932), Wright wrote savagely about the architectural and social miseries of New York and promoted his Broadacre City (1934–35), a countermodel of dispersed, automobile-oriented settlement.[2]

Yet despite his antiurban fervor, Wright was seduced by New York City, by its media power, cultural weight, and brazen ambition. For his first building project in the city, St. Mark's-in-the-Bouwerie Towers (1927–31), he reinvented the structure of the high-rise, replacing the standard skeletal frame with a centralized system of open building plates cantilevered from a structural core (fig. 2). The unorthodox structures gave pause to the client, the Reverend William Norman Guthrie, and the free-standing towers were at odds with Manhattan's urban form;[3] the proposal did not move forward. Wright received no other major New York City commissions until Hilla Rebay wrote him in 1943 about her idea for "a temple of spirit—a monument."[4] Wright pursued the Guggenheim Museum for the last sixteen years of his life (1943–59) with astonishing perseverance and vigor. In 1954, he even took up residence in the Plaza Hotel in New York in order to monitor and promote the project; the hotel suite he redesigned became known as Taliesin East.[5] The city that he had for decades anathematized was also where he staged his epic last triumph.

The Guggenheim embodies Wright's tortured relationship with New York City. It was a self-conscious architectural icon, attracting visitors in its own right rather than for the treasures within, as with the Metropolitan Museum of Art, the Museum of Modern Art, or the New York Public Library, and it was sui generis, unlike the Empire State Building, which despite its record-breaking height conformed to the generic skyscraper format. People came to see the Guggenheim Museum's spiraling form, promenade on the ramp, and experience the spatial drama of the interior. It was both magnetic and diffident, a self-contained, opaque, windowless diva utterly uninterested in its environs: "belligerent strangeness" was architectural critic Ada Louise Huxtable's apt phrase.[6]

The Guggenheim Museum is typically seen as a building that goes against the grain of New York. In a city where buildings are subsumed into the wall they form along the street, the museum is a sculptural object. Its curving shape is at odds with the city's rectilinear format. Yet the tension between the Guggenheim and the vernacular urbanism of New York intensifies the aesthetic force of Wright's building. The New York context is decisive: the Guggenheim's spiral draws energy from its setting, depends on it for contrapuntal effect, and reveals a new dimension of Manhattan's gridiron plan.

The Site

In June 1943, when Wright was invited to design the Guggenheim Museum, there was no building site. Wright came to New York that month to meet the patron, Solomon R. Guggenheim, and his curator, Rebay, and soon thereafter, the contract was drawn. The lack of a site factored significantly into its terms. Site acquisition was budgeted at $250,000, out of a total budget of one million dollars, an amount sufficient to purchase a 50- to 75-foot lot, depending on the location, and to build in a typical manner. If the site cost less than the allocation, the difference would be applied to construction. If there were no site by July 1944, the contract would be canceled. Thus Wright had an incentive to find a relatively inexpensive property and to find it fast.

At that time, there was no better guide to New York real estate than Robert Moses, who held the position of Commissioner of Parks and City Construction Coordinator, giving him oversight of metropolitan development. Moses and Wright represented opposite poles of American thought about urbanism, nature, and planning, although their larger-than-life personalities and egos put them on common ground. In their verbal jousting over the years, Moses cast himself as a mole, grounded and focused narrowly on the job at hand, and Wright as a skylark, soaring above reality. Bemused to discover they were cousins by marriage, these two polemical figures collaborated on the Guggenheim project, which tapped a common strength: an indomitable determination to accomplish ambitious goals. After touring the city with Moses, Wright was left with a positive impression of the man who transformed the capital of the twentieth century: "He has the future of New York not only in mind but has it in hand too, as has no one else."[7]

In July 1943 and over the next few months, Moses showed Wright several sites in Manhattan. Two properties that covered the block front from Sixty-ninth to Seventieth Street on Park Avenue were ample enough to appeal to Wright, but at an estimated cost of half a million dollars, they were double the budget. Rebay seemed to favor a property on West Fifty-fourth Street, perhaps because it was near the first Museum of Non-Objective Painting, which was located at 24 East Fifty-fourth Street from 1939 to 1947. But the adjacent Museum of Modern Art created an identity problem, and the lot, owned by the Rockefeller family, was expensive: when Wright inquired, the price jumped from $350,000 to $550,000, and the property was soon withdrawn from the market. Wright vetoed a nearby 60-foot sliver of land between Fifty-second and Fifty-third streets that would have buried his building midblock, "leaving us only a look-out opposite M.[useum] of M.[odern] A.[rt]."[8] Moses came up with another site: the former mansion of J. P. Morgan Jr., at the southeast corner of Madison Avenue and Thirty-seventh Street next to the Morgan Library, which interested Wright more than the other Manhattan options.[9] But none of these possibilities inspired him. As he explained to Guggenheim, these "locations are the NOW, more or less. They are not the future and they tie us down to the conventional idea of the Art Museum on hard pavements."[10]

The site both Wright and Moses preferred occupied eight acres in Henry Hudson Memorial Park, in the Spuyten Duyvil section of the Riverdale neighborhood of the Bronx.[11] As Wright explained to his client, the site "would form an individual hill crown, rising up from within and above the new municipal park areas which within a decade will be to Greater New York what Central Park is now to little old New York," and it would provide "a unique opportunity to leisurely plan and build a new type of Treasury for works of art, one that would be a haven of refuge for city dwellers."[12] It is no surprise that Wright originally envisioned the Guggenheim Museum as a freestanding object set in a park. He conceived of architecture in relation to landscape and pursued this approach in the Gordon Strong Automobile Objective and Planetarium (1924–25), an unbuilt project in which a spiral form rises from a mountain top. This scheme provided the template from which the Guggenheim design derived.[13] Wright's preference for the Riverdale park was also steeped in his aversion to Manhattan's congestion and his Broadacre mindset; he believed the park setting would be "a genuine relief from the cinder heap old New York is bound to become."[14] By contrast, Moses championed Manhattan and saw it as an extraordinary form of civilization; his mission was to reinforce the central city. But Moses and Wright converged on the Riverdale location because they embraced the reality of automobile-driven metropolitan expansion and saw the value of a magnetic building in an outlying park. "I wish you and Mr. Guggenheim could see both these sites," Wright wrote Rebay. "Only seeing is believing. And this is especially true of the hill-top on the Hudson. The project simmers in my head. I see more clearly how advantageous to us from nearly every standpoint it is to decentralize altogether than get stuck in the thick of traffic."[15]

Anticipating an anxiety about the building's remoteness, Wright stressed its accessibility by train and by the Henry Hudson Parkway, a Moses road project of the 1930s, and he underscored that Rebay's lofty aspirations for the art museum as a "temple of spirit" conflicted with the hustle and bustle of commercial street life.[16] "We are neither a cigar store nor any business," he wrote to Guggenheim. "The sidewalk crowd means less than nothing to our enterprise. We are cultural—in a true educational sense. Therefore we are the natural object of organized pilgrimage."[17]

The idea of a pilgrimage meant nothing to Rebay and Guggenheim; they wanted the museum to be on a Manhattan sidewalk near where their cultivated audience lived. "What [Guggenheim] does not like at all" about the Riverdale site, Rebay reported, "is the Harlem River separating New York from Spuyten Duyvil, and I don't like the toll-tax in-between, which is such a nuisance that more people turn around before, who want to take a drive—people without money, and they are the most, could never see the Museum. The dealers in 57th Street would have won a triumph to see us in the cold."[18]

In December 1943, Wright gave up on the outlying park site. He seemed reconciled with the commission's constraints: his client's preference, the timeline for site selection, the budget, and the realities of New York real estate. "As [it] now appears," he wrote Rebay on December 22, "our desire for prominence in location is incompatible with our means.... A certain ready realism is essential I believe where New-York-real-estate is concerned."[19] A week later, Wright acknowledged the formal implications of a Manhattan location: "Believe that by changing our idea of a building from horizontal to perpendicular we can go where we please."[20] He expanded on the point to Guggenheim:

It now seems probable that our desire for a horizontal building is incompatible with real estate values in that part of New York where you would be pleased to see the museum built, as real estate values thereabout are all predicated upon the possibilities of the tall-building.

I can see a tall building of a new type perfectly appropriate to our purpose having monumental dignity and great beauty, requiring about half the ground area we have been looking for.[21]

FIG. 3 Panoramic photo of Fifth Avenue at Eighty-ninth Street, New York, 1911. Milstein Division of United States History, Local History and Genealogy, New York Public Library, Astor, Lenox and Tilden Foundations

A. M. HUNTINGTON   McLANE VAN INGEN   No. 1080   EAST
       No. 1083   No. 1081   89th St.
              C. S. PHILLIPS
                  No. 1082

In October 1943, Wright had been commissioned to design the S. C. Johnson & Son, Inc. Research Tower in Racine, Wisconsin, and in December he produced the first scheme, for a seventeen-story building. That project helped ease Wright's necessary conceptual shift from the horizontal to the vertical dimension for the museum. With the new formal orientation in mind, Wright was prepared for "prospecting," as he put it.[22] He began designing for an imaginary corner lot in Manhattan, about 125 by 90 feet, tempting Guggenheim with the idea of a modern ziggurat, which he first mentioned in January 1944.[23]

The allure of Wright's visualization did the trick. In March 1944, Rebay found a Fifth Avenue site, at the south corner of Eighty-ninth Street. It was the first of three purchases that by 1951 would give the entire block front from Eighty-eighth to Eighty-ninth Street to the museum. In 1944, however, the Eighty-ninth Street corner lot was imagined as the complete site, not a beachhead. This location was farther north than Rebay and Guggenheim had wanted, but Wright saw its potential: "I would look favorably on the Fifth Avenue site because a building should be dated at least 10 years ahead of present conditions and that means that all the

No. 1073   WM. W. FULLER   ROB'T C. LEWIS
                         No. 1072   No. 1071

frontage on Central Park will be preferred place for dignified or important buildings…. Why not step aside and be safe and serene on the border of Central Park
which ensures light, fresh air and advantages in every way but one. And that is *congestion.*"[24] When it came down to it, the frontage on Central Park satisfied Wright's
appeal to nature.

    At the time, upper Fifth Avenue was being transformed by one of New York's
characteristic growth spurts. Beginning in about 1920, four- and five-story townhouses were replaced by high-rise apartment buildings. The Guggenheim block
is a typical New York real-estate story, mirroring the trends elsewhere on the avenue. A block-by-block photographic survey of Fifth Avenue shows how the future
Guggenheim site looked in 1911 (fig. 3), and a map from 1916 records the subdivision of the block front into seven lots, ranging in width from 25 to 35 feet (fig. 4).
A six-story structure was built on the lot at the Eighty-ninth Street corner in 1908
(fig. 1).[25] While that building resembles grand, single-family residences on Fifth
Avenue, it was probably a multifamily dwelling, and it was relatively short-lived.
By 1929, it was demolished, and the corner lot was in the hands of a development

FIG. 4 Map detail showing Fifth Avenue between Eighty-eighth and Eighty-ninth streets, 1916. Map by G. W. Bromley & Co. Lionel Pincus and Princess Firyal Map Division, New York Public Library, Astor, Lenox and Tilden Foundations

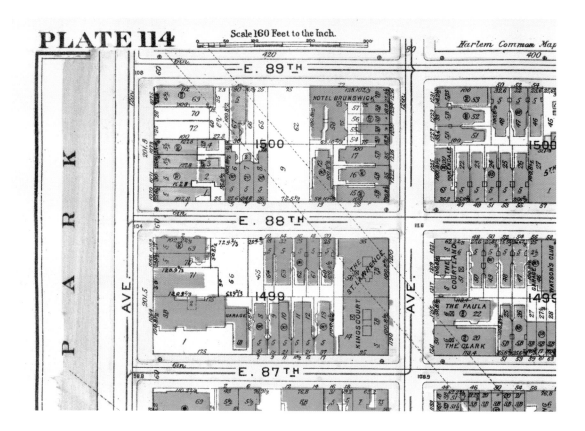

company with plans to build a nineteen-story, 210-foot-tall apartment building. But the tenement-house commissioner blocked the plan, and the Eighty-ninth Street corner lot and the next two, which were undeveloped in 1911, remained vacant until the museum was built.[26] On the south end of the block stood four townhouses, each five stories (fig. 5). By 1944, the five-story building on the Eighty-eighth Street corner had been replaced by a thirteen-story apartment building (fig. 6). The block was filling in and growing taller.

Before Wright's coiled innovation landed on Eighty-ninth Street, upper Fifth Avenue was emerging as a precinct both for museums and for millionaires, and the Guggenheim reinforced that trend. Lenox Library, between Seventieth and Seventy-first streets, and the Metropolitan Museum had set the tone in the late nineteenth century. Lenox Library was replaced by the Frick mansion, which opened as a museum in December 1935, and in 1940 the National Academy of Design arrived on the block between Eighty-ninth and Ninetieth streets and added to what the *New York Times* termed "the growing colony of art institutions along Fifth Avenue."[27]

Once it possessed a foothold on the block, the Guggenheim Foundation began to think more expansively. The Eighty-ninth Street property covered more than half the block front—145 feet on Fifth Avenue—and took up 125 feet on Eighty-ninth Street. In August 1946 it purchased the townhouse at 1071 Fifth Avenue, which was next to the south corner lot. The lot was L-shaped, with a 30-foot facade on the avenue and a perpendicular extension fronting on Eighty-eighth Street, such that

the property wrapped around the corner apartment building. The townhouse at 1071 Fifth Avenue became the second home of the Museum of Non-Objective Painting, which moved there in 1948 from its original quarters on East Fifty-fourth Street.

The final purchase came in April 1951, when Wright persuaded the Guggenheim heirs to acquire the Eighty-eighth Street corner property, thereby giving the museum the entire block front.[28] Wright drove the acquisition, enlisting the real-estate firm Douglas Gibbons in the negotiation and traveling to England to lobby Eleanor Castle Stewart, Guggenheim's daughter, to make the purchase of what he disparagingly called the "hang-nail at the corner."[29] William Zeckendorf, the deal-making developer who provided the site for the United Nations, handled the sale. The acquisition transformed the project.

With each land expansion, Wright redesigned the building. In 1944, he concentrated the spiral coil on the only part of the block available at the time, the 145-foot property at the north end. In 1951, he flipped the coil to the south end of the block, where the site had maximum depth, moved the Monitor to the north end, and decompressed the composition. The full-block expansion allowed Wright to accentuate the horizontal dimension with the thick, continuous band at the second story. A sweeping view down the avenue shows how that wall section responds to the plane of the street wall and in so doing accents the rotundity of the rising form above. The Guggenheim's trustees approved Wright's design in February 1952, setting the stage for the anticipated battle over city approval.

Building Code

After the first decade of the Guggenheim project, from 1943 to 1952, when the site and design were in flux, the museum entered a second phase, from 1952 to 1956, when Wright's ideas were tested by the disciplines of budget and building code. Wright, who was generally intolerant of criticism and felt his artistic genius trumped other considerations, pilloried small-minded code officials who failed to understand his innovative structural ideas. Newspaper headlines happily embraced the simplified storyline that Wright was spinning. "Wright's Plan for Guggenheim Museum Be-deviled by Archaic Building Code," reported a real-estate newspaper.[30] But the bureaucrats were not opposed to Wright's design; on the contrary, code officials did what they could to advance Wright's project.

To tackle the challenges of building in New York, Wright pursued a two-pronged approach: he relied on architect Arthur Cort Holden to obey the rules of the buildings department and on Robert Moses to outsmart them. Wright did not imagine he could succeed without Moses; as he forewarned Rebay in 1945, "*Our* permit will not be one we will get by standing in line at the City Hall—but a special permit with Moses's help and the good-will of the Building Commission, which we have because our building is a high specialty."[31] The truth turned out to be otherwise, as Holden spearheaded the permitting process.

Holden, born in 1893, charted an impressive career that advanced urban design and planning as fundamental matters of public policy.[32] A housing and planning reformer and partner at the firm Holden, McLaughlin & Associates, his two intellectual poles were signaled by his training at Columbia University, where he received a bachelor of architecture degree and a master's in economics in 1915.[33] Associated with the settlement house movement on the Lower East Side in the 1920s, he became chief consultant to the Lower East Side Chamber of Commerce, which under the leadership of Joseph Platzker was a think tank that dealt with slum conditions, depressed land values, and high vacancy rates. Holden supported pooling property to allow improvements at the scale of an entire city block to occur, and he published proposals to assemble blocks on the Lower East Side at the same time that Wright was working on his St. Mark's towers. Wright's proposal for a four-story apartment complex surrounding the church on Second Avenue and Tenth Street included aggregating the private backyards on the block and reorganizing them as a collective garden; it exemplified the privately directed block reorganization that Holden championed. Given the harmony between their approaches and their mutual focus on the Lower East Side, it seems likely that the two men were familiar with each other's work, though not in direct contact in the late 1920s while St. Mark's was underway.[34]

FIG. 7 Plot diagram by Arthur Cort Holden of the Guggenheim Museum site, including the annex, December 17, 1948. Arthur Cort Holden Papers, Box 16 and Folder AM 81-201, Manuscripts Division, Department of Rare Books and Special Collections, Princeton University Library, Princeton, New Jersey

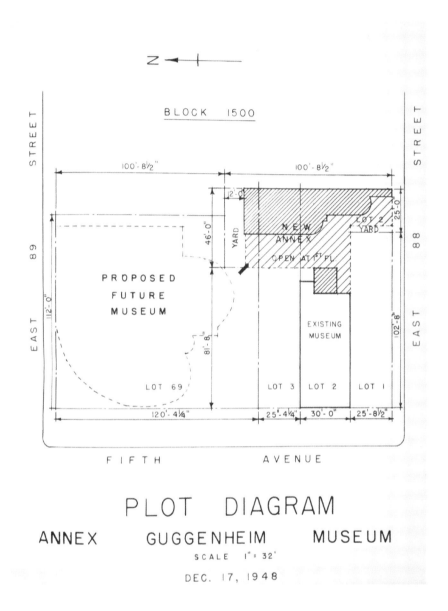

Wright and Holden established a working relationship in 1947. William Clay Irons Jr., the builder Moses had recommended to Wright as an advisor about building costs, had in turn recommended Holden to serve as Wright's local architect.[35] The suggestion resonated because Wright had come into contact with Holden at precisely this time. An active alumnus of Princeton University, Holden was chair of the Conference on Planning Man's Physical Environment for the university's bicentennial celebration in 1947, and he invited Wright and Moses as blockbuster speakers for the occasion. Later that year, Wright invited Holden to a meeting in Guggenheim's art-filled suite at the Plaza Hotel, which extended the entire length of the building's Fifth Avenue facade. Wright explained that Guggenheim was prepared only to build the annex on Eighty-eighth Street, adjacent to the corner apartment building and connected to the rear of 1071 Fifth Avenue (fig. 7). Wright had the plans and said, as Holden described some years later, that "he would like to have me study them and see that they conformed with the New York building code and make such recommendations of what would need to be changed for exit facilities or anything that I could inform him about. He agreed that we should associate on the work and that I was to help in expediting the thing through the Building Department."[36]

Wright's designs for the annex did not reckon with the fire safety code. He should have known better: Wright had a similar problem with St. Mark's, which had had a single means of egress. Holden developed alternative schemes for stairs and exits that conformed to the building code, and Wright endorsed a solution in November 1948. In this instance, Wright was flexible, but he was rarely so; his prevailing impulse was to turn the code review into a dramatic standoff. When Holden informed Wright that a structural engineer licensed in New York had to sign the structural calculations, Wright protested, as if this requirement was unexpected or irregular. "We do our own engineering," he railed, "and, if that isn't good enough for the big-city police, we won't build there at all.... Is all this complexity due to your having struck a snag of some kind at City Hall that needs special work upon it?"[37] To which Holden replied: "I hope I haven't created the impression that the New York Building Department has not been cooperative because they have been cooperative to the nth degree, giving us—on your account—the courtesy of a preliminary and preparatory examination of the plans, which from a strict point of view of routine regulations would not be permitted until we actually filed the plans and paid the required fee.... We have struck no snag at City Hall. So far we have received only interest and suggestions to facilitate cooperation."[38] Holden did his best to keep the project on track, but Guggenheim died in November 1949, and Rebay cancelled the annex in 1950, both before the matter of a local structural engineer was settled.

As soon as the foundation's trustees approved the new, full-block design in February 1952, Wright reappointed Holden as architect of record and charged him to obtain a building permit for the museum.[39] Despite Wright's grandstanding over structural engineering, and despite the unorthodoxies of the building's expanding spiral, Holden told Wright he was less concerned about the engineering design standards than required egresses and land coverage. Wright felt the latter could be easily waived because the museum "was bringing the open space of the park across Fifth Avenue."[40]

Holden's ties to New York power brokers and years of experience made it easy for him to guide the permitting process. He personally knew Building Commissioner Barney Gilroy and solicited his advice on how best to handle Wright's unusual design, which was sure to require variances. Gilroy brought into the discussions Arthur Benline, superintendent of buildings for the Borough

THE GUGGENHEIM MUSEUM: THE NEW YORK CONTEXT

of Manhattan, and Isidore M. Cohen, an engineer and rabbi and, in Gilroy's esti-mation, "one of the ablest, if not the ablest examiner" in the buildings department. Gilroy asked Cohen to take a special interest in the project:[41] in Holden's words, "Barney Gilroy said to him, 'Can you do a little extra work on the side? Can you take a special interest in this? Here's a special type of building and it's very inter-esting what we might we able to make of it.'"[42] Cohen agreed to play an advisory role and subsequently met informally with Holden to suggest a way forward. "I think this was very, very helpful," Holden recalled, "because after we had one or two conferences he pointed out to me that there were certain features that could be adapted that wouldn't require any formal rulings if Mr. Wright agreed to them," and Cohen outlined how to obtain approvals for the nonconforming elements of the design.[43] "The problem, simply stated," Cohen explained, was that Wright's "design for the Guggenheim Museum is unique in the City's construction experi-ence."[44] But he was eager to find solutions, and Benline "said that he would follow the procedure personally, and provide for an examination especially for the review of the engineering principles that had been incorporated in the structural design."[45]

Next, Holden arranged for the city officials to meet with Wright in March 1952, a month before Holden filed the building plans, docket number New Building 27 of 1952. The first gatekeeper was the Department of Buildings, and with a push from Gilroy to expedite the review, examiner Cohen produced his report on May 14. He listed thirty objections, many trivial and easily remedied. Yet Wright resisted: "I suggest we make very few—if any—changes before we appeal. Our project nips 'at the bud' the blossoms of disaster in which 'the code' flowers.... The various escape enclosures they outline by code only make danger instead of ensuring safety."[46]

Holden organized a less combative response. Nineteen items were removed by compliance, meaning Wright responded to the concerns. Objections 27 and 28, however, were important: the examiner stated that the design of reinforced concrete members should be based on the generally accepted theory of flexure as applied to reinforced concrete, and that the mix, strength, and allowable working stresses should likewise comply with the code. At two meetings in September and October 1952, William Wesley Peters, the project manager and Wright's son-in-law, presented five books of structural calculations to the examiner, and he approved them. He also approved use of metal mesh as reinforcement in the concrete, which Wright had used in the Johnson Research Tower.[47]

The next step was to appeal the remaining eleven objections to the Board of Standards and Appeals.[48] Several objections had mostly to do with fire codes; thus Holden's appeal, filed December 12, advanced a new theory of fire safety. He argued that the "usual provisions for public safety both in structure and exit requirements, as set forth in the building code, are neither as appropriate nor as effective as the methods created by the architect to meet the needs of the special design" of the building.[49] The standard approach targeted the spread of fire by flue action; the code anticipated floors connected by staircases and shut off by self-closing doors. Wright, on the other hand, argued that the safety provisions of the museum depended on openness: "the rotunda…provides the best possible means for the dispersion of superheated gases that might be generated by a fire; and that the complete dispersion of such gases is a protection equal to (1) the protection afforded by confining such gases in a narrow flue, or (b) the maintenance of enclosed shaft for stairs from which it is the aim to exclude harmful gases."[50] Other requested variances—for example, to permit construction of the grand ramp without doors—stemmed from Wright's description of the ramp as a safe form of egress.

Wright had little patience for this scrutiny. He drafted a cover letter to the application to the Board of Standards and Appeals, which began: "Architecture, may it please the court, is the welding of imagination and common sense into a restraint upon specialists, codes and fools."[51] (At the prompting of Harry F. Guggenheim, Solomon's nephew, who became chairman of the foundation's board of trustees in 1950, he removed the reference to fools in the submitted letter.) In August 1953, after appearances by Wright and Holden, they unexpectedly withdrew the appeal "without prejudice" because Wright decided to rework the designs, mostly to reduce construction costs and address structural issues. The architectural historian William Jordy has explained in depth the alterations at this stage, which affected the stair tower, the dome, and the ramp.[52] Some changes were precipitated by the concerns of the Board of Standards and Appeals, but the board did notably accept the essence of Wright's fire safety argument about the ramp and did not constrain the openness of the rotunda.

During this period of revision, the trustees of the Guggenheim Foundation lost confidence in Holden and replaced him with an engineer named Jacob Feld, who managed the last phase of review by the Board of Standards and Appeals. "I feel very certain," Holden said of the episode, "that advice had been given to Mr. Wright by someone that, if he expected to get along in New York, he had 'to pay the tolls.' At any rate, I subsequently found out that the Guggenheim had arranged to retain in consultation a Mr. Feld whom 'those in [the] know' had found it wise to retain in similar 'appeals.'"[53] In fact Feld had been recommended by Moses, who had used him in connection with hearings before the Board of Standards and Appeals for the New York Colosseum, one of Moses's most controversial projects.[54] Holden was an advocate of Wright's aesthetic vision, whereas Feld was an operative insensitive to the Guggenheim design who, according to Holden,

unnecessarily sacrificed Wright's glass-enclosed elevator: "Both I. M. Cohen and I recognized the importance of this element of the design and while we both agreed to hold it in abeyance, both of us agreed that ultimate approval could be obtained. After Mr. Feld was retained by the Trustees, I had no further conferences or contacts with the Department [of Buildings], but neglect to follow through in order to obtain approval for the glass enclosed elevator, I believe was a tragic mistake."[55]

The revised design was completed in March 1954, whereupon the museum's new director, James Johnson Sweeney, requested adjustments to accommodate museum functions, such as painting storage. Revisions for Sweeney, not code issues, caused delays at this stage. In March 1956, thirteen years after Rebay's initial approach, the building permit was issued. Demolition and site work began in May, and groundbreaking followed in August.

Wright's attack on the building code as the enemy of his art was a useful rhetorical stance. It cast the building as a heroic undertaking, mobilized public support, and masked other problems, including an escalating budget and the hostility of Sweeney, who fundamentally disliked Wright's design. The code did indeed compel Wright to solve significant egress, fire safety, and structural issues, but these were not unique to building in New York, and the Buildings Department was unusually collaborative. In truth, New York City officials were delighted to have a celebrity building by Frank Lloyd Wright.

On the Grid

When Robert Moses learned that the first model of the Solomon R. Guggenheim Museum had been destroyed in transport in spring 1947, he prodded Wright to rethink the design. "When you make the new Museum model why not concede something to the surroundings—however little you may like them," Moses wrote. "After all, the eclectic buildings in the neighborhood and especially along Fifth Avenue, are going to be with us for a long, long time."[56] Wright protested, insisting that the Guggenheim "considers the neighborhood and the Park more generously in every way than any building on the Avenue."[57] Obviously the museum is unlike the buildings around it, which are straight-walled extrusions from rectangular ground plots. But the degree to which the Guggenheim does in fact respond creatively to the New York grid has long been underappreciated.

One traditional critique of the city's grid plan was its failure to create privileged sites for monumental architecture. The repetitive, antihierarchical pattern of land division subordinated New York's buildings to the overpowering logic of the grid, whereas in Washington, D.C., for example, streets and vistas were organized to accentuate certain buildings. The grid's founding fathers made the antimonumental effect of their plan an implicit goal, justifying it in 1811 in relation to the need for residential dwellings, a cellular building form based on incremental repetition. As the age of civic monuments dawned in the mid-nineteenth century, Frederick Law Olmsted lamented the incapacity of New York to position a building at the climax of an axial view or to step out from the grid to claim public attention.[58]

The vernacular of New York came to be dominated by the street wall and the infinite view, both forms of architectural self-abnegation. The monumental buildings of New York usually achieve their standing by interrupting the grid: they occupy a superblock, such as Pennsylvania Station; they step back from the street wall, such as the New York Public Library; or they surround themselves with open ground, such as the Frick Collection. All three tactics are evident in designs for the American Museum of Natural History, and the campuses of Lincoln Center and Columbia University, which contain several monuments on reformatted superblocks.

The Guggenheim Museum, on the other hand, did not make its mark through the standard devices. The monumental character of the museum resides in its three-dimensional, sculptural form erupting from the cramped framework of the grid. The skyscraper, the paradigmatic New York urban form, complies with gridiron logic and, as Rem Koolhaas has noted, its sky-high crowning features are where it becomes exuberant.[59] The Guggenheim brought that expressive freedom down to street level and demonstrated a hitherto undeveloped capacity of the grid to accommodate a sculptural object.

Another quintessential characteristic of New York City is the excitement of its streets. A walk on the avenue directs your attention to the shopfront up close as well as to the distant vista, where space is stretched out and framed by street walls. Wright internalized the street in the museum's grand interior ramp. A theme of

Wright's antiurban writings is the lack of spatial expression in the city, a joyless flatness embodied by the cellular unit of a typical office or apartment. The presence of the stylish, glass-curtain wall buildings of High Modernism in New York—Lever House, the Seagram Building, the United Nations—reinforced the sense that the Guggenheim was an outlandish, anti–New York concoction. But in its own subversive way, the museum absorbs and reinterprets the keynotes of the city in Wright's distinctive organic language: the walking avenue becomes a spiral ramp, and the slit of space defined by the avenue's street walls is reshaped as a womblike volume.

The idea of the Guggenheim as interiorized urban space is reflected in the Elmer Holmes Bobst Library (1967–73) at New York University, designed by Philip Johnson and Richard Foster and located on the south side of Washington Square Park. A floor-to-ceiling atrium dominates the interior, and crosswalks that wrap around it offer views across the void. The intention was to create an enclosed town square for the university community, but the space is intimidating, not embracing; and in contrast to the dynamism of Wright's ascending and expanding spiral, the geometric order of Bobst is static. These discordant reverberations of the Guggenheim in a building downtown underscore not just the remarkable beauty of Wright's design but also its propulsive energy and the way it transfigures the elements of New York's urban poetics: grid, street, and motion.

Robert Moses disliked the Guggenheim Museum. "I venture to predict that long after the public has wearied of Frank Lloyd Wright's inverted oatmeal dish and silo with their awkward cantilevering, their jaundiced skin and the ingenious spiral ramp leading down past the abstractions which mirror the tortured maladjustments of our time, the Metropolitan will still wear well."[60] And yet, despite his personal disapproval, Moses recognized its star quality, which he considered good for New York: "I agree that your building will attract immense attention and that alone—if there were nothing else, which I don't in the least assert—would make it worthwhile for New York and a great contribution by the Guggenheim Foundation."[61]

On March 31, 1959, nine days before he died, the ever-vigilant Wright objected to a temporary fence to be erected outside the museum as it approached completion. The idea was to protect the building from vandalism, but Wright considered it vandalism to obstruct the building and fence it off from the street and the people. He scolded, "Do not discount the importance of the place the structure will occupy in the public esteem."[62] He might well have added, "And in the world's image of New York City."

Notes

1 "Text of Moses Remarks," *New York Times*, October 22, 1959, p. 40.

2 Wright promulgated his ideas about Broadacre in three books: *Architecture and Modern Life* (New York: Harper and Brothers, 1938), *When Democracy Builds* (Chicago: University of Chicago Press, 1945), and *The Living City* (New York: Horizon Press, 1958). Also see David G. De Long, "Frank Lloyd Wright and the Evolution of the Living City," in *Frank Lloyd Wright and the Living City*, ed. De Long (Weil am Rhein, Germany: Vitra Design Museum, 1998), pp. 14–51.

3 Hilary Ballon, "From New York to Bartlesville: The Pilgrimage of Wright's Skyscraper," in *Prairie Skyscraper: Frank Lloyd Wright's Price Tower*, ed. Anthony Alofsin (Bartlesville, Okla., and New York: Rizzoli, 2005), pp. 100–13.

4 Hilla Rebay to Frank Lloyd Wright, June 1, 1943, in *Frank Lloyd Wright: The Guggenheim Correspondence*, ed. Bruce Brooks Pfeiffer (Fresno: The Press at California State University; Carbondale and Edwardsville: Southern Illinois University Press, 1986), p. 4.

5 Jane King Hession and Debra Pickrel, *Frank Lloyd Wright in New York: The Plaza Years, 1954–1959* (Salt Lake City: Gibbs Smith, 2007.)

6 Ada Louise Huxtable, "That Museum: Wright or Wrong?" *New York Times*, October 25, 1959.

7 Wright to Solomon R. Guggenheim, July 14, 1943, in Pfeiffer, *The Guggenheim Correspondence*, p. 10.

8 Wright to Rebay, July 23, 1943, in ibid., pp. 13–14.

9 Wright to Rebay, July 26, 1943, in ibid., p. 15.

10 Wright to Solomon R. Guggenheim, July 14, 1943, in ibid., p. 12.

11 Wright incorrectly stated in one letter that the site was 80 acres, probably as a typo; see ibid., p. 10. Robert Moses corrected Wright in a letter of July 16, 1943, ficheid M129A05, Frank Lloyd Wright Foundation Archives, Scottsdale, Ariz. (hereafter cited as FLW Archives).

12 Wright to Solomon R. Guggenheim, July 14, 1943, in Pfeiffer, *The Guggenheim Correspondence*, p. 10.

13 On the Gordon Strong Automobile Objective, see Mark Reinberger, "The Sugarloaf Mountain Project and Frank Lloyd Wright's Vision of a New World," *Journal of the Society of Architectural Historians* 43, no. 1 (March 1984), pp. 38–52; and De Long, "Frank Lloyd Wright: Designs for an American Landscape, 1922–1932" in De Long, ed., *Designs for an American Landscape, 1922–1932*, exh. cat. (New York: Harry N. Abrams, 1996), pp. 80–100.

14 Wright to Solomon R. Guggenheim, July 14, 1943, in Pfeiffer, *The Guggenheim Correspondence*, p. 10.

15 Wright to Rebay, July 23, 1943, in ibid., p. 14.

16 On the Henry Hudson Parkway and Moses's approach to metropolitan planning, see Hilary Ballon and Kenneth T. Jackson, ed., *Robert Moses and the Modern City: The Transformation of New York* (New York: W. W. Norton, 2007).

17 Ibid., 11.

18 Wright citing Rebay in a letter to Moses, July 26, 1943, FLW Archives, ficheid M129D05.

19 Wright to Rebay, December 22, 1943, in Pfeiffer, *The Guggenheim Correspondence*, p. 24.

20 Wright to Rebay, December 30, 1943, in ibid., p. 25.

21 Wright to Solomon R. Guggenheim, December 31, 1943, in ibid., p. 25.

22 Wright to Rebay, January 20, 1944, in ibid., p. 41.

23 On January 26, 1944, Wright wrote to Rebay, "I find that the antique Ziggurat has great possibilities for our building. You will see. We can use it either top side down or down side top." Ibid., p. 43.

24 Wright to Rebay, March 13, 1944, in ibid., pp. 44–45.

25 "In the Real Estate Field," *New York Times*, March 25, 1908.

26 "Court Restricts Fifth Avenue Building," *New York Times*, June 29, 1929.

27 On the Frick house in relation to the development of Fifth Avenue, see Ballon, *Mr. Frick's Palace: The Council of the Frick Collection Lecture Series* (New York: The Frick Collection, 2009). On the National Academy, see "Academy of Design Gets New Home," *New York Times*, June 12, 1940.

28 "Guggenheim Fund to Build Museum," *New York Times*, April 17, 1951.

29 Wright to Harry F. Guggenheim, August 6, 1951, in Pfeiffer, *The Guggenheim Correspondence*, p. 149.

30 Undated clipping, ca. 1956, from "Metropolitan Buildings," Arthur Cort Holden Papers, Box 16, Folder 8, Manuscripts Division, Department of Rare Books and Special Collections, Princeton University Library, Princeton, N.J. (hereafter cited as Holden Papers).

31 Wright to Rebay, May 12 and June 2, 1945, in Pfeiffer, *The Guggenheim Correspondence*, pp. 61–62. Emphasis in the original.

32 Holden's civic leadership roles were significant: he was chairman of the board of the New York Urban League from 1922 to 1931, a member of Mayor La Guardia's Committee on City Planning from 1934 to 1938, and a leader in the New York chapter of the American Institute of Architects from the 1930s through the 1950s, including a stint as director of the New York region from 1949 to 1952. In 1957, he received the Medal of Honor from the New York chapter of the AIA. Holden represents the trajectory of mainstream progressive thinking about planning and housing in the mid-twentieth century. By the 1950s, he was supportive of urban renewal and eminent domain. See Joel Schwartz, "Tenement Renewal in New York City in the 1930s: The District-Improvement Ideas of Arthur C. Holden," *Journal of Planning History* 1, no. 4 (November 2002), pp. 290–310.

33 Holden had previously received a bachelor's degree in literature from Princeton University, from which he graduated in 1912.

34 Holden recalled that he and Wright first met in the late 1930s at a meeting on housing chaired by Charles Abrams; see Arthur C. Holden, "Frank Lloyd Wright: Some Notes on a Friendship and an Association," dictated at Washington, Conn., December 1979–May 1980, Holden Papers, vol. 2.

35 Ibid., Box 17, Folder 2, p. 9.

36 Transcript of a tape-recorded interview with Holden, January 20, 1971, Holden Papers, Box 17, pp. 5–6.

37 Wright to Holden, November 9, 1949, Holden Papers, vol. 1.

38 Holden to Wright, November 15, 1949, Holden Papers, Box 16, Folder 1.

39 Wright to Holden, March 4, 1952, Holden Papers, Box 16, Folder 1947–1956.

40 Holden, "File for Record, Interview of To-day's date, with Frank Lloyd Wright RE Plans for Construction of Permanent Museum," February 6, 1952, Holden Papers, Box 16, Folder 1947–1956.

41 Transcript of a tape-recorded interview with Holden, January 20, 1971, p. 10.

42 Ibid.

43 Ibid., pp. 10–11.

44 Holden to Wright, February 26, 1953, Holden Papers, vol. 2.

45 Holden, "Frank Lloyd Wright: Some Notes on a Friendship and an Association," p. 14.

46 Wright to Holden, July 3, 1952, Holden Papers, Box 16, Folder 1947–1952.

47 Dept. of Housing and Buildings, Objections, New Building Application, February 26, 1953, Holden Papers, Box 17, Folder 2.

48 For an inventory of the thirty objections and how they were addressed, see notes by Holden to Wright, November 10, 1952, Holden Papers, Box 17, Folder 1.

49 "Typewritten Statement as required by: Paragraph Q2. Appeal from Administrative Decision and Paragraph N. Application for Variation of Requirements of the Zoning Resolution Concerning Guggenheim Museum of Non-Objective Painting, 1071 Fifth Avenue, Frank Lloyd Wright, Architect, New Building Application No. 27 of 1952, Holden McLaughlin & Associates, Consulting Architects and Applicant," Holden Papers, vol. 2, p. 1.

50 Ibid., p. 8.

51 Wright to Board of Standards and Appeals, February 14, 1953, in Pfeiffer, *The Guggenheim Correspondence*, p. 184.

52 William H. Jordy, "The Encompassing Environment of Free-Form Architecture: Frank Lloyd Wright's Guggenheim Museum," in Jordy, *American Buildings and Their Architects*, vol. 5, *The Impact of European Modernism in the Mid-Twentieth Century* (Garden City, N.Y.: Doubleday, 1972; repr., New York: Oxford University Press, 1976), pp. 279–359.

53 Holden, "Frank Lloyd Wright: Some Notes on a Friendship and an Association," p. 27.

54 Ballon and Jackson, *Robert Moses and the Modern City*, pp. 263–67.

55 Holden, "Frank Lloyd Wright: Some Notes on a Friendship and an Association," p. 33.

56 Moses to Wright, March 27, 1947, FLW Archives, ficheid M160C04.

57 Wright to Moses, April 4, 1947, FLW Archives, ficheid M160E01.

58 Frederick Law Olmsted, "The Misfortunes of New York," in Olmsted, *Civilizing American Cities: Writing on City Landscapes*, ed. S. B. Sutton (New York: Da Capo Press, 1997), pp. 43–51.

59 Rem Koolhaas, *Delirious New York: A Retroactive Manifesto for Manhattan* (New York: Oxford University Press, 1978).

60 "Moses Gets Prize from Art Society," *New York Times*, May 21, 1959.

61 Moses to Wright, September 16, 1953, FLW Archives, ficheid M232A08.

62 Wright to Medley Whelpley, March 31, 1959, in Pfeiffer, *The Guggenheim Correspondence*, p. 301.

WRIGHT'S GUGGENHEIM MUSEUM AND LATER MODERNIST ARCHITECTURE

Joseph M. Siry

Now why not let walls, ceilings, floors become seen as component parts of each other, their surfaces flowing into each other to get continuity in the whole, eliminating all constructed features just as Louis Sullivan had eliminated background in his ornament in favor of an integral sense of the whole. Here an ideal began to have consequences.

—Frank Lloyd Wright, *An Autobiography*[1]

OF ALL FRANK LLOYD WRIGHT'S ARCHITECTURAL WORKS, the Solomon R. Guggenheim Museum, with its tall, spiral-ramped main gallery, most vividly embodies his ideal of spatial and material continuity. First identifying this ideal in his mentor Louis Sullivan's curvilinear ornament, Wright proposed to realize it in the three-dimensional totality of his architecture. This concept, also associated with the term "plasticity," was central to his theory of organic form, which opposed the rectilinear architecture of the classical tradition and the International Style. Before and while he designed the Guggenheim, Wright experimented with continuity in the spiral ramp as a simultaneously spatial and structural form, a uniquely modern innovation made possible by the new material of steel-reinforced concrete. These experiments culminated in the Guggenheim, whose form likely stimulated younger contemporaries like Eero Saarinen, Louis Kahn, and I. M. Pei, and whose ramp is a modern symbol that inspired later variations in the works of Richard Meier, Frank O. Gehry, and Zaha Hadid. This essay traces the idea of the circular ramp in Wright's work prior to the Guggenheim, its realization in the museum's geometry and construction, and modernist responses to the building over the half century since 1959.

Wright and the Ramp, 1924–52

The most internationally prominent early use of steel-reinforced concrete ramps in modernist architecture was for automobile buildings, such as those designed by Albert Kahn for the Ford Motor Company near Detroit, which dated from 1909 to 1926. Kahn himself showed his structures to Wright, who recalled in 1931: "I had seen his Ford factory. I had seen the industrial buildings which he had designed and for which I have always had a great respect."[2] Kahn's firm designed many early,

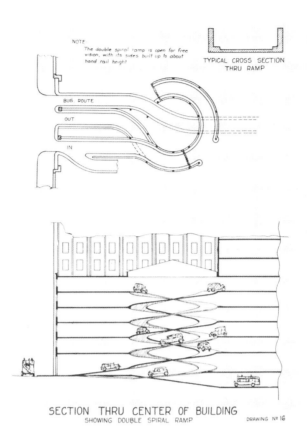

notable multistory parking garages all over the United States, such as Detroit's Fort Shelby Garage (1921–22), where ramped floors extended two-thirds of the building's 130-foot length. On these floors, cars were parked with the aisle in the center, making the ramp about 50 feet wide between columns (fig. 2). This plan allowed cars to be driven continuously from the ground to the top floor. In 1927, Kahn wrote that some automobile-service buildings "are two or three stories high, depending on ramps rather than on elevators for transportation of cars from floor to floor. In truth, the extensive use of ramps in this type of building is a striking example of modern adaptation to changing conditions."[3] As Wright surely saw, the ramped garage was a building type wherein novel functional, spatial, and structural ideas were shaping a new architecture that not only accommodated but, via its ramps, simulated continuous movement. The Guggenheim's continuity would also be both material and experiential.

By the mid-1920s, the urban parking garage was an established building type, often a freestanding structure with street frontage, distinct from an enclosed facility in a larger commercial building. As Kahn noted, one solution for urban garages was to ramp entire floors at a minimal grade of 4 percent (approximately the same as the Guggenheim's ramp) to enable cars to both park and drive on the same sloping surfaces. Yet there were variations on garages whose floors were largely flat yet which included internal ramps, usually through their central core. Some garages included double-spiral ramps, as shown in one 1926 design intended as a prototype for privately funded multiple-floor garages (fig. 3). This projected building, approximately 400 by 200 feet in area and six stories in height, would have housed upward of two thousand automobiles at a time. Such a design "results

FIG. 4 Frank Lloyd Wright,
Gordon Strong Automobile Objective
and Planetarium (unbuilt), Sugarloaf
Mountain, Maryland, 1924–25.
Perspective (presentation drawing).
Graphite pencil and colored pencil
on tracing paper, 50 x 78 cm.
Frank Lloyd Wright Foundation,
Scottsdale, Arizona 2505.039

in economy of space, and ease and continuousness of operation, for the reason
that the cars are going in and out of the building always in the same direction, and
ascending and descending in the same circular area occupied by the ramp."[4] Spiral
ramps were upheld on circular rings of ten freestanding concrete columns set at
about 30-degree intervals, just like the Guggenheim's structural piers set 30 degrees
apart around its circle. As shown in a typical cross section at fig. 3's upper right,
each ramp was to be "open for free vision, with its sides built up to about hand rail
height," like the Guggenheim's later, smaller-scale ramp for pedestrians.[5]

Such contemporaneous solutions were likely in Wright's mind when he
designed his unbuilt project for Chicago businessman Gordon Strong, an Automobile
Objective and Planetarium (1924–25) atop Sugarloaf Mountain in Maryland (fig. 4).
Intended as a recreational destination for motor trips by residents from nearby
Washington, D.C., and Baltimore, this unprecedented structure was "to provide a
maximum of facility for motor access to and into the structure itself," with storage
for up to five hundred cars inside the structure on the top of the mountain and one
thousand cars in adjoining storage sheds on the mountain's slope.[6] Wright took
the idea of the double-spiral automobile ramp, heretofore set inside a tall garage
building, and expressed it externally as the full architectural volume. His Automobile
Objective also merged parking and movement along its spiral as the Guggenheim
would merge art exhibition and visitor movement along its ramp.[7]

Strong and Wright both viewed the project as historically inspired by the
squared, stepped pyramid at Saqqâra, Egypt, and the ziggurats of ancient Assyria

and Babylonia. (Wright later termed the Guggenheim an inverted ziggurat.)[8] Yet Wright defended the design with reference not to a specific precedent but rather to the idea that ancient architectural variations on the spiral as a form found in nature derived ultimately from the effects of gravity. Invoking a spiral spring, a snail shell, an eggbeater, and a screw, Wright told Strong: "Every carpenter that drives a screw proves me standardized and unoriginal. Every spiral spring shows me up. I have found it hard to look a snail in the face since I stole the idea of his house—from his back. The spiral is so natural and organic a form for whatever would ascend that I did not see why it should not be played upon and made equally available for descent at one and the same time."[9] Wright viewed his project as a variation on the spiral theme "because a principle involved with organic integrity in all human experience of which the fabulous Tower of Babylon, the leaning Tower of Pisa and the crown of Gordon Strong's 'Sugarloaf' are conspicuous examples, is at work in them all!"[10] Thus Wright presented the idea as both modeled on nature and historically informed, yet not superficially historicist, as if the Automobile Objective were a modern variant on a form that transcended time. He later saw the Guggenheim in similar terms.

Wright returned to the ramp in his later unbuilt projects for civic centers: Monona Terrace, in Madison, Wisconsin (1938–59), and Pittsburgh Point Park (1947–48), as well as a self-service garage for Edgar Kaufmann Sr. in downtown Pittsburgh (1949–50). The latter two designs postdated Wright's original 1943 studies for the Guggenheim Museum, and, like the museum, they were to be large constructions of a continuous circular spiral form in reinforced concrete, unlike anything yet built. The unrealized status of these projects frustrated Wright. As he later wrote to Kaufmann, "What counts with me are *buildings built*, not plans drawn and set aside."[11] In the years he was pushing to build the Guggenheim, Wright would realize the circularly curved ramp at a smaller scale in his son David Wright's house (1950–52) near Phoenix (see page 169) and Max Hoffmann's automobile showroom (1954–55) on the ground floor of 430 Park Avenue, New York (see page 190, lower right).[12]

The earliest spiral ramp built by Wright that approximates the function and form of the Guggenheim is in his remodeling of the V. C. Morris Gift Shop at 140 Maiden Lane in San Francisco (fig. 5).[13] The shop sold contemporary table furnishings and gifts for the home, especially modern glassware, china, silver, and linens, with a separate department for books and fine prints. Wright prepared drawings dated 1948, and the remodeling of the two-story building was completed in 1949. On a small site with party walls on either side, Wright rebuilt the street front in brick, eliminating its plate-glass show windows. Inside he opened the floor between the first and second story and joined the two by means of a circular ramp with a display of merchandise and artworks along its length on counters, in cases, and set on shelves in circular or semicircular recesses along the ramp's curving wall. About the width of a residential staircase, the ramp begins to the right of the tunnel-like entrance and rises into a 25-foot-high rotunda below the skylit ceiling.

The violation of the planar floor is also the fundamental idea behind the Guggenheim, embodied in a series of spirals where the unity of the space and its display of objects on multiple levels is revealed once inside. In the museum, the effect suggests the totality of the collection on view in one space, even though only a small part of it would be shown at any one time. As with the Guggenheim, the Morris shop was almost wholly removed from visual contact with the outside, placing visitors and objects in a self-contained world removed from the street. The new store received five hundred to fifteen hundred visitors per day, as if it were an exhibit of Wright's architecture, which the Guggenheim was to become.[14]

Perhaps the most telling difference between the interior of the Morris Gift Shop and the Guggenheim is in their construction methods. The Guggenheim's wider multilevel expanding spiral ramp is supported on piers (called webs) around the rotunda's periphery. Yet, as the structural plan shows, the Morris's ramp—smaller in diameter, circular rather than spiral, more steeply inclined, and rising only one story—is held on thirty-two steel beams arrayed radially around its circumference (fig. 6). The radial beams frame into channel beams around the circular ramp's inner circumference. Around the ramp's outer circular edge, the radial beams either frame into outer circular channel beams or are anchored to the side walls or to peripheral steel beams or struts bolted to the existing second-floor joists. The construction ties the ramp into the existing building's framing. Some radial beams rest on a quadrant of curving concrete wall to the rear, as shown on the right half of fig. 6 in the ramp-framing plan. No radial piers or columns uphold the ramp, which appears to ascend or descend as if floating in space. This effect is reinforced by the ceiling of circular "domes" of white translucent Plexiglas and the floral display globe suspended from the ceiling over the ramp, which Wright referred to as "the floating flower disc."[15] In the Morris Gift Shop, Wright was clearly looking ahead to such an effect in the Guggenheim, which was to have a skylit dome of translucent glass tubes like those in his earlier S. C. Johnson & Son, Inc. Administration Building (1936–39) in Racine, Wisconsin. As Wright's friend Edgar Kaufmann Jr. wrote: "There is an unaccountable feeling of spaciousness in this smallish rectangle, closed in on four sides. The center of the shop is quite free and open. Around it sweeps a slow majestic ramp which seems to unroll space like the symbolic red carpet."[16] Wright would realize this idea on an expanded scale in the Guggenheim.

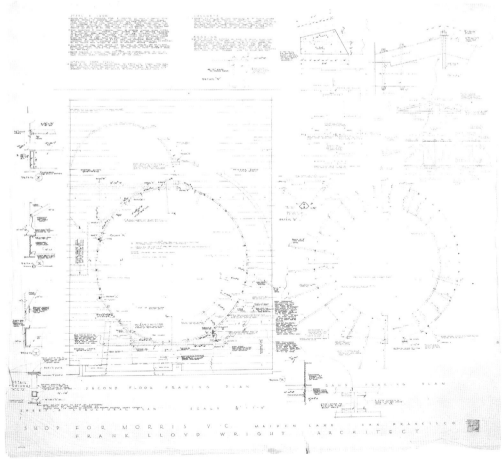

The Idea of Continuity in the Guggenheim's Design and Construction
Designed beginning in 1943 and built from 1956 to 1959, Wright's museum went
through at least six sets of plans, and the final building did not exhibit all the
features he had hoped it would. But he did realize the essential idea of structural
and spatial continuity in the main gallery's "grand ramp," as he called it. This
gallery's spiral of steel-reinforced concrete was among Wright's most radical and
technically challenging schemes, posited in opposition to Manhattan's rectilinear
steel-framed skyscrapers. At the time it was also the boldest American attempt
to create a sculpturally free architecture of reinforced concrete. Wright saw the
Guggenheim's spiral as a cantilever, the form that signified his democratic ideal
for modern architecture. He wrote grandly of steel in tension: "It is just like the
democratic principle that we subscribe to; that is why I have always referred to
this as the architecture of democracy: the freedom of the individual becomes the
motive for society and government."[17] He sought a new type of museum whose
curved interior space would enhance visitors' appreciation of the nonobjective modern paintings inside. Wright disliked the sequence of discrete rooms in
most museums, where rectilinearly framed paintings were subservient to rectilinear interiors, whereas the paintings in the Guggenheim would be set freely in
three-dimensional curvilinear space.[18] The Guggenheim was to be an ultimate
demonstration of organic architecture, with its emphasis on continuity of form
analogous to that in nature. This effect depended on how its geometry related
to its construction process. As Kaufmann Jr. wrote of the museum: "All through
his career Wright had been experimenting also with ways to vary planes enclosing space, not by giving them merely interesting textures or even quasi-structural
convexities and concavities, but by exploring the various ways in which the planes
could express the character, the quality, of the space enclosed or modulated by
them. As always his interest in materials, in expressive forms and treatments, was
rooted in a more profound devotion to the very essence of his architecture, to
space itself."[19]

    In September 1945, just after World War II ended and following nearly two
years of design, Wright exhibited a model of the proposed museum as a monolithic
structure whose main circular gallery (then planned for the site's north side rather
than the south side where it was eventually built) had an unbroken floor surface
that would stretch in a continuous spiral rising about seven stories from a subterra-
nean theater to a shallow glass-domed roof. Like the nonobjective painters whose
work featured varied geometric shapes, Wright had long valued the symbolic power
of pure forms totally unrelated to representation: "Certain geometric forms have
come to symbolize for us and potently to suggest certain human ideas, moods, and

sentiments," he wrote in 1912, "as for instance, the circle, infinity; the triangle, structural unity; the spire, aspiration; the spiral, organic progress; the square, integrity."[20] More than any other form, the spiral signified both spatial and temporal continuity. His phrase "organic progress" also implies both natural growth and human aspiration. He proclaimed of the 1946 design, "For the first time in the history of architecture a true logarithmic spiral has been worked out as a complete plastic building: a building in which there is but one continuous floor surface: not one separate floor slab above another floor slab, but one, single, grand, slow wide ramp, widening as it rises for about seven stories—a purely plastic development of organic structure."[21] Here Wright invoked the mathematically exact logarithmic spiral that expands geometrically in diameter out from its central point of origin. His spiral for the Guggenheim is not, strictly speaking, logarithmic because its diameter increases not geometrically but rather more gradually as it rises. Yet the metaphor of the outwardly expanding spiral was symbolically compelling. As architect Frederick J. Kiesler observed of Wright's 1946 design, this discovery of the spiral's "perpetual renascence…indeed seems to be the secret of the spiral's irresistible hypnotism: continuous rebirth in new planes without losing contact with former ones. An expansion of steps without a halt. Continuous motion from within its own force. Power of birth and re-birth."[22] Like the Automobile Objective, the Guggenheim's spiral demonstrates a principle everywhere evident in nature, from the shape of galaxies to the tendrils of the vine leaf, and an idea recurrent in historic architecture that was susceptible to renewal.

Wright's concept of an inverted ziggurat alludes to the modern structural capacity of cantilevered steel-reinforced concrete to create continuous space unlike that of the ancient inward-stepping temples of solid stone tiers. To experience spatial continuity in the Guggenheim, visitors were to ascend via the elevator to the topmost tier and walk down the ramp to view the art around its periphery. They were to feel the natural condition of their bodies drawn along by the force of gravity, so that their procession would be linear, if not determinate, along the galleries. As the visitor strolls, the ramp circles the interior court around a volume that grows larger toward the bottom, with its diameter increasing from 50 to 64 feet. By contrast, the diameter of the outer circular wall decreases from 125 feet at the top to 95 feet at ground level, so that the outer gallery bays become shallower as one walks down. Making a total of six complete circular turns down to the ground floor, the ramp descends 11 feet with each revolution, with its slopes averaging a 4 percent grade.

As Wright announced the design in 1945, the spiral form's realization would depend on its material continuity. Since his fire-resistant, steel-reinforced concrete Imperial Hotel (1912–23) in Tokyo had survived the Great Kanto earthquake in 1923,

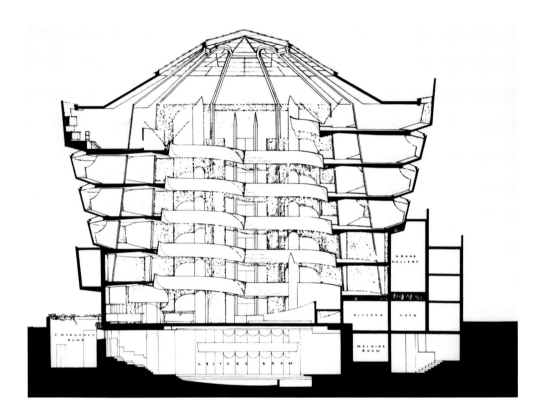

Wright had preferred this system as more permanent and expressive than the steel frame.[23] So he first imagined his museum in concrete, and the final design was crafted in this material:

> Here for the first time architecture appears plastic, one floor flowing into another (more like sculpture) instead of the usual superimposition of strati-fied layers cutting and butting into each other by way of post-and-beam construction....The structural calculations are thus those of the cantilever and continuity rather than the post-and-beam formula. The net result of such construction is a greater repose and an atmosphere of the unbroken wave—no meeting of the eye with angular or abrupt changes of form.[4]

Because of its unusual geometry as a self-supporting structure, the Guggenheim was difficult for the City of New York to evaluate with existing building codes. Yet Wright and a succession of consulting engineers and collaborators, including Jaroslav J. Polivka, Jacob Feld, William Wesley Peters, and Mendel Glickman, rede-signed the project through its long approval process for construction in a modified form.[25] After Wright interviewed a number of possible builders, he selected young George N. Cohen's Euclid Contracting Corporation, which before then had built a number of major projects in reinforced concrete. Having graduated from Cornell University in civil engineering in 1927, Cohen became thoroughly absorbed in the project's innovations, which he described as "one of the most unusual concrete buildings ever constructed."[26] Wright usually selected a consistent unit dimension for the plan of each of his buildings, and in the Guggenheim, all lines, radial points, and axes on the plans were located with respect to an 8-foot-square modular unit dimension. To build the spiral, Cohen and his project manager Charles W. Spero set the central point as the center of the main gallery. Points at each level were measured relative to the central vertical axis marked by a mast with a nail at true center from which the builders "could establish angles and chords for circular construction. Having this center from which to work, [they] easily ran out lines to establish interior and exterior ramp points, parapets and the like."[27]

In Cohen and Spero's modified version of the spiral, the radially oriented concrete web piers (set at 30-degree intervals around the circular ring at each level) are widest at the top, where the ramp's width increases to over 50 feet (fig. 7). At all levels, ramps cantilever in from the webs by 14 feet 6 inches and taper to a minimal depth. Concrete slabs span between the webs. In September 1957, while visiting the site, Wright said: "It is all one thing, all an integral, not part put to part. This is the principle I've always worked toward." Wright "pranced over a bundle of thin, orange-rusty steel rods which two workmen were about to carry away to become reinforcing rods in the concrete. He pointed to them. 'We can do these things now, build as in Nature,' he explained, 'because we can use steel this way now. Just these thin rods. They are the tendons and muscles of the building; the concrete is the fatty tissue and the flesh; the rubberized, waterproof paint is the skin. Reinforced concrete makes this all possible.'"[28] The idea of continuity recurs throughout the building in specially formed concrete elements like planters, fountains, circular columns, arches, and balconies, all of which "blend smoothly into the whole structure as though they truly belong to it, which they do."[29]

To create uniform continuity along the poured-concrete spiral ramp, Wright gave meticulous instructions as to the composition, color, and size of stone aggregate and sand, seeking a mix that would flow evenly around the steel-wire mesh and steel-bar reinforcing. The building required an architectural concrete designed with "a plasticizing admixture" added to a stiff or dry mix, with slump tests (measures of the concrete's stiffness that see how far the mix deforms outward when it empties from a small pail turned upside down) kept at 3 to 4 inches. Moreover, "control of concrete for uniform strength, the inherent shape of the structure, the arrangement of reinforcing, and the planned extent and location of pour sections, all contributed to the elimination of cracking, a quality so essential for architectural concrete."[30] Since the shapes of the component parts were so unusual, "great care had to be exercised in the design and erection of the formwork," which included "varying thickness and types of plywood, prestwood and metal molds" to translate Wright's intent into the material.[31] The image of continuity would have been marred if there had been vertical joints to accommodate thermal expansion along the spiral, so "expansion joints were carefully omitted."[32]

Ultimately, no matter where the eye fell, the concrete's perfect smoothness sustained an image of abstraction consistent with the nonobjective art along its ramp inside. Since the closely spaced ramps made pouring of the outer ramp walls between conventional wood forms impracticable, the exterior curved walls of the "grand ramp" were made of gunite or concrete sprayed onto steel reinforcement against outer plywood formwork. Gunite's potential to create seamless surfaces was essential. All gunite was to "be screeded to a dense, smooth, level surface (floated if necessary)," like plaster, to create curving planar continuity.[33] All pours for the ramp's floor were to merge as seamlessly as possible with areas of gunite for the wall surfaces. Wright specified that "there is to be no 'trim' in this structure. Ceilings and walls meet each other on precise lines of intersection."[34]

Wright's Guggenheim and Mid-Century Architecture

Wright's emphasis on material continuity and organic form in curvilinear reinforced concrete was part of an international architectural dialogue. In this era, Spanish engineer Eduardo Torroja was widely admired as a master of construction in thin-shell concrete vaults with large-span curvatures and cantilevers. Thin-shell concrete was then among the most rapidly developing structural techniques. In July 1949, Wright, speaking at the Carnegie Institute of Technology in Pittsburgh, said that architects might well take notice of the work of Torroja, who "has expressed the principles of organic construction better than any engineer [he knew]."[35] Torroja, who was lecturing at the University of California, Berkeley, as part of a national tour, wished to meet Wright, so their mutual friend Polivka, based in Berkeley, arranged a visit to Wright's home and studio, Taliesin West in Scottsdale, Arizona.[36] In 1951 Polivka began to cotranslate Torroja's major work, published in 1958 as *Philosophy of Structures*. There Torroja quoted Wright and published Wright's and Polivka's 1949 project for the concrete Butterfly Bridge as the southerly crossing of San Francisco Bay to Oakland, the northerly one being the San Francisco–Oakland Bay Bridge, opened in 1936. In July 1951, Wright asked Torroja: "Would like to consult you concerning the Guggenheim Museum. May send you the engineering drawings to check—if you will."[37] Torroja replied: "Of course I shall be delighted to be of help in the way you suggest, with reference to the Guggenheim Museum, or, indeed, on any other matter. It is an honour for me to collaborate with you, and to become acquainted with any of your designs is always a worthwhile lesson."[38]

It is not known if he advised Wright about the Guggenheim, yet Torroja was a leading practitioner of the experimental design in cantilevered concrete that Wright proposed for the museum. In his own work Torroja emphasized "that one should admit the intuition of forms aesthetically perfect to be constructed in materials of greater strength aptitude than the usual ones."[39] He held that if enveloping surface materials did contain thicknesses necessary for stability, then these thicknesses should be made visible. In advocating such expression of structure, he quoted Wright as saying, "It is this quality of depth that alone can give life to architecture."[40] Torroja added that "the designer must be continually reminded of the necessity to make it easy for the observer to sense and to feel these thicknesses.... The designer must never forget that in construction it is not only what the sight encompasses that is seen, but its whole extension in space."[41] In the Guggenheim, Wright's structurally expressive forms created such a fully spatial effect.

As a cantilevered spiral ramp of monumental scale, Wright's Guggenheim had no close analogy in realized works of its era or later, but sculptural exploration of concrete was central to some of the best-known works of the time, such as Eero Saarinen's variation on the thin-shell vault, the Kresge Auditorium (1950–55) at the Massachusetts Institute of Technology, Cambridge; the David S. Ingalls Hockey Rink (1956–58) at Yale University, New Haven, Connecticut; and the Trans World Airlines (TWA) Terminal (1956–62) at Idlewild (later John F. Kennedy) Airport, New York. Saarinen had been in contact with Wright since the early 1930s, when Wright visited his father Eliel Saarinen at Cranbrook Academy of Art in Bloomfield Hills, Michigan.[42] In June 1953 Eero wrote to his wife-to-be, art critic Aline Bernstein Louchheim, about Wright: "I have always had too little appreciation for him. I have recognized certain great contributions he made in his early career—contributions which most of modern architecture is partly based upon—but I have never liked his form."[43] Yet in December 1959, two months after the Guggenheim opened and eight months after Wright died, when many were assessing his historical importance, Saarinen said: "Frank Lloyd Wright's influence comes from another era; his forms do also. It is my prediction that he will influence the world of architecture more through his principles than his outward form. At the same time, one has to remember his great influence early in the century and realize that he will go down in history as one of the great giants of our time, just as Michelangelo did."[44]

Wright kept in touch with Eero and Aline Saarinen during the Guggenheim's construction. He also toured the site in September 1957 with Aline, who published a resulting interview in the *New York Times*, where she had earlier advocated for the museum's construction when, to her, the foundation appeared to delay it. She noted that the museum "has been called structurally the most daring and revolutionary building in New York."[45] Wright appreciated the piece, and Aline soon after wrote to him: "I do want to tell you personally how very beautiful I found the

FIG. 8 Eero Saarinen, TWA Terminal, Idlewild (later John F. Kennedy) Airport, New York, 1956–62

Museum and what a privilege it was to walk through it with you."[46] In May 1958, when the Guggenheim's director, James Johnson Sweeney, proposed to paint the interior "dead-white—thus tearing the inside from the outer walls of the organic building," Wright wrote to Aline for her aid in opposing this step.[47] In September, he told her: "Tell your young architect [Eero] that I hope he will do something someday that I like. This is a friendly hope not easily achieved."[48]

Wright may not have been impressed with Saarinen's work up to that time. Yet Wright's admiring supporter, Kaufmann Jr., was, like most of the architectural world and the public, wholly taken with the TWA Terminal (fig. 8). Saarinen had begun work on the design in February 1956, just as the Guggenheim's construction was about to begin. Like the museum's ramps, the terminal's multiple thin-shell vaults demanded a high level of expertise from its structural engineers and contractors in the design and crafting of the concrete and its wood formwork.[49] Kaufmann praised it in modernist terms like those he used to describe Wright's Guggenheim:

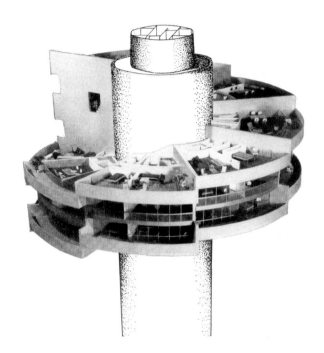

"Eero Saarinen's T.W.A. building at Idlewild is one of the few major works of American architecture in recent years that reaches its full stature *as an interior*. However memorable the outside shape, it is but a carapace for the channels of life within.... Space is defined by a full orchestration of curved forms, unfamiliar, but immediately comprehensible thanks to their bilateral correspondence around an open, unmistakable center. Light permeates this space from every direction and is reflected from the off-white and pale-gray surfaces.... Space, form, and light merge into one effect."[50] When Saarinen began working on the terminal, the Guggenheim was the outstanding project of the moment in the field of sculpturally monumental concrete. His explorations of such spatially expressionistic use of this material recall the museum that his wife praised, and whose progress he, too, undoubtedly followed.

When the Guggenheim opened in October 1959, it had been among the most discussed postwar buildings in the United States and elsewhere. In April 1960, Bruno Zevi, the leading Italian advocate of Wright's work, noted on the first anniversary of Wright's death that "his genius, however, is still alive and working, and will remain so in the coming decades. His New York Museum is now the focus of the international debate on the future of architecture."[51] In New York, the Guggenheim's influence had extended beyond museums. Perhaps the earliest notable design that responded to its example was an unbuilt project of 1949 by I. M. Pei for William Zeckendorf for a helical spiral apartment building twenty-two stories high in which a circular plan with eight wedge-shaped spaces would be supported on eight radiating concrete fins (figs. 9, 10). It aimed to provide flexible subdivision between the wedge-shaped segments to create apartments of different

sizes as tenant demands varied over time. The helix was not a continuous ramp;
rather, each wedge-shaped segment was set 5 feet above the preceding one and
5 feet below the one above along their shared circular curvature. Initially envisioned
for a site overlooking the East River, the building would have a constant diameter
of 102 feet, so it was not an expanding spiral like Wright's outspreading Guggenheim.
Pei's central space was a utility core rather than an atrium, but the outer rings featured living spaces 25 feet deep opening onto balconies that ringed the exterior.
In this aspect, the scheme echoed Wright's widely publicized S. C. Johnson & Son,
Inc. Research Tower (1943–50) in Racine. Base walls and floor slabs would be poured-
in-place concrete, but the vertical structural fins above the ground level would be
precast and prestressed, allowing great economies in prefabrication but not seeking the material continuity central to Wright's organic ideal at the Guggenheim.
Overall, Pei's project addressed utility and efficiency, effectively borrowing the idea
of the helix, which Wright saw in transcendent spiritual terms, for a commercial
project that responded to questions of cost and marketability.[52]

Wright's museum does come to mind as one source for Pei's most prominent
essay in the type, the East Building of the National Gallery of Art in Washington, D.C.
(1968–78, fig. 11). Pei's East Building recalls the Guggenheim's idea of a public hall

where ground- and upper-level galleries surround a geometrically dynamic skylit atrium, but the galleries are not part of the main space as in Wright's building. Pei used interlocked triangles, generated from the site's shape, to plan the primary path of movement into and then turning through the main space before going up or down into its adjuncts. Like the Guggenheim, the East Building offers a spectacular interior as the major attraction, so that the architecture itself provides the first aesthetic experience for visitors. Pei's building recalls the Pantheon-like rotunda at the center of John Russell Pope's adjacent National Gallery of Art (1935–41). But like Wright's Guggenheim, Pei's East Building is modernistic in its non-right-angled geometry, its large spans of architecturally precise concrete, and its truss-framed skylights, although its marble walls relate to Pope's building of Indiana limestone. Yet Wright's transcendent aim of material continuity, and his controlling analogy of architecture as a natural organism, are not central to Pei's approach. As with his helical apartments, in the East Building Pei adapted a concept that recalls the Guggenheim but integrated it with other programmatic, contextual, and technical concerns removed from Wright's.[53]

Among mid-century American architects, perhaps the most creative figure was Louis Kahn (no relation to Albert), whose relationship to Wright was likely important but has not been well documented. Kahn admired Wright's work and made a key visit in 1959 to the Johnson Administration Building. To his students at the University of Pennsylvania, Kahn praised Fallingwater (1934–37), at Mill Run, Pennsylvania, even as he urged them to be analytically critical of this masterpiece. In 1937, Kahn had worked with one of Wright's former assistants, Henry Klumb.[54] Kahn kept a 1954 clipping announcing Wright's design for Beth Sholom Synagogue in Elkins Park, just north of Philadelphia, when Kahn was entering into a relationship with the nearby congregation Adath Jeshurun to design its synagogue, which was, in the end, not built to his plans.[55] Questioning Beth Sholom's symbolic premise as an architectural image of Mount Sinai, the site of the revelation of the Ten Commandments, Kahn reportedly told students that one "can't do…an architecture school representing an Ionic column or a synagogue representing Mt. Sinai."[56] In 1955, Kahn praised Wright's early work as "the most wonderful true architecture Amerique," but, compared to Le Corbusier, "Wright is more arbitrary, personal, experimental and disdainful of tradition."[57] Likening Wright to the composer Richard Wagner, Kahn added, "We need a Bach in Architecture, like Brunelleschi, like Bramante."[58]

Kahn saw Wright's Johnson Research Tower as a compelling work of architecture, but also as an individual statement, in contrast to Kahn's view that a laboratory building should first of all be designed to function well. In 1953 he told students at Yale:

FIG. 12 Louis Kahn, Phillips Exeter Academy Library, Exeter, New Hampshire, 1966–72. View of book-stacks and ceiling beams

Architecture should start a new chain of reactions. It shouldn't just exist for itself; it should throw out sparks to others. That is really the judgment of a piece of art, that power. If the Tower has this power to throw out sparks, to make you want to build one of these things, then I believe it functions. If it doesn't necessarily function as an experimental laboratory, then Wright should be fired by the Johnson Co. The form itself does excite us. If you can define one building as sculpture separated from architecture.[59]

Kahn's first laboratory, the Richards Medical Research Building (1957–61) at the University of Pennsylvania, is a set of brick towers with cantilevered traylike floors. As Vincent Scully and William Jordy note, Wright's corner brick towers for staircases and air-intake and exhaust plenums at the Larkin Company Administration Building (1902–06) in Buffalo were likely one source for towers for such functions at the Richards Building.[60]

Kahn's buildings do not imitate the Guggenheim, yet his Phillips Exeter Academy Library (1966–72) in Exeter, New Hampshire (fig. 12), may bear some of its lessons. Though functionally and structurally distant from the Guggenheim, the library features a low entrance as preface to the large central, open atrium surrounded by multistory, circular, concrete arches that frame views of the five levels of book-stacks on all sides. As one glimpses the art displayed on the Guggenheim's ramps on emerging into the tall main gallery, so too Kahn described his aims at Exeter: "I made the outer depth of the building like a brick doughnut, independent of the books. I made the inner depth of the building like a concrete doughnut, where

FIG. 13 Louis Kahn, Kimbell Art Museum, Fort Worth, Texas, 1966–72. View of lobby. Kimbell Art Museum, Fort Worth, Texas/Art Resource, New York

the books are stored away from the light. The center area is a result of the two contiguous doughnuts; it's just the entrance where the books are visible all around you through the big circular openings. So you feel the building has the invitation of the books."[61] Looking up in the atrium, one sees X-shaped concrete beams whose vertical depth, greater than structurally necessary, modulates the light coming not from a domical skylight but from high clerestory windows all around. Kahn presents the library's treasures in a heroically scaled architectural form, analogous to Wright's presenting his museum's spatial totality as the setting for the displayed art.

While Kahn's aesthetic was unlike Wright's, their comments on the importance of natural light for art are remarkably similar. In June 1958, amid concern that the Guggenheim would not be appropriate for showing paintings, Wright wrote a defense, accompanied by new interior perspectives showing paintings mounted along the ramp's bays (see page 88, fig. 15; page 118, fig. 1; and pages 124–25, figs. 6–8), in which he stressed how the gallery would create "a new unity between beholder, painting and architecture."[62] In the closing section, entitled "LIGHT," he wrote:

> But the charm of any work of art, either of painting, sculpture or architecture is to be seen in normal, naturally changing light. If only the light be sufficient enough to reveal the painting these changes of light are natural to the gamut of painting as to all other objets d'art and thus most interesting to the studious observer…. Instead of light fixed and maintained in two-dimensions, this more natural lighting for the nature of a painting is a designed feature of the new Solomon R. Guggenheim Art Museum.[63]

FIG. 14 Richard Meier, High Museum of Art, Atlanta, 1980–83. View of central atrium

FIG. 15 Richard Meier, High Museum of Art, Atlanta, 1980–83. Perspective of central atrium from West Galleries. Mixed media, 119.4 x 119.4 x 4.8 cm framed. Richard Meier & Partners Architects LLP, New York

By 1960, when Wright's statement was first published, Kahn had built his first museum, the addition to the Yale University Art Gallery (1951–53). His subsequent Kimbell Art Museum (1966–72) in Fort Worth, Texas, while very different from the Guggenheim, is premised on the same conviction about the importance of seeing works of art exhibited in natural light (fig. 13). This priority had been set by the Kimbell's director, Richard F. Brown, who required that

> natural light should play a vital part in illumination.... The visitor must be able to relate to nature momentarily from time to time—to actually see at least a small slice of foliage, sky, sun, water. And the effects of changes in weather, position of the sun, seasons, must penetrate the building and participate in illuminating both art and observer.... We are after a psychological effect through which the museum visitor feels that both he and the art he came to see are still part of the real, rotating, changeable world.[64]

With a broad collection of premodern art and sited in a large park in a region known for strong sunlight, the Kimbell Museum presented a notably different problem than Wright's, yet Kahn's concerns were similar: "I can't define a space really as a space unless I have natural light. And that because the moods which are created by the time of day and seasons of the year are constantly helping you in evoking what a space can be if it has natural light and can't be if it doesn't. And artificial light—be it in a gallery, be it even in an auditorium—loses one a great deal."[65] For the single floor of the Kimbell's galleries, Kahn's celebrated long-span concrete cycloidal vaults, with crowning slots for daylight carefully modulated through perforated aluminum reflectors, can be seen in part as a critique of the Guggenheim. With this solution for the sunlit museum, Kahn created a structurally modern space for viewing art enhanced by natural light, as if he had respected those functional criteria that Wright had been accused of neglecting at the Guggenheim, just as Kahn had criticized the Johnson Research Tower as willful and not functional. In this way, the Guggenheim was perhaps influential as a negative example. As Stanford Anderson wrote of Kahn's work, "It is often the case that those who follow can learn more by questioning the works of the great master than by trying either to emulate or explain them."[66] One can imagine that Kahn took a comparable stance toward Wright's rotunda.

Wright's Guggenheim and Architecture Since 1980

Stimulating younger minds both to emulate and to question it, Wright's Guggenheim inspired other architecturally engaging museums, such as those of Richard Meier, who in 1978 designed the Guggenheim's Aye Simon Reading Room in a space off the rotunda. Meier later recalled of Wright's building:

> Two things stand out in my mind as being influential and enlightening for me as an architect. The first is when the building was under construction and I had a chance to see the site with William Short. They were just installing the dome, and the sight was truly awe inspiring. The other came later, when I was asked to renovate the broom closet into what is now the Aye Simon Reading Room. I remember walking into that space that had only been used for janitorial purposes and realizing that there was nothing in this building that was not inextricably connected. If you look on the plans, you see that Wright had designated this space to be used as an architectural archive. But every detail, no matter how insignificant, was an integral part in making up the whole building.[67]

Meier adapted the idea of the curvilinear ramp in his High Museum of Art (1980–83) in Atlanta. As he himself said, the High Museum was both an homage to and critique of the Guggenheim, and the differences are telling. Sited on the southwest corner of Peachtree Street, the city's main north-south artery, at Sixteenth Street, the High houses a significant collection of mainly American art. The building has four quadrants, one of which is displaced and pivoted outward to form an auditorium, leaving in its place the focal 67-foot-tall skylit atrium with its quarter-circular entrance wall facing southeast (fig. 14). The ramped atrium is framed by a

FIG. 16 Richard Meier, Getty Center for the Arts, Malibu, California, 1984–97. View into main entrance hall, looking south

squared building, unlike Wright's circular freestanding rotunda. Along the inner and outer faces of a curved interior wall parallel to the atrium's quarter-circular glass face are a series of ramps with open metal railings that connect the upper-level galleries. The ramps do not form circular spirals but rather ascend and descend, pendulum-like, back and forth along the curving wall, giving varied glimpses into the galleries (fig. 15). Of Wright's Guggenheim, Meier wrote, "The ramp is made to double as a gallery, inducing a propelling motion that is inappropriate to contemplative viewing. The sloping floor plane, ceilings, and walls not only are uncomfortable but, by suppressing the right-angle datum, make the display of paintings especially difficult. In Atlanta, the separation of circulation and gallery space overcomes these problems while maintaining the virtue of a central space governing the system of movement."[68] What Wright unified (exhibition and movement) in one continuous structure, Meier separated for programmatic propriety in deference to the art, whose galleries were spatially opposite the ramp system across the atrium. Neither a self-contained rotunda nor an exhibition area, the High's atrium is a social area in which moving spectators become actors in this major space, visible from every level of the galleries. In other words, Wright's hall is more a statement about the organic nature of built form, whereas Meier's atrium is more about the sequential experience of the exhibited art in discrete spatial layers, as in the older tradition of floor-by-floor or room-by-room museums that Wright had wanted to supersede.

A comparably domical space as the introductory hall to a museum recurs in Meier's Getty Center for the Arts in Malibu, California (1984–97, fig. 16). Though

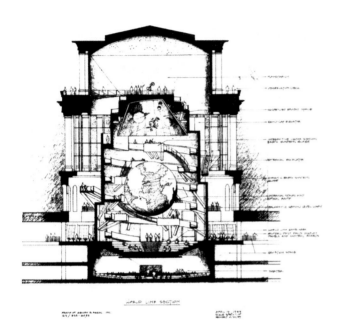

there is no ramp circling the interior, this building also appears to refer to Wright's,
but, like the High, the Getty's entrance hall lacks the Guggenheim's thematic motif
of the concrete cantilevered structure as daring construction. The hall echoes the
Guggenheim as a white-walled, skylit, circular space, but more at the level of visual
image than of built form. As a lobby, the Getty entrance hall, like the High's, does
not present art so much as welcome the public, while Wright conceived his gallery
as the spatial complement to the Guggenheim's particular collection of nonobjective painting. In the benign Southern California climate, Meier's goals differed.
He wanted the Getty to "incorporate the free flow of space, the relationship between
building and garden."[69] This is the effect of the hall, which serves as an open,
transitional space between the center's forecourt and the galleries around the rear
court. As in the High, the structure overhead varies around the central rotunda,
whereas Wright's aim was a seamless continuity. It is as if the visitor to the Getty's
rotunda moves through a memory of the Guggenheim on the way to the art.[70]

Frank Gehry's oeuvre also includes both sympathetic and critical reinterpre-
tations of Wright's Guggenheim, which was completed just at the time when Gehry
began his independent practice.[71] In subsequent museum projects, both built and
unbuilt, Gehry explored the basic idea of the skylit atrium surrounded by cantilevered balconies, staircases, and ramps, as in the Aerospace Museum of California,
Los Angeles (1982–84), and the competition design for the Neues Museum, Berlin
(1994). His closest unbuilt approximation of Wright's rotunda was his World Link
for the Federal Triangle Competition in Washington, D.C. (1989), where a series of
circular spiral ramps and internal stairs through six levels surrounded a "dynamic
earth systems globe"[72] above a tiered amphitheater and below a suspended exhibition space in the ceiling, with the whole hall closed to natural light (fig. 17). The
ramps and stairs are upheld by angled beams projecting from walls, unlike Wright's

FIG. 19 Frank O. Gehry, Guggenheim
Museum Bilbao, Spain, 1991–97.
Three-dimensional digital rendering
of steel frame for southwest gallery.
Gehry Partners, LLP, Los Angeles

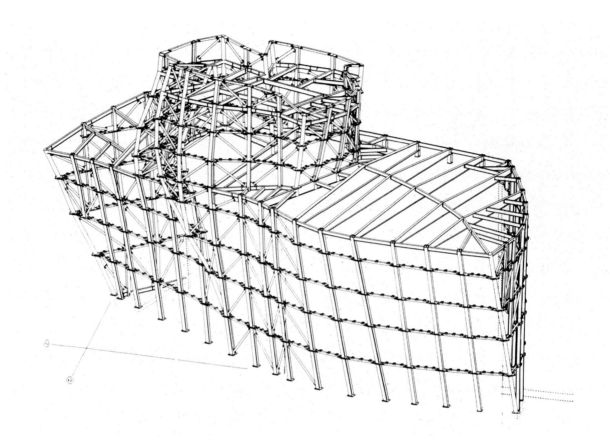

webs and cantilevers.[73] Earlier Gehry had adapted the idea of the interior spiral
in his Vitra Design Museum in Weil am Rhein, Germany (1987–89). Yet, as Francesco
dal Co has observed, this museum is composed of a series of skylit spaces on different
levels that are not internally visible as a unified whole but rather are discontinuous
and even labyrinthine.[74] Varied display rooms and connecting paths are externally
expressed in a collage of volumes roofed in titanium-zinc panels and clad in white
stucco (fig. 18). Thirty years after Wright's Guggenheim, Gehry produced a creatively
critical commentary on his ideals of organic wholeness and unity. For Meier, as
for Gehry, Wright's museum was an admired precedent, yet it functioned for both
of them as a stimulus to innovation in later museum projects that they fashioned
in conscious opposition to some of its principles.

Gehry set a central skylit atrium amid his vocabulary of curvilinear forms at
the Guggenheim Museum Bilbao, Spain (1991–97)—in his words, "an awesome
assignment in the face of Mr. Wright's New York Guggenheim."[75] Comparisons
with Wright's Guggenheim partly shaped its critical reception. As different as
the two buildings are, they both show the importance of structural and material
continuity as a controlling theme in what might be called an organic tradition
in modern architecture. William J. Mitchell has noted that what makes Gehry's
Guggenheim so momentous is its digitally designed construction.[76] At the heart
of the project is its skeletal structure of steel fashioned in tall, broad curving planes
using universal joints to connect units that served less as conventional columns,
beams, and bracing and more as a planar network of finite elements whose

FIG. 20 Frank O. Gehry, Guggenheim
Museum Bilbao, Spain, 1991–97

structural analysis was done by computers (fig. 19).[77] Though different from Wright's
steel-reinforced concrete, Gehry's construction echoes Wright's nonrectilinear
form, rendered at a large scale to achieve the poetry of a natural, animate object.
His use of extremely thin titanium panels as a cladding for his sinuous steel frame
heightens this effect, creating a kind of skin whose sheen and flutter the architect
meant to evoke the image of a living organism, like a fish (fig. 20). Wright might
have appreciated these effects, though he would have likely objected to a reliance on
steel not set in monolithic concrete and to the conceptual and material separation of
the frame and its covering as inconsistent with his aim of organic unity.

 Both Wright's and Gehry's Guggenheims explore what may be the central question of modern architecture: how to create an experientially innovative space with
technically novel construction. This overarching theme of modernism has been
a staple issue for its historiography, from the Crystal Palace of the mid-nineteenth
century through the work of masters like Ludwig Mies van der Rohe, Le Corbusier,
and, of course, Wright himself.

 When, in 1986, Wright's Guggenheim received the American Institute of
Architects' (AIA) Twenty-five Year Award as acknowledgment of its continuing
importance, one critic wrote, "It embodied the sum of all that Wright tried to
do in his lifetime and served as an emblem for most of the architectural issues
dominating the time at which it was designed—that in fact involve us still."[78] What
were those issues of the 1950s that still resonate half a century later? Perhaps the
most important is modern architecture's potential to achieve spatial and structural

FIG. 21 Zaha Hadid, Arts Center
for Frank Lloyd Wright's H. C. Price
Company Tower (unbuilt), Bartlesville,
Oklahoma, 2002. Computer rendering. Zaha Hadid Architects, London

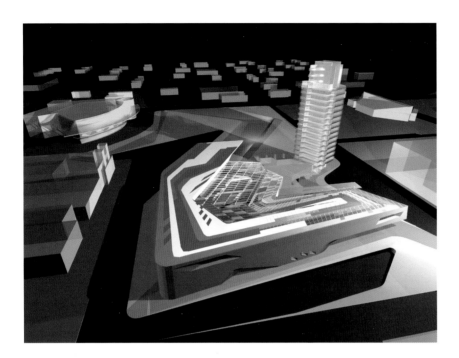

freedom beyond its inherited conventions of orthogonality, from ancient Greek temples to modern steel frames. Spanish architect Santiago Calatrava has described Wright's Guggenheim as "the manifestation of the search for an expression of liberty, an architectural ideal, where the lyric and the poetic transcend space and form."[79] To put it another way, the building's most prophetic quality is the embodiment of its architect's ideal of plasticity. To Wright, this meant abandoning the rectilinear frame as conventional construction, from the log cabin to the apartment towers that framed his museum on Fifth Avenue. As he said to the AIA in 1954:

> The old architecture has gone. You see, the old architecture was a box and the corners of that were the supports.... The box form is now the old thinking and the old thought, and what you hear of as the International Style is, of course, the old box with its face lifted. You make the box walls of glass and you look into the box. Has the thought changed? Never! The same old thought; no real dissidence. That is not modern architecture, that is only contemporary. There is a distinction I wish you'd remember because it's a valid one and it's a genuine basic structural reason for what we call organic architecture.[80]

Apart from works by Meier and Gehry that evoke the original Guggenheim, Wright's organic ideal underlies the work of another leading contemporary architect, Zaha Hadid, who has pursued what she terms "the incomplete project of modernism."[81] Like Gehry's in 2001, Hadid's work was comprehensively exhibited in Wright's museum in 2006. Four years earlier she had designed a project for an arts center whose sinuous curves wrap around the base of Wright's H. C. Price Company Tower (1952–56) in Bartlesville, Oklahoma, expanding on the geometry of his building (fig. 21).[82] Of her work, Hadid wrote: "The expressive-organic language of architecture…is neither arbitrary [n]or idiosyncratic. Rather, it represents the fulfillment of a longstanding dream of architecture to gain the fluidity, pliancy and adaptability of natural systems. The aesthetic proposed here portends the future in as much as this new language of architecture projects the full potential of the new, state-of-the-art, digital design and manufacturing capabilities."[83] In this light, Sullivan's and Wright's organic ideal anticipated a future for architecture that their work first explored and that is just now reaching another level of expressive vitality. This future is being created with digital technologies that enable architects to envision and realize forms more complex than, but partly inspired by, those that Wright pioneered in his unique Guggenheim. Wright's museum remains among the most influential buildings of the twentieth century. As it was being built, it attracted criticism. When Cohen asked Wright about it, the architect told his builder not to worry, as, fifty years hence, the world would proclaim the work's greatness.[84]

Notes

The first two parts of my essay, on the sources, design, and construction of the Guggenheim Museum, build on two foundational studies: William H. Jordy, "The Encompassing Environment of Free-Form Architecture: Frank Lloyd Wright's Guggenheim Museum," in Jordy, *American Buildings and Their Architects*, vol. 5, *The Impact of European Modernism in the Mid-Twentieth Century* (Garden City, N.Y.: Doubleday, 1972; repr., New York: Oxford University Press, 1976), pp. 279–359; and Neil Levine, *The Architecture of Frank Lloyd Wright* (Princeton, N.J.: Princeton University Press, 1996), pp. 298–363, 367–74. I thank one of my Wesleyan University students, Brian R. Colgan, for putting me in touch with Judge Rhoda J. Cohen, daughter of the Guggenheim's builder, George N. Cohen, some of whose reminiscences of her father's work with Wright are noted below.

1   Frank Lloyd Wright, *An Autobiography* (1932), in Bruce Brooks Pfeiffer, ed., *Frank Lloyd Wright: Collected Writings*, vol. 2, *1930–1932* (New York: Rizzoli, 1992), p. 206.

2   Wright, "American Architecture Today" (1931), quoted in Pfeiffer, ed., *Frank Lloyd Wright: Collected Writings*, vol. 3, *1931–1939* (New York: Rizzoli, 1993), p. 55.

3   Albert Kahn, "Sales and Service Buildings, Garages and Assembly Plants," *Architectural Forum* 46, no. 3 (March 1927), pp. 210–11. Kahn noted that "the plan of the Richards-Oakland Service Building, now under construction in Detroit, shows a typical example of the use of ramps."

4   Hugh E. Young and Eugene S. Taylor, *Solving the Traffic Problem* (Chicago, 1926), p. 16.

5   Ibid., p. 20.

6   Gordon Strong to Wright, September 22, 1924, ficheid S010B07, Frank Lloyd Wright Foundation Archives, Scottsdale, Ariz. (hereafter cited as FLW Archives). As Wright likely began active work on the design in late fall 1924, Strong drew his attention to data gathered by the Ramp Buildings Corporation of New York, which covered "practically every detail of garage construction," including the optimal grade for automobile ramps and their minimal necessary widths for straight runs and turns by single cars and two lanes of vehicles, which required more turning space. Strong to Wright, November 14, 1924, FLW Archives, ficheid S010C04. Publications of the Ramp Buildings Corporation included "Building Multi-Floor Garages for Storage Efficiency and Operating Economy" (1925), "The Modern Garage with Particular Reference to d'Humy Motoramps for Interfloor Travel" (1925), "The Modern Multi-Floor Garage" (1929), and "Planning the Modern Parking Facility" (1948). David G. De Long, "Frank Lloyd Wright: Designs for an American Landscape, 1922–1932," in De Long, ed., *Frank Lloyd Wright: Designs for an American Landscape, 1922–1932*, exh. cat. (New York: Harry N. Abrams, 1996), p. 130n187, notes that Strong's specifications for ramps recalled those in Harold F. Blanchard, "Ramp Design in Public Garages," *Architectural Forum* 35, no. 5 (November 1921), pp. 169–75.

7   Shannon Sanders McDonald, *The Parking Garage: Design and Evolution of a Modern Urban Form* (Washington, D.C.: Urban Land Institute, 2007), p. 36, notes that Wright's project "granted the ultimate wish of every parking garage designer: to completely merge the ramp and the parking area, maximizing the number of parking spaces and integrating storage space and traffic flow."

8   Wright to Hilla Rebay, January 26, 1944, in Pfeiffer, ed., *Frank Lloyd Wright: The Guggenheim Correspondence* (Fresno: The Press at California State University; Carbondale and Edwardsville: Southern Illinois University Press, 1986), p. 42, quoted in Levine, *The Architecture of Frank Lloyd Wright*, p. 322.

9   Wright to Strong, October 20, 1925, FLW Archives, ficheid S011A06.

10 Wright to Strong, October 20, 1925, FLW Archives, ficheid S011A07.

11 Wright to Edgar J. Kaufmann Sr., August 2, 1954, FLW Archives, ficheid K114A06.

12 On the unbuilt project "How to Live in the Southwest" and the David Wright House, see "Frank Lloyd Wright: This New Desert House for His Son Is a Magnificent Coil of Concrete Block," *House and Home* 3, no. 6 (June 1953), pp. 99–107. On the Max Hoffmann automobile showroom, see "Frank Lloyd Wright Designs a Small Commercial Installation," *Architectural Forum* 103, no. 1 (July 1955), pp. 132–33.

13 See "The New Curiosity Shop," *Architects' Journal* 110 (November 10, 1949), pp. 512, 516, 639; Edgar J. Kaufmann Jr., "Wright Setting for Decorative Art," *Art News* 48, no. 10 (February 1950), pp. 42–43; "F. LL. W.'s Store," *Architectural Forum* 48, no. 4 (April 1950), pp. 54, 60; Elizabeth B. Mock, "China and Gift Shop for V. C. Morris," *Architectural Forum* 92, no. 2 (February 1950), pp. 79–85; Levine, *Architecture of Frank Lloyd Wright*, pp. 367–74.

14 By 1957 Lillian Morris wrote to assure Wright, "The building will be kept in its entirety and integrity whether continuing as a store or as a museum, for which it is known." Morris to Wright, July 16, 1957, FLW Archives, ficheid M263B05.

15 Wright to Julius Shulman, January 21, 1953, FLW Archives, ficheid S227C05. All of the Plexiglas was manufactured by Rohn and Haas Company of Philadelphia, as described in Burnap Post to Wright, March 16, 1950, FLW Archives, ficheid R070A01.

16 Kaufmann Jr., "Wright Setting for Decorative Art," pp. 42–43.

17 Wright, address to Taliesin Fellowship, published as "A New Sense of Space," in Olgivanna Lloyd Wright, *Frank Lloyd Wright: His Life, His Work, His Words* (New York: Horizon Press, 1966), p. 155.

18 Wright, "The Solomon R. Guggenheim Museum" (1958), quoted in Pfeiffer, ed., *Frank Lloyd Wright: Collected Writings*, vol. 5, *1949–1959* (New York: Rizzoli, 1995), pp. 245–48.

19 Kaufmann Jr., "The Form of Space for Art—Wright's Guggenheim Museum," *Art in America* 46, no. 4 (Winter 1958–59), p. 77.

20 Wright, "The Japanese Print: An Interpretation" (1912), in Pfeiffer, ed., *Frank Lloyd Wright: Collected Writings*, vol. 1, *1894–1930* (New York: Rizzoli, 1992), p. 117. On Wright's heightened interest in varied geometric forms in his decorative art after his first European trip of 1910, see Anthony Alofsin, *Frank Lloyd Wright: The Lost Years, 1910–1922, A Study of Influence* (Chicago: University of Chicago Press, 1993).

21 Wright, "The Modern Gallery" (1946), in Pfeiffer, ed., *Frank Lloyd Wright: Collected Writings*, vol. 4, *1939–1949* (New York: Rizzoli, 1994), p. 281. The spiral "is a curve which, starting from a point of origin, continually diminishes in curvature as it recedes from that point; or, in other words, whose radius of curvature continually increases." D'Arcy W. Thompson, *On Growth and Form*, vol. 2, 2nd ed. (1917; repr., Cambridge: Cambridge University Press, 1942), p. 748. The term "logarithmic spiral" refers to the first mathematical definition by Jacob Bernoulli in 1691. Frederick J. Kiesler, "Notes on the Spiral-Theme in Recent Architecture," *Partisan Review* 13, no. 1 (Winter 1946), p. 98, quoted Bernoulli's idea of the logarithmic spiral where "the length of radii vectors making equal angles with one another are in geometric progression."

22 Kiesler, "Notes on the Spiral-Theme in Recent Architecture," pp. 98–100.

23 Joseph M. Siry, "The Architecture of Earthquake Resistance: Julius Kahn's Truscon Company and Frank Lloyd Wright's Imperial Hotel," *Journal of the Society of Architectural Historians* 67, no. 1 (March 2008), p. 99.

24 Wright, "Frank Lloyd Wright's Masterwork," *Architectural Forum* 96, no. 4 (April 1952), p. 144. In introducing the project in 1946, Wright had similarly said: "The main structure is monolithic throughout, pre-stressed steel in high tension reinforcing high pressure concrete." Wright, "The Modern Gallery," p. 282. While he first designed the Guggenheim in pre-stressed reinforced concrete, estimated quantities and costs of reinforcing steel were so high that he studied a welded-steel system as an alternative that would use less steel.

25 On the initial project developed in models to 1946, Wright was aided by Jaroslav J. Polivka's "interesting structural work and research on models," as noted in "New York Modern Art Gallery Models," *Architect and Engineer* 166 (August 1946), p. 8. Polivka "was working out stresses on a model built to scale of" the museum. *Berkeley (Calif.) Daily Gazette*, May 10, 1949, FLW Archives, ficheid P101E02. In December 1955, when the New York City Board of Standards and Appeals ruled that Wright's design could be built, it was noted that "Jacob Feld, New York City, is consulting engineer. This is the first time that Wright has employed an outside consultant." "Approve Spiral-Ramp Museum," *Engineering News–Record* 155 (December 29, 1955), p. 24. Jordy, *American Buildings and Their Architects*, p. 319, reports that Feld did not continue through to the project's completion and that structural calculations for the Guggenheim were by William Wesley Peters and Mendel Glickman, who was Wright's longtime collaborator from the 1930s until his death. In later years, Wright often worked with local representatives, in this case architects Arthur Cort Holden and William H. Short, the latter an eventual partner of Robert Venturi.

26 George N. Cohen, "Frank Lloyd Wright's Guggenheim Museum," *Concrete Construction* 3 (March 1958), p. 10. Cohen's firm had previously built "the three-mile reinforced-concrete deck of the Tappan Zee Bridge, the Staten Island Ferry Terminal's foundation, the East Harlem General Hospital's foundation, and a section of the Brooklyn-Queens Expressway," as well as parking

garages. "Guggenheim's Euclid," *New Yorker* 33, no. 13 (May 18, 1957), p. 24. See "George Cohen, 66, A Design Expert," *New York Times*, October 6, 1972. Wright chose Cohen after being introduced to him by Wright's former apprentice Edgar Tafel, who had designed the Cohens' house in suburban New York. Rhoda J. Cohen, telephone conversation with author, June, 11, 2008.

27 Charles W. Spero, "Forms Mold Sculptured Concrete," *Construction Methods and Equipment* 40 (April 1958), p. 140.

28 Wright, quoted in Aline B. Saarinen, "Tour with Mr. Wright," *New York Times Magazine*, September 22, 1957, pp. 23, 69.

29 Cohen, "Frank Lloyd Wright's Guggenheim Museum," p. 10. Cohen noted that concrete with lightweight expanded shale aggregate was used throughout the ramps and floors, while a heavier stone concrete was used for the interior walls to assure a smooth finish, in "Guggenheim's Euclid," p. 23. Yet, to insure structural consistency, all concrete was designed for maximum loads of 3,500 pounds per square inch.

30 Cohen, "Frank Lloyd Wright's Guggenheim Museum," p. 10. Jordy, *American Buildings and Their Architects*, p. 323, notes the difference between Wright's approach to smoothly finished concrete surfaces and Le Corbusier's rough textured *bêton brut* of the postwar era. By contrast, Wright specified that all visible slabs "be finished on the exterior by rubbing with Carborundum [a trademark for an abrasive of silicon carbide crystals] stone to remove form marks. Fill and neatly patch any minor honey-combing…. Any large honeycombing or voids shall be sufficient cause to require all parts of the work damaged thereby to be removed and rebuilt." The contractor was to "immediately after removing the forms, remove all joint marks, bellies, projections, loose materials, and cut back all metal form ties, and point up all voids with cement mortar," before rubbing with Carborundum preparatory to receiving the sand-finished paint, also meticulously described. "Specifications for the Museum for the Solomon R. Guggenheim Foundation," Division 4: Concrete Work, pp. 3, 15, FLW Archives.

31 Cohen, "Frank Lloyd Wright's Guggenheim Museum," p. 10.

32 Ibid. Wright also described the original design as "a monolith without joints." Wright to Rebay, July 17, 1945, in Pfeiffer, *Guggenheim Correspondence*, p. 64, quoted in Levine, *Architecture of Frank Lloyd Wright*, p. 328. An analysis of the Guggenheim's structure in 2006–07 revealed vertical crack patterns in the spiral's concrete and other surfaces due partly to the intended lack of thermal expansion joints. See "Face-Lift for an Aging Museum," *New York Times*, April 17, 2007, and "The Restorers' Art of the Invisible," *New York Times*, September 10, 2007.

33 "Specifications, Archeseum for the Solomon R. Guggenheim Foundation Memorial, February 1956," Division 5: Gun-Placed Concrete, p. 2, FLW Archives. Gunite could be a stuccolike insulation, but its

proportions of cement, water, and aggregate could be varied to make a structural material with an ultimate strength like that of poured-in-place concrete. Walls of the spiral gallery above the first floor are structural gunite applied on layers of steel mesh and reinforcing bars over T-frames that are tied into the structure, with 5 inches sprayed against outer plywood formwork from inside the building. On Fifth Avenue, the north-south wall over the entrance between the north monitor and the main south gallery is structural-strength gunite on steel mesh stretched on a steel truss. Yet the inside faces of outer poured-in-place concrete walls (meaning exterior walls enclosing interior heated space) were also insulated with a three-inch coating of nonstructural gunite. Cohen, "Wright's Guggenheim Museum," p. 12. Wright had used structural gunite in his Community Christian Church in Kansas City (1939–42), Mo.; see Siry, "Beth Sholom: Frank Lloyd Wright and Modern Religious Architecture" (manuscript).

34 "Specifications, Archeseum for the Solomon R. Guggenheim Foundation Memorial, February 1956," Division 5: Gun-Placed Concrete, p. 2, FLW Archives.

35 Wright, quoted in "News; People," *Architectural Forum* 91, no. 1 (July 1949), p. 14. Eduardo Torroja published an account of his work as *The Structures of Eduardo Torroja: An Autobiography of Engineering Accomplishment* (New York: F. W. Dodge Corporation, 1958).

36 Early in 1950, awaiting Wright's updated structural design for the Guggenheim, Polivka wrote to Wright: "I just received a letter from Professor Torroja, Madrid, Spain, that he is going to pay a visit to the States and will come also to Berkeley to talk over various matters (about the middle of April). You will remember Torroja is the man [from] the book of whom you admired so much when I took it with me to Taliesin West last April [of 1949], and you were not able to buy. Now I am writing him to bring with him a copy of his book for you. As I wrote you previously, Torroja admires your Butterfly-wing bridge, and would like to meet you when in the States. Please let me know what shall be done in this respect." Polivka to Wright, March 11, 1950, FLW Archives, ficheid P109B06. Polivka to Wright, April 14, 1950, FLW Archives, ficheid P110A05, noted the Taliesin trip.

37 Wright to Torroja, July 16, 1951, FLW Archives, ficheid T049C10. On the bridge design, see Elizabeth B. Mock, *The Architecture of Bridges* (New York: Museum of Modern Art, 1949), pp. 120–21; Wright, *Taliesin Drawings: Recent Architecture of Frank Lloyd Wright, Selected from His Drawings* (New York: Wittenborn, Schulz, 1952), pp. 58–61; and Torroja, *Philosophy of Structures*, ed. Jaroslav J. Polivka and Milos Polivka (Berkeley: University of California Press, 1958), pp. 102–4.

38 Torroja to Wright, July 26, 1951. FLW Archives, ficheid T049D02. Two years later, Wright drafted a cable to Torroja in Madrid: "Would you come immediately for about two weeks. Preliminary consultation several large projects—expenses only guaranteed satisfactory fee if projects realized." FLW Archives, ficheid T055E07.

39 Torroja, *Philosophy of Structures*, p. 272.

40 Ibid., p. 273.

41 Ibid.

42 When Eliel Saarinen died in July 1950, Eero Saarinen notified Wright the next day. Eero Saarinen to Mr. and Mrs. Frank Lloyd Wright, July 3, 1950, FLW Archives, ficheid S188A06.

43 Eero Saarinen praised Wright's ideas about landscape, organic form, the nature of materials, and spatial continuity and freedom. Eero to Aline B. Louchheim (later Saarinen), June 1953, quoted and paraphrased in Eeva-Liisa Pelkonen and Donald Albrecht, eds., *Eero Saarinen: Shaping the Future* (New Haven, Conn.: Yale University Press in association with the Finnish Cultural Institute, New York; Museum of Finnish Architecture, Helsinki; National Building Museum, Washington, D.C.; and Yale University School of Architecture, 2006), p. 334.

44 Eero Saarinen, lecture, Dickinson College, Carlisle, Penn., December 1, 1959, quoted in Pelkonen and Albrecht, *Eero Saarinen*, p. 347.

45 Aline B. Saarinen, "Tour with Mr. Wright," p. 23. On Aline's earlier critique of then-Guggenheim director Rebay's policies and the Guggenheim Foundation's delay in realizing its building, see Levine, *Architecture of Frank Lloyd Wright*, p. 337, citing Louchheim, "Museum in Query," *New York Times*, April 22, 1951.

46 Aline B. Saarinen to Wright, October 2, 1957, FLW Archives, ficheid S272D07.

47 Wright to Aline B. Saarinen, May 24, 1958, FLW Archives, ficheid S282B08.

48 Wright to Aline B. Saarinen, September 23, 1958, FLW Archives, ficheid S286D05. Levine, *Architecture of Frank Lloyd Wright*, p. 481n32, notes that Wright's mid-1950s work, such as the cylindrical forms in revised designs for Monona Terrace in Madison, Wisc., resemble Saarinen's work, such as the Kresge Chapel at MIT.

49 On the formwork, see "Shaping a Two-Acre Sculpture," *Architectural Forum* 113, no. 2 (August 1960), pp. 117–21.

50 Kaufmann Jr., "Inside Eero Saarinen's TWA Building," *Interiors* 121, no. 12 (July 1962), p. 86. Emphasis in original.

51 Bruno Zevi, "L'incessante polemica sul Museo Guggenheim," *L'Architettura* 5 (April 1960), p. 14. Zevi's major works include *Frank Lloyd Wright* (Milan: Il Balcone, 1947), the introduction to which was published as "Frank Lloyd Wright and the Conquest of Space," *Magazine of Art* 43, no. 5 (May 1950), pp. 186–91; and *Towards an Organic Architecture* (London: Faber and Faber, 1950).

52 "Apartment Helix," *Architectural Forum* 92, no. 1 (January 1950), pp. 90–96.

53 Paul Goldberger, "The Guggenheim Effect," *Guggenheim Magazine* 13 (Fall 1999), pp. 45–49, notes Wright's Guggenheim's import for later museums like I. M. Pei's East Building and Edward Larrabee Barnes's Walker Art Center in Minneapolis (1971), with its squared spiral of galleries around a structural core rather than an atrium space.

54 De Long, "The Mind Opens to Realizations," in David B. Brownlee and De Long, *Louis I. Kahn: In the Realm of Architecture*, exh. cat. (Los Angeles: Museum of Contemporary Art; New York: Rizzoli, 1991), p. 27. Carter Wiseman, *Louis I. Kahn: Beyond Time and Style, A Life in Architecture* (New York: W. W. Norton, 2007), p. 86, cites Charles Dagit's account of Kahn's critique and praise for Fallingwater. Vincent Scully notes that Kahn was moved by his visit to the S. C. Johnson & Son, Inc. Administration Building, in fall 1959, in Scully, *Louis I. Kahn* (New York: George Braziller, 1962), pp. 30–31. On Wright and Kahn, see Robert McCarter, *Louis I. Kahn* (London and New York: Phaidon, 2005).

55 Kahn's Beth Sholom clipping was noted in De Long, "The Mind Opens to Realizations," p. 56, cited in Susan G. Solomon, "Secular and Spiritual Humanism: Louis I. Kahn's Work for the Jewish Community in the 1950s and 1960s" (Ph.D. diss., University of Pennsylvania, 1997), p. 117n52. Clippings from the *Sunday Bulletin* of May 23, 1954, and *Time* of May 31, 1954, the same month in which Adath Jeshurun reportedly contacted Kahn for their project, are in 030.II.A, box 60, folder 31 and box 66, folder 6, Louis I. Kahn Collection, Architectural Archives, University of Pennsylvania (hereafter Kahn Collection).

56 Kahn, to a class at the University of Pennsylvania, according to notes taken by Tim Vreeland, in an unmarked file, box 122, Kahn Collection, cited in Sarah Williams Goldhagen, *Louis Kahn's Situated Modernism* (New Haven, Conn.: Yale University Press, 2001), p. 152.

57 Kahn, notebook (K12.22), 1955–ca. 1962, Kahn Collection, quoted in De Long, "The Mind Opens to Realizations," p. 79.

58 Ibid.

59 Kahn, "On the Responsibility of the Architect," *Perspecta 2: The Yale Architectural Journal* (1953), pp. 47–50, reprinted in Alessandra Latour, ed., *Louis I. Kahn; Writings, Lectures, Interviews* (New York: Rizzoli, 1991), p. 53.

60 Scully, "Wright, International Style and Kahn," *Arts Magazine* 36, no. 6 (March 1962), p. 71, and Jordy, *American Buildings and Their Architects*, p. 369. Kahn delivered a key lecture, "Architecture: Silence and Light," in the auditorium of Wright's Guggenheim Museum on December 3, 1968. It was originally published in Arnold Toynbee et al., *On the Future of Art* (New York: Viking Press, 1970), pp. 20–35. The museum sponsored this book's publication.

61 Kahn, quoted in "The Mind of Louis Kahn," *Architectural Forum* 137, no. 1 (July–August 1972), p. 77.

62 Wright, "The Solomon R. Guggenheim Museum" (June 1958), incorporated into *The Solomon R. Guggenheim Museum* (New York: Horizon Press, 1960), reprinted in Pfeiffer, *Frank Lloyd Wright: Collected Writings*, vol. 5, p. 245.

63 Ibid., p. 248.

64 Richard F. Brown, "Pre-Architectural Program," in Kimbell Art Museum, *In Pursuit of Quality: The Kimbell Art Museum* (Fort Worth, Tex.: Kimbell Art Museum, 1987), appendix 2, p. 326. When asked if he would have

gone to Wright for a museum building, Brown said: "No. Wright hardly considered the amenability of what he would design for contemporary art.... Wright would have created another monument in terms of [a] tradition he had already established." "Kahn's Museum: An Interview with Richard F. Brown," *Art in America* 60, no. 5 (September–October 1972), p. 44.

65 Kahn, "Discussion in Kahn's Office," *Perspecta 7: The Yale Architectural Journal* (1961), p. 14, reprinted in Robert Twombly, ed., *Louis Kahn: Essential Texts* (New York: W. W. Norton, 2003), p. 108.

66 Stanford Anderson, "Louis Kahn in the 1960's," in "Louis I. Kahn," special issue, *A & U: Architecture and Urbanism* (Tokyo, 1975), p. 301.

67 Richard Meier, quoted in "The Architecture World Pays Tribute to Frank Lloyd Wright's Guggenheim," *Guggenheim Magazine* 5 (Spring–Summer 1994), p. 5. On the Aye Simon Reading Room, see Kenneth Frampton, *Richard Meier* (Milan: Electa, 2003), pp. 102–3.

68 *Richard Meier Architect, 1964/1984* (New York: Rizzoli, 1984), p. 297. See also *High Museum of Art: The New Building, a Chronicle of Planning, Design, and Construction* (Atlanta: High Museum of Art, 1983), pp. 20–21.

69 Meier, "On the Road Again" (1989), in *Architecture: Shaping the Future—A Symposium and Exhibition with Ricardo Legorreta, Fumihiko Maki, Richard Meier, Richard Rogers* (La Jolla: University of California, San Diego, 1990), p. 33, quoted in Frampton, *Richard Meier*, p. 190.

70 A trace of the spatial experience if not the structure of Wright's ramp occurs in Meier's building for the Getty's Institute of Art History and the Humanities. Entrance to this circular building is on its upper level, with a curving ramp leading down to the library's upper study level around a glass-walled central circular outdoor court. Yet the ramp does not continue through the multiple levels below that partly encircle the court. On both the Getty museum and institute, see Frampton, *Richard Meier*, pp. 192–211.

71 Frank Gehry's first noted work, the Steeves House (1958–59) in Brentwood, California, was partly inspired by Wright's houses. See Francesco dal Co and Kurt W. Forster, *Frank O. Gehry: The Complete Works* (New York: Monacelli Press, 1998), pp. 66–67.

72 Dal Co and Forster, *Frank O. Gehry*, p. 416. The Federal Triangle Competition project featured a crowning suspended exhibition space with images of the planets and stars. As shown in the 1945 model, Wright proposed that atop the Guggenheim there be "an observatory where an adequate astronomical telescope will be installed for general study of the cosmic order." Wright, "Modern Gallery" (1946), in Pfeiffer, *Frank Lloyd Wright: Collected Writings*, vol. 4, p. 283.

73 Dal Co and Forster, *Frank O. Gehry*, p. 416. In his Frederic C. Hamilton Wing of the Denver Art Museum, opened in 2006, Daniel Libeskind also included a staircase that spirals up in angled segments from the entrance through a four-story skylit atrium lobby.

74 Dal Co, "The World Turned Upside Down: The Tortoise Flies and the Hare Threatens the Lion," in ibid., p. 56.

75 Gehry, quoted in "The Architecture World Pays Tribute to Frank Lloyd Wright's Guggenheim," p. 5.

76 William J. Mitchell, "Roll Over Euclid: How Frank Gehry Designs and Builds," J. Fiona Ragheb, ed., *Frank Gehry*, exh. cat. (New York: Solomon R. Guggenheim Museum, 2003), pp. 352–63.

77 Hal Iyengar, Larry Novak, Robert Sinn, and John Zils, "The Guggenheim Museum, Bilbao, Spain," *Structural Engineering International* 6, no. 4 (November 1, 1996), pp. 227–29.

78 Andrea Oppenheimer Dean, "Wright's Guggenheim Museum Receives AIA's 25-Year Award," *Architecture: The AIA Journal* 75, no. 3 (March 1986), p. 16.

79 Santiago Calatrava, quoted in "The Architecture World Pays Tribute to Frank Lloyd Wright's Guggenheim," p. 5.

80 Wright, address to Detroit Chapter, American Institute of Architects, May 27, 1954, quoted in Patrick J. Meehan, ed., *Truth Against the World: Frank Lloyd Wright Speaks for an Organic Architecture* (New York: John Wiley & Sons, 1987), p. 320.

81 Zaha Hadid, quoted in Patrik Schumacher, *Digital Hadid: Landscapes in Motion* (Basel: Birkhäuser, 2004), p. 20.

82 See Kevin Lerner, "Zaha Hadid Develops Design for Museum Adjacent to Wright's Price Tower," *Architectural Record* 191, no. 6 (June 2003), p. 30; Joseph Giovannini, "Hadid in America: A Lightness of Being," *Art in America* 91, no. 11 (November 2003), pp. 58–63; Alexandra and Andreas Papadakis, eds., *Zaha Hadid: Testing the Boundaries* (London: Papadakis Publisher, 2005), pp. 90–94; and *Zaha Hadid: Thirty Years in Architecture*, exh. cat. (New York: Solomon R. Guggenheim Museum, 2006), p. 132. Hadid and Gehry had both previously designed exhibitions for the rotunda. She created the setting for the show of early Soviet avant-garde art *The Great Utopia* (1992); Gehry designed *The Art of the Motorcycle* (1998).

83 Hadid, on her design for the Fine Arts Center, University of Connecticut, quoted in Schumacher, *Digital Hadid*, pp. 66–68. Hadid developed these ideas in such projects as an unrealized design for the Guggenheim Museum, Taichung, Taiwan (2003), an ever-changing event space, in which the large-scale moving architectural elements enable transformations of galleries that would be visible spectacles on the exterior, taking the ideal of plasticity to another level. On this project, see Papadakis and Papadakis, *Zaha Hadid*, pp. 72–81; and *Zaha Hadid: Thirty Years*, pp. 132–33.

84 Rhoda J. Cohen, conversation with author, June 11, 2008. She also noted that Wright had insisted that Cohen's name be inscribed on the Guggenheim's exterior.

FIG. 1 Visitors to the Solomon R. Guggenheim Museum's inaugural exhibition, New York, October 1959

COMPETING VISIONS OF THE MODERN ART MUSEUM AND THE LASTING SIGNIFICANCE OF WRIGHT'S GUGGENHEIM

Neil Levine

TO SAY THAT THE GUGGENHEIM MUSEUM is one of Frank Lloyd Wright's most important, striking, and characteristic buildings would raise few eyebrows. But to say that its influence in the field of museum design "has been phenomenal" and "revolutionary," as the architectural historian Victoria Newhouse wrote in her insightful *Towards a New Museum* (1998), might at first seem at odds with the historical reception of the building as not only seriously flawed in terms of function but also as waging war on the very art it was intended to house—an "art-defying architecture," as Philip Johnson put it.[1] This essay addresses the museum's significance as a museum of modern art and its role in defining that typology.

FIG. 2 Philip L. Goodwin and Edward Durell Stone, Museum of Modern Art, New York, 1938–39. Facade, aerial view. Museum of Modern Art, New York

The art museum as a type, whether for modern or any other kind of art, did not play a role of any importance in the formative development of the modern movement in architecture. From the late 1910s through the 1920s, when modern architecture established itself as a new way of building for the twentieth century, its most recognized landmarks were in other areas. Either because of their association with traditional patronage and programming or their long history of representation by accepted forms of academic monumentality, museums were especially resistant to a modernist approach. That changed, though only gradually and spottily, in the 1930s and early '40s as museums devoted exclusively to modern and contemporary art made their claims for a form of building appropriate to their new needs. All three major "form-givers" of modern architecture—Le Corbusier, Ludwig Mies van der Rohe, and Frank Lloyd Wright—played primary roles in this envisioning process.[2]

Le Corbusier's Expandability

The first museum dedicated solely to modern and contemporary art was New York's Museum of Modern Art (MoMA). Founded in 1929, it occupied rented space until 1939, when it moved into the purpose-built structure designed the year before by Philip L. Goodwin and Edward Durell Stone. The six-story midtown building gave a new face to museum architecture as well as a new plan conception that would have major consequences for the field (fig. 2). Unlike most earlier museum buildings, MoMA was neither a freestanding structure nor a monumental one- or two-story one. Its entrance, directly on street level, was located asymmetrically in relation to the main ground-floor space, while the upper floors of galleries and offices were sheathed in a flat, unimposing metal, glass, and white-marble curtain wall. Most important for the development of the museum type, the gallery floors were treated like commercial loft space, with no permanent hierarchical divisions and merely a column grid to serve as an underlying and neutral structure for a system of movable partitions, which could be realigned at will in response to the needs of a growing collection and program of changing exhibitions. Natural lighting was mostly replaced by artificial lighting, which could be freely adapted to the partition system in use.

Just about one year after the Museum of Modern Art came into existence, Le Corbusier produced his first design for a museum for contemporary art, in response to a call for "the creation in Paris of a museum of living artists" by the art critic and publisher Christian Zervos in his Paris-based avant-garde journal *Cahiers d'art*. Asking "why France, which for half a century has produced or attracted the best painters and the best sculptors in the entire world, does not possess any museum of contemporary art," Zervos declared it "urgent to create a museum of contemporary art [in France] so as to safeguard at least an important part of its current artistic creation."[3]

Although Le Corbusier's response to Zervos's demand gives no direct evidence of his friend and admirer's posture of competitiveness with New York, the design the architect developed by the end of 1930 was deliberately defined by a concern for the limited possibilities for private funding in France, while at the same time exploiting that concern to create a radical solution to the problem posed (fig. 3).[4] First, Le Corbusier rejected building in the city proper and proposed the cheaper idea of "a potato or beet field" in the suburbs. Then, instead of offering the vision of an actual building as such, complete in all its parts, he laid out the "idea" of a modular structural system, a kit of parts composed of "standardized posts, fixed or movable partition-membranes, [and] standardized ceilings" that could be put up singly or in groups, in increments over time as funds became available. The museum was to grow in a spiral around a space 14 meters square that would eventually serve as the central entrance hall of the institution (figs. 3–5).[5]

Le Corbusier had just previously employed the spiral form in his 1928–29 design for a historical World Museum, intended as the centerpiece of the utopian Mundaneum, planned to complement the League of Nations in Geneva (see page 97, fig. 6). But whereas that design, like the earlier Wright project for the Gordon Strong Automobile Objective and Planetarium (1924–25; see page 42,

FIGS. 3–5 Le Corbusier with
Pierre Jeanneret, Museum of Living
Artists (Musée d'Art Contemporain)
(unbuilt), Paris, 1931. Plans, first
through third stages (details). India
ink on vellum, 71 x 102 cm; 71 x 86 cm;
68 x 89 cm (left to right). Fondation
Le Corbusier, Paris

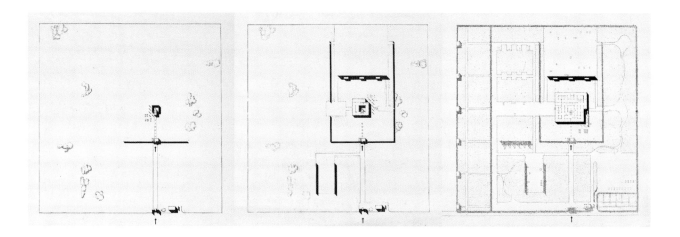

fig. 4) directly referenced the multistory, stepped-back ziggurats of ancient
Mesopotamia, the Museum of Living Artists (Musée d'Art Contemporain)
abstracted and flattened the historicizing image into a planimetric condition.[6]
Rejecting the representational altogether, the spiral now became simply a diagram
for accommodating the continuous expansion of the structure in what the architect
described as "the true form of harmonious and regular growth."[7] Its geometry
had no direct effect on circulation or spatial flow. The exterior walls of the existing
galleries were merely temporary and were to be removed when new units were
added. The expanded space was treated as a freely planned, open, loftlike whole,
divided into display areas by movable partitions similar to the Goodwin and Stone
solution for New York's MoMA.

Because the Museum of Living Artists would be perennially under construction,
the building was justified, in the architect's thinking, in having "no facade." To mask
the fact that it might appear too much like a "construction site," Le Corbusier took
pains to ensure that the visitor would never "see anything but the interior of the
museum."[8] Access to the central hall was by means of a tunnel entered through a
gate in the wall surrounding the structure. The experience of looking at the works
of art would thus take place in a closed environment. The "theoretically perfect
lighting" assured by lay light strips running the length of the galleries would provide, according to the architect, a perfectly glare-free, shadowless luminosity.[9]

Le Corbusier described the overriding concerns in his first modern art museum
design as fundamentally practical. His stated goal was first and foremost to find a
way of building without incurring major expenses at the outset. Once the system was
conceived, he then thought mainly of museological issues, like movable partitions
for flexibility and increased wall space, even and adequate lighting, and provision
for expansion. He maintained that his solution was a "curator's paradise," providing
"life [and] mobility instead of [the] ankylosis and hopeless fixity" characteristic of the
"stone palaces" of the traditional museum.[10]

The 1931 Museum of Living Artists became Le Corbusier's ideal museum-type, to which he returned time and again.[11] The version that gave it the name by which it is best known, the Museum of Unlimited Growth (Musée à Croissance Illimitée), was produced in 1939 for the French-Algerian port city of Philippeville (now Skikda), near Constantine (fig. 6). While the concept remained the same, a number of things differentiate this unbuilt design from its prototype. First, the building is raised on *pilotis* so that the visitor can enter the central "hall of honor," with its ramp leading up to the gallery level, without having first to disappear into a tunnel. While the building could be perceived from the outside as unfinished by virtue of the projecting floor and ceiling beams, the architect this time highlighted the situation by constructing "appendices" extending out from two opposite sides of the enclosed square. Serving as a canopy over the entrance path and a bridge linking the second-floor exhibition space to the surrounding garden, these elements were eventually to be incorporated as part of the transverse orienting spaces meant to overcome the "labyrinthine" aspect of the earlier spiral design.[12]

While refusing to sacrifice the flexibility provided by the free disposition of partitions, the architect sought to give a sense of orientation by reducing the ceiling height in bay-wide spaces cutting across the main flow of the exhibition areas. Set in from the corners and connecting to the appendices, these lower and less evenly lit spaces were to mark stopping points in the visitors' "peregrinations."

FIG. 7 Le Corbusier, National Museum
of Western Art, Tokyo, 1956–59.
View of entrance hall. Fondation
Le Corbusier, Paris

Their "swastika"-like disposition gave a dynamism to what otherwise might have
resulted in a static, classical, cross-axial arrangement.[13] The plan's pinwheeling
movement became the norm for the architect's later variations on the type.

It was not until the 1950s that Le Corbusier got the opportunity to build
his ideal museum, but in its realization he preserved only the basic form of the
earlier concept rather than its principle of expandability. Both the City Museum
in Ahmedabad, India, designed in 1952 and completed in 1958, and the National
Museum of Western Art in Tokyo, designed in 1956 and completed in 1959, eliminated the evidence of the "unfinished" represented in the earlier projects by the
outer spiral turning the corner. In the Tokyo example, Le Corbusier made the most
important alteration to his museum type in the lighting system. First, he enclosed
the entrance hall and used the central column to support a tall, triangular skylight,
transforming what had previously been a negative space into a double-height
gallery for exhibiting sculpture in a highly dramatic fashion (fig. 7). The balconies
projecting into this central atrium from the galleries brought additional light
into those spaces while providing points of orientation for visitors.

The major innovation, however, occurred in the circuit of galleries themselves
(fig. 8). Le Corbusier dropped deep lighting chambers from roof monitors down

FIG. 8 Le Corbusier, National Museum of Western Art, Tokyo, 1956–59. Preliminary section (detail). India ink, pencil, and colored pencil on tracing paper, 75 x 135 cm. Fondation Le Corbusier, Paris

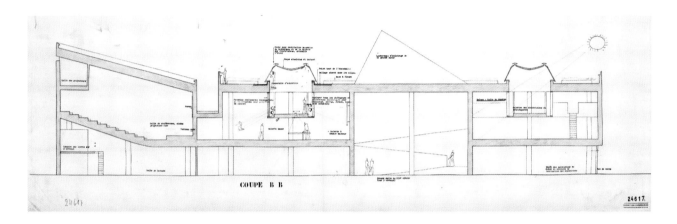

into the exhibition spaces. Supported on the intermediate row of vertical posts, these "electricians' galleries," as he called them, modulated and redirected the natural light from above while at the same time providing space for the manipulation of the artificial-lighting equipment.[14] By these means, the Museum of Unlimited Growth became more a well-regulated machine for viewing works of art than a diagram for future expansion. Depending now mainly on the outer walls paralleling the lighting chambers for hanging space, the museum also lost the earlier flexibility of movable partitions and presented a more directed and rigidly defined path to the museumgoer.

The Corbusian museum, as it finally materialized in Tokyo at the very end of the 1950s, was a blank, square box raised on pilotis, its four linear, skylit galleries joined to one another in a pinwheeling fashion around a central atrium court. Appearing almost entirely closed to the outside world and rejecting any significant form of representational expression, the interior, aside from the dramatic entrance hall, was likewise treated in a functionally direct way derived from the technical priorities of lighting and display. The raw reinforced-concrete structure maintained a material continuity between interior and exterior, the only relief being the precast concrete panels with exposed pebble aggregate.

Mies's Transparency

The Miesian museum was different enough so as nearly to seem the exact opposite of the Corbusian paradigm. Mies first proposed a museum design in 1943 that he realized partially in Houston, Texas, in the 1950s, then fully in Berlin in the following decade. The architect's Museum for a Small City was the response to a commission by *Architectural Forum* in February 1943 for an issue to be published in May devoted to the creation of an ideal American small city for the postwar period. Mies was asked to do a church but chose to do a museum.[15] The site he was given was at the heart of the town center. The sketchy perspective of the pavilion-like

FIG. 9 Ludwig Mies van der Rohe,
Museum for a Small City, 1943. Plan.
Pencil on illustration board, 76.2 x
101.6 cm. Ludwig Mies van der Rohe
Archive, Museum of Modern Art,
New York, Gift of the architect

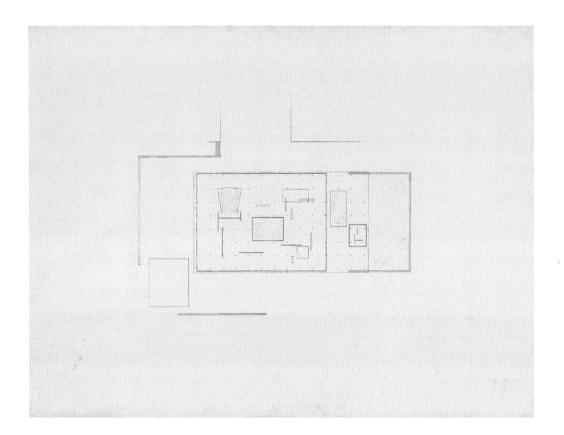

building, however, placed it in an idealized setting against a backdrop of mountains, distinctly more rural than the urban one it was supposed to occupy. The natural setting was critical to Mies's idea for the museum.

The building's design was based on the architect's earlier German Pavilion for the 1929 International Exhibition in Barcelona, where the products of German industry and art were displayed in an atmosphere of extraordinary elegance and refinement. For the museum design, Mies returned to the pavilion's open plan, in which a regular grid of cruciform-shaped columns rises from a podium-like base to support a continuous flat ceiling and roof (fig. 9). The museum, Mies wrote, was "conceived as one large area, allow[ing] for every flexibility in use."[16] Between the floor slab and the roof plate is a sheer glass wall, completely transparent and revealing both the interior of the building and the mountains beyond.

The only visible interruption in the horizontal plane defining the upper limit of the enclosed space is occasioned by the exposed roof trusses from which the auditorium ceiling is hung. The roof plate itself continues, to the left, beyond the glass-enclosed exhibition space to provide cover for a self-contained structure housing administrative offices. With its large rectangular opening to the sky, the indoor-outdoor patio-like area serves as a transition zone between the glass-walled museum and a garden court, further to the left, enclosed only by a low masonry wall. A reflecting pool visible from the interior of the museum fills the upper right-hand corner of the podium.

FIG. 10 Ludwig Mies van der Rohe, Museum for a Small City, 1943. Interior perspective. Cutout photographs and photo reproductions on illustration board, 77.5 x 102.9 cm. Ludwig Mies van der Rohe Archive, Museum of Modern Art, New York, Gift of the architect

The interior space of the glass-enclosed structure is defined by a free play of partitions for the hanging of paintings and bases for the placement of sculpture. These are set at right angles to one another, allowing for a flow of movement and space through and around them. The only curved or angled planes define the walls of the auditorium. The three larger rectangles to the left of that represent, at the bottom of the plan, the print department; in the center, a large skylight; and at the top, "a shallow recessed area," as Mies wrote, "around the edges of which small groups [of visitors] could sit for informal discussions."[17] This would have been one of the earliest conversation pits and surely the first one designed for such a public situation.

Mies represented the interior space of the museum by means of collage. The two that were reproduced in *Architectural Forum* show how works of art would be accommodated and experienced in the building's space. While "small pictures would be exhibited on free-standing walls,"[18] a major question in the architect's mind was how to display modern, mural-sized paintings. The most celebrated recent example of such was the nearly 12-foot-high by 26-foot-wide *Guernica* (1937), Pablo Picasso's depiction of the German Luftwaffe's bombing of the eponymous Basque town during the Spanish Civil War. Mies took it as a test case. Noting that the painting "has been difficult to place in the usual museum gallery," the architect claimed that it could "be shown to greatest advantage" in his Museum for a Small City by virtue of the fact that it would "become an element in space against a changing background."

In one of the collages, *Guernica* is placed in the middle ground, off center, and is framed by figures by Aristide Maillol: *Night* (1902–09), on the right, in front of it and impinging on its lower right-hand corner, and *Monument to Cézanne* (1912–25), well behind it, in the distance on the left (fig. 10). Looking as if reclining by the seashore, the latter appears in front of a photograph of water, most likely the pool on the podium outside. Behind the downcast profile view of *Night* and occluded in large part by the Picasso painting is a photograph of foliage, perhaps an aspect of the surrounding hills Mies said the artworks would be seen against.[19] The difference in size of the photographs, combined with the placement of the artworks in front of them, define a perspectival scene in which *Guernica*, the main actor in the drama, is isolated in space and time, like an event still unfolding and in which we, the spectators, are directly involved.

The expansive, universal space of the Museum for a Small City is revealed to be one in which works of art are granted a unique sense of power and autonomy. Each establishes its own individual presence while at the same time being brought into meaningful dialogue with others and with the spectator. In the other of Mies's collages, a much-enlarged and unframed image of Paul Klee's painting *The Colorful Repast* (1928) hangs in space between a rear view of Maillol's *Torso of a Young Girl* (1930) and, far off to the right, the same sculptor's figure of *Chained Action* (1906), striding toward the painting but looking the other way. The headless (and thus eyeless) torso acts as a repoussoir figure offering the beholder a vantage point from which to assume the act of perception. The figure of *Chained Action*, restrained as if by an unseen force, creates a sense of tension implying that each work of art ultimately demands to be seen on its own and in its own right. In the *Guernica* collage, where Maillol's *Night* serves as the repoussoir figure, the reclining figure of the *Monument to Cézanne*, far in the background and behind the painting, impels us to read the dialogue between the works of art against the background of the external world of nature.

The radical transparency of the museum space to the natural world outside was a bold move on Mies's part that contravened conventional museological wisdom. For Mies, the issue clearly went beyond the problems such openness posed regarding adequate wall space, conservation, lighting, security, etc. He stated that "the first problem is to establish the museum as a center for the enjoyment, not the interment of art" and that "in this project," by means of transparency, "the barrier between the art work and the living community is erased."[20] His purpose thus went well beyond the usual functional and programmatic criteria set by museum professionals. His idea was to rewrite the program of the modern museum in terms of avant-garde modern art, which, since the 1910s, had called for breaking down the barriers between art and everyday life.

In contrast to Le Corbusier's obsession with standardization as the basis for expandability, Mies's initial museum design might at first seem downright elitist

FIG. 11 Ludwig Mies van der Rohe,
Neue Nationalgalerie, Berlin, 1965–68.
Potsdamer Strasse facade

in terms of its material elegance and rarefied spatiality. But while Le Corbusier
talked little, if at all, about the interaction between the museumgoer and the
works of art exhibited and envisioned his ideal museum essentially in self-reflexive,
instrumental terms, Mies (delusionally or not) saw his Museum for a Small City
as a fundamentally populist enterprise. It was, he said, for "the enjoyment, not the
interment of art." Such an intention no doubt explains his provision of the previously mentioned conversation pit, a relatively large area half the size of the print
room and about a third of the size of the auditorium, where "small groups could
sit for informal discussions." It also explains the ultimate rationale he gave for
the expansive, open interior of the museum's design. "The entire building," he
wrote in the final sentence of his text in *Architectural Forum*, "would be available
for larger groups, encouraging a more representative use of the museum than
is customary today, and creating a noble background for the civic and cultural
life of the whole community."[21]

After World War II, when Mies, like Le Corbusier, got the opportunity to build
his ideal museum, the results show a decided turning away from the anti-elitist,
everyday rhetoric of the Museum for a Small City in favor of a neoclassical monumentality—which is to say, the museum as temple of art. Many critics and scholars
have remarked on the general move toward classicism in Mies's work of the 1950s
and '60s, and the museum program, combined with the specific circumstances the
architect faced in his first real commission for one, provided the perfect platform
for such an expression.

When he was commissioned in 1954 to design the Cullinan Hall addition for the Beaux-Arts style Museum of Fine Arts, Houston (completed in 1958), Mies filled in the open space of an existing garden court with a single, clear-span, 30-foot high, nearly 100-foot-square room whose ceiling was hung from transverse plate girders supported on the exterior by steel columns forming part of the curving glass-curtain wall. He also designed a system of flexible display panels to help the museum's director manage the overpowering space. When James Johnson Sweeney took over in Houston in 1961, soon after leaving the Guggenheim, he found that suspending paintings directly from the ceiling on wires was a more satisfactory way of dealing with the problem.[22]

Mies apparently so liked Sweeney's solution that a system of suspended panels was adopted for the exhibition of Piet Mondrian's paintings that inaugurated the Neue Nationalgalerie in Berlin, which the architect designed in 1962–65 and saw to completion in 1968 (fig. 11). Set like a temple on a podium approached by a wide central flight of steps, the nearly 170-foot-square, 26-foot-high main hall intended for temporary exhibitions of modern and contemporary art is completely enclosed by glass and its space entirely clear of internal structural supports. The deep, rigid plate roof is carried aloft by tapered steel columns, two to a side, inset from the corners so as to increase the sense of interior space flowing outward in all directions. The galleries devoted to the permanent collection of nineteenth- and twentieth-century art (along with the museum's administrative offices) were placed in the basement in the podium so that the upper-level, light-filled, universal space for temporary exhibitions would always remain the representational space of the museum-as-temple for the modern cult of art.

Wright's Sociability

Unlike the museum designs of Le Corbusier and Mies, which evolved from ideal conceptions to real solutions, Wright's only museum, the Guggenheim, was from the beginning a response to a real program. That is not to say it was not projected by the architect as an "ideal" solution to the problem of exhibiting a unique collection of twentieth-century abstract paintings called "non-objective" by the museum's director and prime mover, Hilla Rebay. Indeed, it was.[23] But it was never purely speculative or theoretical, and the built building, despite the fact that it took more than sixteen years to materialize, was always the goal in sight. Originally designed between the fall of 1943, shortly after Mies's Museum for a Small City, and the end of 1945, the building was constructed between 1956 and 1959, at precisely the same time as Le Corbusier's Tokyo museum.[24]

Speaking as the client, Rebay made it clear to Wright at the very outset that something out of the ordinary was required. Declaring that "functionalism does not agree with non-objectivity," she implored the architect to make the Guggenheim "a temple of spirit, a monument." The type of paintings to be shown, she added, were not traditional "easel paintings" and therefore had to be "organized into space" in an unprecedented way.[25] The architect rose to the bait and embraced the challenge of creating an appropriately "new unity between beholder, painting, and architecture."[26] Wright's rejection of the frame, as well as the entire notion of the painting as framed object placed against an upright wall, would be comparable to Mies's thinking. Beyond these points, however, the similarity between the Guggenheim and the Museum for a Small City ends.

In addition to reforming the way artworks were displayed and perceived, the Guggenheim Museum was designed to be a monument, and a spectacular one at that. Its light-colored, reinforced-concrete, spiraling form expands outward as it rises to create a dynamic, floating, unstable image that is in stark contrast to its apartment-house neighbors (fig. 12). Its demonstratively modern shape is as far removed from the nearby Metropolitan Museum of Art's Beaux-Arts classicism as it is from the Museum of Modern Art's International Style modernism. Its sculptural exuberance was also clearly a rejection of Corbusian facadelessness and Miesian transparency.

With the Guggenheim, Wright returned to the three-dimensional spiral he first used for the Strong Automobile Objective but adapted it to its new purpose by inverting it and turning it inside out. Widening and opening out as it ascends rather than narrowing and closing in on itself, the shape, in Wright's view, transformed the "pessimistic" pyramidal form into one of "pure optimism."[27] Turned inside out, the spiral became the continuous interior gallery circuit of which the exterior was now the public cast. Its dynamic abstract shape announced the type of art to be encountered within. From a strategic and practical point of view, the inversion had a profound effect on how the interior of the structure was intended to meet the needs of its new program.

First, the gradual widening of the vessel allowed for an ample dome providing natural light to even the lowest levels of the space. Second, the open, full-height atrium court now became a major device of orientation, visible from all parts of the surrounding structure. And third, as is made particularly evident in the cutaway model that gave the public its first glimpse of the building-to-be in September 1945, the circulatory spiral gallery space was conceived in terms of a visitor circuit intended both to provide a series of overviews of the museum and a relaxing descent through it (see page 157, lower right). A hydraulic elevator enclosed in a

FIG. 12 Frank Lloyd Wright, Solomon R. Guggenheim Museum, New York, 1943–59. View from Fifth Avenue and Eighty-eighth Street

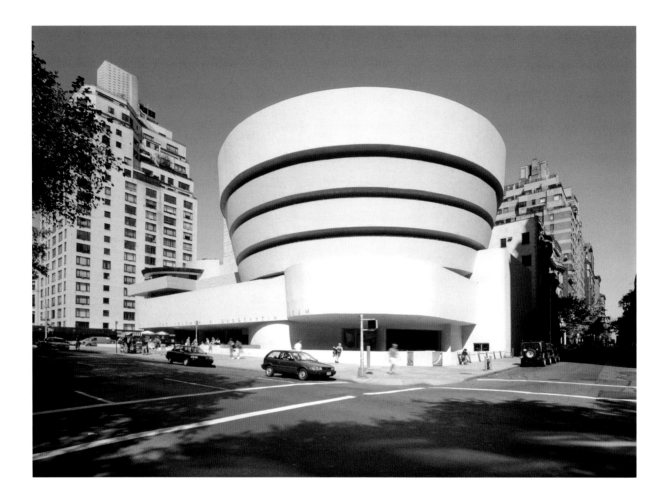

glass tube was to have slowly lifted the visitor up to the roof where a revolving, spherical glass "cosmic observatory" would have served as the starting point for the movement of visitors down the ramp to the generous social spaces, with cafe, restaurant, and bookstore on the lower levels and a cinema-theater in the basement. "After refreshments," as Wright explained, the visitor could easily take the elevator up again "to come back for more museum."[28]

Although many important changes were made to the design between 1945 and 1956—not the least of which was the elimination of the glass elevator tube— the fundamental spatial and circulatory pattern of the museum remained constant in informing the unique museumgoing experience the building affords. Four basic ideas in this spatial concept should be noted. First, the central atrium court is not just a representational entrance hall, as in Le Corbusier's Tokyo museum and earlier classical examples, but functions also as a combined vertical axis and omnipresent orientation node. Second, the circulation system was top down, resulting in a continuous loop always returning to its point of origin. Third, though the circulation path and gallery space are one and the same and inflexible in terms of directionality, the openness to the atrium court provides constant views across the space to works of art both preceding and succeeding one's own position in the circuit (fig. 13). Fourth, and finally, the gallery ramp itself was designed so as to

integrate into a single structural form all requirements of display, with the result
that the building as a whole becomes the expanded frame for the works of art,
each thus "'framed' by its *environment*," as Wright put it.[29]

　　To visualize how the ramp-gallery system was intended to work, it is important to look at a sectional detail of the outside wall (fig. 14). Provision for lighting,
display, and security are all accounted for in an integrated system, in contrast to
Le Corbusier's light chambers, which are inserted into the Tokyo gallery space as
completely independent, monofunctional objects. In Wright's design, the floors,
walls, and ceilings flow into one another and are angled in relation to one another
in three dimensions. The walls are tilted back to allow for paintings to be leaned
against them rather than hung on them. A hollow space at the top of this angled
plane is faced with glass both inside and out to allow natural light to wash the wall.
A mirror within that space, along with fixtures for artificial lighting, supplements
the natural light. Finally, the angled base that joins the gallery-ramp floor to the
wall provides a built-in security device to keep visitors from approaching the paintings too closely.

While many of the features of the original design of the Guggenheim were not carried out for economic, legal, and programmatic reasons, the overriding atrium court and spiraling gallery-ramp concept held sway. The design posed extraordinary demands for those like Sweeney, who, having replaced Rebay in 1952, sought to accommodate the building to an exacting connoisseurly approach to exhibiting works of art—an approach in his case formed over many years of involvement with the Museum of Modern Art. The angled floors and walls eliminate the fixity of horizon line and parallel ground plane. The resulting sense of instability undermines the traditional museum's reliance on the exclusive power of the eye in the act of perception and calls into play, in a most forceful way, the physicality of bodily movement through space and in time: the kinesthetic thus replaces the purely optical.

Once the museum was completed—after Wright's death—Sweeney, for his part, did whatever he could to adapt what he had inherited to his own vision. He masked the natural light coming in through the skylight band, supplemented the now exclusively artificial lighting with fixtures attached to the ceiling, and, most significantly, projected the paintings out from the angled walls on rods that held the canvases suspended in space, upright, and in much closer proximity to the beholder's eye. (Sculpture, which was not part of the original Rebay program, was placed on specially angled bases.) Little did Sweeney realize, however, that the definition of art as a two-dimensional rectangular painting or a three-dimensional sculptural object standing on a base, for which the Guggenheim seemed to pose such great problems, was about to be eroded by completely new, freer conceptions of what constitutes art, which sometimes even dispensed with the physical object itself.

Despite his misgivings about Wright's design from the point of view of a museum professional, Sweeney accurately sensed the unique contribution of the building to the larger question of the modern museumgoing experience. Writing soon after the Guggenheim opened to the public, he very perceptively commented on the building's novel effect on the changing museum audience. The "'great-room' character, which permits the accommodation of 1,200 to 1,500 visitors at once under, as it were, a single ceiling," he stated,

> is the most individual and gratifying feature of this building as an art museum. And its effect on the public is immediately noticeable. There is no sense of cloistered contemplation. There is a sociability in participation evident on all sides among the spectators. The play of light and color from one side of the building to the other and the mobile rhythms of the ramp parapets awaken a liveliness in the visitor....

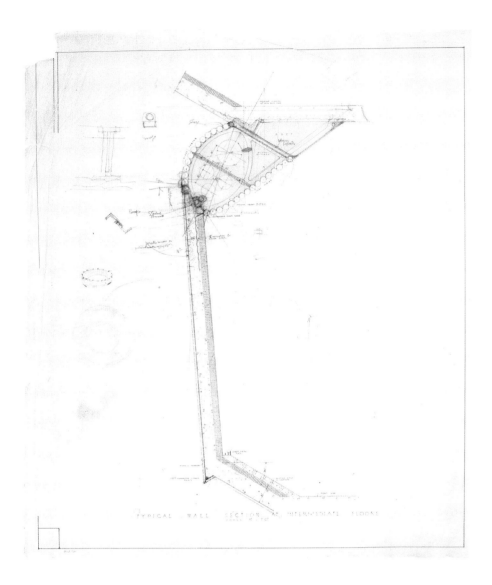

It is in this social aspect that Frank Lloyd Wright's building has struck its most original museum note.[30]

Although he could not foresee the changes in art that were to come, Sweeney understood that the Guggenheim Museum embodied a changing art world. Modern art in particular was becoming popular in ways it had never been before and, as a result, was bringing new audiences to museums such as the Guggenheim—indeed, "streams of visitors," as Sweeney noted, who would not necessarily approach the works on display with a traditional dedication to "cloistered contemplation" and who might even come simply for the architectural experience of the building itself.[31] Wright had earlier written to Sweeney, in one of his futile attempts to win the hostile director over to his side, asking him for his help in preserving "the integrity of a new, more liberal idea of the nature of a public museum." This "new kind of museum," Wright told Harry F. Guggenheim, who took over for his uncle Solomon as chairman of the Guggenheim Foundation in 1950, was meant to be "a more broad and enjoyable one."[32]

FIG. 15 Frank Lloyd Wright, Solomon R. Guggenheim Museum, New York, 1943–59. Interior view ("Reception"), 1958. Graphite and colored pencil on tracing paper, 64 x 102 cm. Frank Lloyd Wright Foundation, Scottsdale, Arizona 4305.092

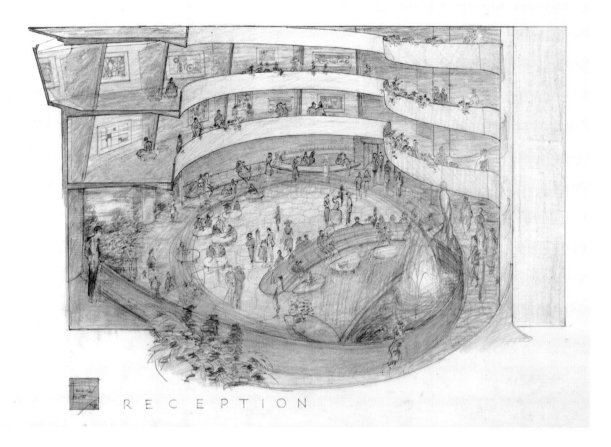

RECEPTION

The architect's drawings of the interior done while decisions were being made whether to follow his or Sweeney's method of installation represent Wright's conception of his "new kind of museum" as one in which populist social interaction and public entertainment have replaced the more elitist types of individual contemplation and private aesthetic experience then associated with the art museum. In the drawing titled "The Masterpiece," a couple and a single individual take in the painting from a distance, sitting casually on low stools (see page 118, fig. 1). In the foreground, there is a standing family group, including two children, one of whom shows no interest whatsoever in the art on the wall and plays with a yo-yo that dangles over the parapet wall. In the adjacent bay, there is another small family group somewhat more intent on the art in front of them. In the perspective titled "Reception," meanwhile, we see the nonobjective paintings on the walls serving primarily as a cultural pretext and backdrop for the otherwise-directed activities of the visitors, who appear mainly to be looking at one another across the skylit court before descending to the gathering place at ground level for conversation and refreshments (fig. 15). The museum seems like a place for fun and socializing rather than a didactic art-historical or aesthetic experience. If Wright was a philistine when it came to modern art, his lack of obeisance to it surely enabled him to project a concept of a modern museum for modern art that would resonate with the expanded role the building type would by the end of the twentieth century be called upon to play—tourist attraction, entertainment center, destination point.

While Wright's Guggenheim was ultimately much more influential on museum design than the models offered by the two other "form-givers" of modern architecture, the evidence would not be fully apparent for some time. Still, neither Le Corbusier's instrumentalized, facadeless Museum of Unlimited Growth nor Mies's transparent, templelike universal space ever had the impact that their architecture in general did. Among the few close adherents to the Corbusian plan-type are I. M. Pei's Everson Museum of Art in Syracuse, New York (1961–69), and the East Building of the National Gallery of Art in Washington, D.C. (1968–78), despite the fact that the latter clearly owes as much to Wright as to Le Corbusier in the dynamic circulation pattern of its main atrium (see page 54, fig. 11). Perhaps the two best-known museums to more or less follow the Miesian paradigm are Louis Kahn's Yale University Art Gallery in New Haven (1951–53) and Renzo Piano and Richard Rogers's Pompidou Center in Paris (1974–78), although in the latter, once again, the Guggenheim made its influence forcefully felt in the "ludic" environment the architects created as a way to encourage the "democratization of art and culture."[33]

Marcel Breuer's Whitney Museum of American Art in New York (1963–66) and Edward Larrabee Barnes's Walker Art Center in Minneapolis (1966–71) clearly reflect, respectively, the outward form and the spatial diagram of the Guggenheim. But it was the intangible quality of the spectacular and experiential novelty of the Guggenheim, as predicted in the East Building and the Pompidou, that would prove to be the lasting contribution of Wright's design to the late-twentieth- and early-twenty-first-century modern art museum. Perhaps not merely coincidentally, the poster child for this development is Frank O. Gehry's Guggenheim Museum Bilbao (1991–97; see page 63, fig. 20). It shares its parent institution's sculptural character, which announces the building as a work of art in its own right and creates a tourist attraction bringing scores of visitors to the museum who might not otherwise come. And, like Wright's Guggenheim, Gehry's exudes a sense of fun and entertainment that allows the difficult and demanding art displayed to appear accessible to a broad audience.

Gehry's Bilbao is hardly alone in revealing how Wright's Guggenheim Museum could serve as a model. Zaha Hadid's Contemporary Arts Center in Cincinnati (1997–2003; see page 64, fig. 21) responded to its then director's stated desire that the building provide challenging, processional "spaces as exhilarating, both physically and psychically, as the Guggenheim rotunda," a "fluid space activated by human presence and motion" where one might "leave behind assumptions and conventions."[34] While making no explicit reference to the geometry of the Guggenheim, Hadid sought to create an "architecture [that] facilitates the experience of art as a collective experience" by offering a series of descending "stair-ramps" that allow visitors to "gently walk down like a promenade" and thereby "see each other moving through the building and interacting with the art."[35]

The continuing significance that Wright's Guggenheim holds for contemporary museum architecture transcends the purely formal; at the same time, the museum derives its power from its unique and inimitable formal expression of a new way of thinking about how modern art might be exhibited and experienced, and what that experience might mean. It is therefore the irony of ironies that Sweeney, the building's major nemesis—a man who no doubt wished that the Wright design had never been built in the first place—understood most clearly and from the beginning that it was in its "social aspect" that Wright's Guggenheim Museum struck its "most original museum note."

Notes

1 Victoria Newhouse, *Towards a New Museum* (New York: Monacelli Press, 1998), pp. 221, 259; and Philip Johnson, "Letter to the Museum Director," *Museum News* 38 (January 1960), p. 25.

2 It should be noted that, despite the lack of modern museums in the 1920s, there were numerous designs for new forms and techniques of installation by artists like El Lissitzky and Piet Mondrian, architects like Frederick J. Kiesler, and museum curators and directors like Alexander Dorner.

3 [Christian Zervos], "Pour la création à Paris d'un musée des artistes vivants," *Cahiers d'art*, 5th yr., no. 7 (1930), pp. 337, 339.

4 Le Corbusier and Pierre Jeanneret, "Pour la création à Paris d'un musée des artistes vivants (II). Réponse et projet d'aménagement et d'organisation," *Cahiers d'art* 6th yr., no. 1 (1931), pp. 5–9. The letter explaining the design and forming the text of the article is signed only by Le Corbusier and dated December 8, 1930.

5 Ibid., pp. 9, 6.

6 One wonders if Karel Teige's stinging critique of the monumentality of the Mundaneum project in the Hungarian journal *Stavba* 7 (1928–29), pp. 145–52, had something to do with Le Corbusier's total revision of the utopian scheme.

7 Le Corbusier and Jeanneret, "Pour la création à Paris d'un musée," pp. 9, 6.

8 Ibid., p. 8.

9 Ibid., pp. 8, 9.

10 Ibid., p. 9.

11 Aside from the examples discussed here, other designs based on the type include the Center for Contemporary Aesthetics project (Project C for the 1937 Exposition Universelle), Paris, 1936; the Museum of Unlimited Growth project, St. Dié, France (part of a civic center in the master plan for the city), 1945–46; the International Art Center (Museum of the Twentieth Century) project, Erlenbach, Germany, 1963; Museum, Chandigarh, India, 1964–68; and the Museum of the Twentieth Century project, Nanterre, France, 1965.

12 Le Corbusier, *Oeuvre complète*, vol. 4, 1938–1946, ed. Willy Boesiger (Zurich: Editions Girsberger, 1946), p. 16.

13 Ibid.

14 Le Corbusier, *Oeuvre complète*, vol. 6, 1952–1957, ed. Boesiger (Zurich: Editions Girsberger, 1957), pp. 171, 173.

15 "New Buildings for 194X," *Architectural Forum* 78 (May 1943), pp. 84–85 (includes project description by Mies). See also my "'The Significance of Facts': Mies's Collages Up Close and Personal," *Assemblage: A Critical Journal of Architecture and Design Culture* 37 (December 1998), pp. 70–101, for an analysis of the project in the light of the architect's other designs of the period and their political implications.

The size of the city was to be 70,000 people. The church design was finally created by the New York–based traditionalist Lorimer Rich.

16 "New Buildings for 194X," p. 84.

17 Ibid.

18 Ibid.

19 Ibid.

20 Ibid.

21 Ibid.

22 Franz Schulze, *Mies van der Rohe: A Critical Biography* (Chicago and London: University of Chicago Press, 1985), pp. 300–01, states that hanging the paintings on suspended panels was Mies's idea. "The Museum of Fine Arts, Houston: An Architectural History, 1924–1986," [Museum of Fine Arts, Houston], *Special*

Bulletin, n.s., 15, nos. 1–2 (April 1992), pp. 101–3, however, offers contradictory and compelling evidence that the idea was originally Sweeney's.

Mies later worked closely with Sweeney on the Brown Wing, an addition to Cullinan Hall, which was designed in 1965–69 and completed, after the architect's death and the director's departure, in 1973.

23 Wright referred to the initial design as an "ideal building" in Wright to Solomon R. Guggenheim, December 31, 1943, in *Frank Lloyd Wright: The Guggenheim Correspondence*, Bruce Brooks Pfeiffer, ed. (Fresno: The Press at California State University; Carbondale and Edwardsville: Southern Illinois University Press, 1986), p. 25.

24 For a full discussion of the history and meaning of the Guggenheim, see my *The Architecture of Frank Lloyd Wright* (Princeton, N.J.: Princeton University Press, 1996), pp. 298–363.

25 Hilla Rebay to Wright, June 1, 1943, in Pfeiffer, *The Guggenheim Correspondence*, p. 4.

26 Wright, "Experiment in the Third-Dimension," *The Solomon R. Guggenheim Museum. Architect: Frank Lloyd Wright* (New York: Solomon R. Guggenheim Foundation, Horizon Press, 1960), p. 19.

27 "Optimistic Ziggurat," *Time* 46, October 1, 1945, p. 74. For a fuller discussion of the symbolic aspects of this inversion, see my *The Architecture of Frank Lloyd Wright*, pp. 347–61.

28 Wright, "Experiment in the Third-Dimension," p. 19. Wright liked to describe the process of ascent and descent as "the generous elevator doing the lifting, the visitor the drifting." Wright, "The Solomon R. Guggenheim Memorial Museum: An Experiment in the Third-Dimension," May 3, 1958, MS. 2401.389V, Frank Lloyd Wright Foundation Archives, Scottsdale, Ariz., (hereafter cited as FLW Archives), p. 3.

29 Wright, "Explanatory: The Curved Walls and Broad Base-Band," undated, FLW Archives, MS. 2401.397, p. 1. Emphasis Wright's.

30 James Johnson Sweeney, "Chambered Nautilus on Fifth Avenue," *Museum News* 38 (January 1960), p. 15.

31 Ibid.

32 Wright to Sweeney, January 9, 1959; and Wright to Harry F. Guggenheim, December 27, 1958, in Pfeiffer, *The Guggenheim Correspondence*, pp. 295, 283.

33 Antoine Picon, "Interview with Renzo Piano and Richard Rogers," *Du Plateau Beaubourg au Centre Georges Pompidou: Renzo Piano and Richard Rogers* (Paris: Centre Georges Pompidou, 1987), pp. 12, 15, 42. The Piano and Rogers design also owed much to Cedric Price's 1961 Fun Palace project.

34 Charles Desmarais, "Contemporary Arts Center, Cincinnati. Lois and Richard Rosenthal Center for Contemporary Art," *Zaha Hadid: Space for Art: Contemporary Arts Center, Cincinnati; Lois and Richard Rosenthal Center for Contemporary Art*, ed. Markus Dochantschi (Baden, Switzerland: Lars Müller, 2004), pp. 30–31.

35 Zaha Hadid, in ibid., p. 54.

FIG. 1 Helmle and Corbett, *Temple of Solomon Reconstruction*, ca. 1923. Front elevation, by Albert Flanagan. Watercolor and black ink on paper, mounted on board with gold border, varnished, 42.5 x 43.8 cm. Avery Architectural and Fine Arts Library, Columbia University, New York

HYBRIDIZED HISTORY: THE GUGGENHEIM MUSEUM, THE ZIGGURAT, AND THE SKYSCRAPER

Luis E. Carranza

Our skyscraper? What is it? The triumph of American engineering but the defeat of our architecture. Nineteenth-century steel frames standing now in the middle of the twentieth hidden by facings of thin stone tied on to the steel framework to make fascinating pictures either imitating feudal towers or making boxes of glass.

—Frank Lloyd Wright, "The Address to the Architects' World Congress—Soviet Russia 1937"[1]

CENTRAL TO THE FORM OF THE SOLOMON R. GUGGENHEIM MUSEUM is both Frank Lloyd Wright's fascination with ancient architecture and his ambivalence toward the modern city and its paradigmatic morphology, the skyscraper. Of the former, Wright's interest lay in its "uncontaminated quality," a characteristic that, as Manfredo Tafuri suggests, provided Wright an escape from the influence of European architecture.[2] For Wright and others, the inherent simplicity of some ancient architectural shapes and ornaments also paralleled modern forms of abstraction. Wright had defined them as "mighty, primitive abstractions of man's nature."[3] These forms and their characteristics were used, in turn, in the early development of the American skyscraper. A prominent example is the transformation and revised understanding of the pyramidal shapes that resulted from the application of setbacks to comply with the 1916 New York zoning ordinance, which required tall buildings to be set back from the street to allow

light and air into the streets. In Mexican architect Francisco Mujica's book *History of the Skyscraper* (1929), ancient pre-Hispanic architecture and traditions were proposed as appropriate for the new setback forms. British architect Alfred Bossom, who was equally interested in these connections, prepared drawings of ancient pre-Hispanic buildings and used their forms in his own work. We also find in this period reconstructions of King Solomon's temple and citadel created under the direction of Harvey Wiley Corbett, one of the instigators of the 1916 ordinance (fig. 3). Hugh Ferriss's renderings of the ordinance show a ziggurat whose form looked remarkably like a contemporary skyscraper emerging from the center of the complex (fig. 2).[4]

Wright's interest in ancient forms stood, then, both in the context of a general interest at the time as well as his own admiration for them.[5] With the Guggenheim Museum, Wright chose and transformed the ancient ziggurat, a form that one begins to see in his work as early as the Gordon Strong Automobile Objective and Planetarium (1924–25) at Sugarloaf Mountain, Maryland, with its pyramidal shape and open exterior circulation. As is well known, in a key design study for the Guggenheim, Wright both semantically and formally noted the relationship between the museum's form and the ancient morphology (fig. 4). In it, we see the words "ziggurat," "zikkurat," and "taruggitz" (fig. 5).[6] The inversion of the word itself reinforces the inversion in the Guggenheim of the ziggurat form characteristic of the Gordon Strong project: in the design of the museum, the base is narrower than its top. Despite making the circulation internal to the building, the central logic of the earlier

FIG. 4 Frank Lloyd Wright, Solomon R. Guggenheim Museum, New York, 1943–59. Broken-out section (conceptual drawing). Graphite and colored pencil on tracing paper, 67 x 77 cm. Frank Lloyd Wright Foundation, Scottsdale, Arizona 4305.014

FIG. 5 Detail of drawing's lower-right corner

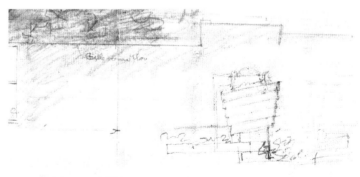

project remains as Wright uses its spiral circulation as the museum's prime organizing system.

That he used the 1924–25 project as a basis for a museum and public building is not surprising. After all, in a letter to Strong, Wright suggests that the "failure" of the design for its particular program and site in Maryland didn't preclude the same form from being used for other purposes, and notes that it is being "contemplated on the other side, in France, only in that case, it is a *museum*."[7] Clearly Wright is refer- ring to Le Corbusier's Mundaneum and World Museum, for which the Swiss architect designed a building whose exterior profile was that of a ziggurat (fig. 6). Additionally, Wright chose to use the Strong project as an important connector for the quadrants of his Living City (1958, fig. 7), a later iteration of his Broadacre City work of the 1930s. In it, the building acts as the community center, with its civic qualities emphasized, as they would be in the Guggenheim.

These modifications not only point to Wright's continual interest in and adap- tations of the ziggurat; they also carry critical implications for form and meaning vis-à-vis modern architecture and the modern city. For Wright, the stepped forms of skyscrapers had become stylistic, lacking a relationship to their purpose, no longer reflecting zoning requirements and the need for light and ventilation in the urban corridors of the modern metropolis. Responding to Boris Iofan's unbuilt Palace of the Soviets (1934–41, fig. 8), for example, Wright criticized its pyramidal setbacks as simply imitating New York architecture: "The Palace suffers likewise from grando- mania of the American type in imitating Skyscraper effects.... [The] perpendicular skyscraping motives are surmounted à la New York setbacks and by a gigantic sculp- ture [of Lenin]."[8]

By inverting the ziggurat-based setback form in the Guggenheim, then, Wright critiques the forms used for skyscraper designs. On the one hand, Wright addresses Strong's criticism of the Automobile Objective and Planetarium, which was that it simply and uncritically adapts the form of the Tower of Babel. Through this inversion, Wright further avoids any formal references to that ancient ziggurat, which has been portrayed as the persistent precedent of the modern skyscraper (quintessentially expressed in Fritz Lang's *Metropolis* [1927]). On the other hand, the new inverted ziggurat form, with its possibility of endless growth upwards—the "optimistic ziggurat," as Wright would call the museum—suggests an attempt to generate an alternative for the modern city based on that very same historical precedent and its transformation.

The resultant form of the museum also becomes a built expression of Wright's recurrent fascination with the prairie. Tafuri suggests that the building's spiral ramp synthetically reproduces the endlessness of the prairie and Broadacre City.[9] In this

FIG. 6 Le Corbusier, Mundaneum and
World Museum (unbuilt), Geneva,
1927–31. Axonometric drawing, 1929.
India ink on vellum, 140 x 110 cm.
Fondation Le Corbusier, Paris

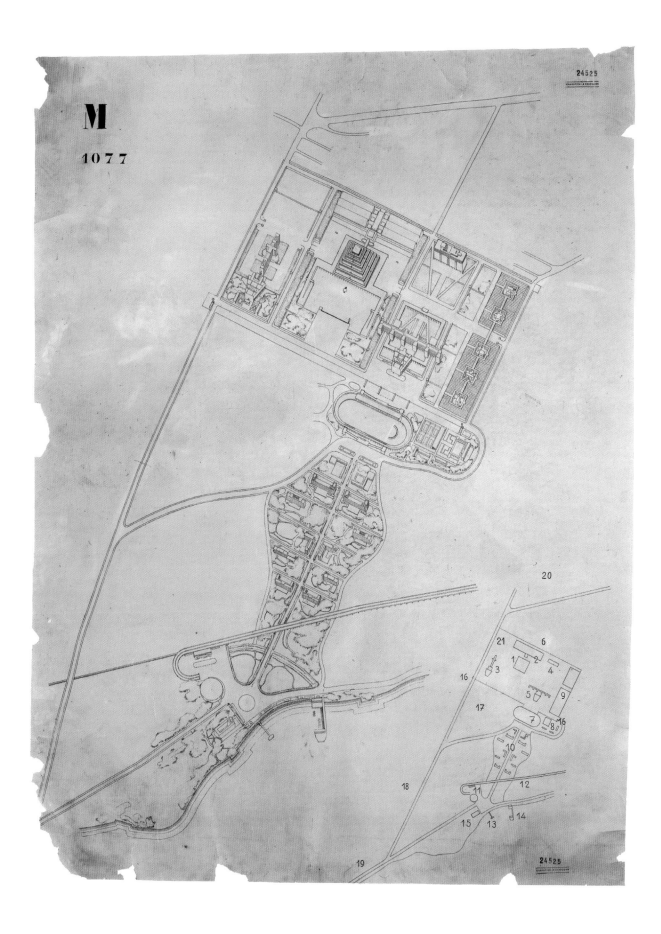

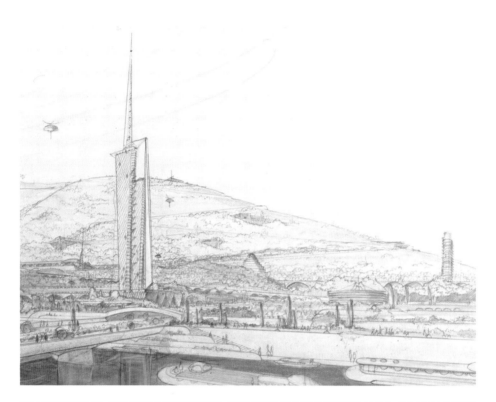

way, the museum's interior space, with its spatial continuity, counters the isolating, repetitive, and boxlike quality of the metropolis and the skyscraper. Additionally, through the inversion of the ziggurat form, Wright makes it impossible to occupy the exterior of the spiral, traditionally the main circulation of that form, and thus expresses his loathing of the modern city by denying any views of the city itself. Wright had done something similar as early as the Larkin Company Administration Building (1902–06) in Buffalo through its use of tall clerestory windows for the workspaces and its centrally focused, multistory atrium. The Guggenheim's atrium and high walls on the outside edge of the ramp also generate an inward orientation. While its exterior form was determined by historical precedent, the interior space became its focus.

Writing in 1922, Adolf Loos noted that the exterior forms of contemporary skyscrapers derived "precisely from monuments that are not habitable, such as the classical model of the tomb for King Mausolos ... and the Gothic church tower."[10] By using the ziggurat as a source, Wright took these fantasized origins and linked the Guggenheim Museum to the contemporary skyscraper. As he had done in the project for Strong and its development for Broadacre City and the Living City, he converted the original uninhabitable precedent into a habitable structure and communal space by carving out the solid mass of the ancient ziggurat. For Wright, the museum, "a 'morgue' no longer," would become instead "a respected, respectful place—a place for quiet comradeship suited for inspection, introspection, and good company concerning both people and things."[11] He created in the Guggenheim Museum a new, hybrid form where tradition and innovation stand in balance.

Notes

1   Frank Lloyd Wright, *An Autobiography* (1932; repr., London: Quartet Books, 1977), p. 573.

2   Manfredo Tafuri, "The New Babylon: The 'Yellow Giants' and the Myth of Americanism," in *The Sphere and the Labyrinth: Avant-gardes and Architecture from Piranesi to the 1970s*, trans. Pellegrino d'Acierno and Robert Connolly (Cambridge, Mass.: The MIT Press, 1987), p. 186.

3   Wright, *A Testament* (New York: Bramhall House, 1957), p. 111.

4   These reconstructions appeared in the article by Eugene Clute, "Dr. Wesley Kelchner's Restoration of King Solomon's Temple and Citadel," *Pencil Points* 6 (November 1925). They were also exhibited at the 41st Architectural League of New York annual exhibition in 1926 along with Alfred Bossom's reconstruction of a Mayan city. See *American Architect* 129, no. 2941 (February 20, 1926).

5   See Luis E. Carranza, "La arquitectura prehispánica en el imaginario moderno," *Arquine* 38 (Winter 2006), pp. 78–91.

6   Wright's use of the German spelling of the word, perhaps, points to a broader interest in early twentieth-century archeological reconstructions of ancient Mesopotamia, characteristic of Walter Andrae.

7   Wright to Gordon Strong, cited in David G. De Long, ed., *Frank Lloyd Wright: Designs for an American Landscape, 1922–1932*, exh. cat. (New York: Harry N. Abrams, 1996), p. 98 (Wright's emphasis).

8   Wright, *An Autobiography*, p. 582.

9   Tafuri, "The Activity of the Masters after World War II," in Tafuri and Francesco Dal Co, *Modern Architecture*, vol. 2, *History of World Architecture* (New York: Electa/Rizzoli, 1976), p. 330.

10 Adolf Loos, "The Chicago Tribune Column" (1923), in *Adolf Loos: Escritos II*, ed. Adolf Opel and Josep Quetglas (Madrid: El Croquis Editorial, 1993), p. 190.

11 Wright, *The Living City* (New York: Horizon Press, 1958), p. 195.

HOLLINGSHEAD COCOON in these 25 beautiful colors

PV010 CREAM	PV080 PALE ROSE	PV145 PALE GREEN
PV020 BUFF	PV090 RUST	PV150 LIGHT GREEN
PV030 TAN	PV100 MAROON	PV160 DARK GREEN
PV040 PEACH	PV130 BROWN	PV170 SKY BLUE
PV050 YELLOW	PV120 MOONMIST BROWN	PV180 BLUE
PV070 ORANGE	PV140 SEA GREEN	PV185 OCEAN BLUE

5

COLOR, FORM, AND MEANING IN THE GUGGENHEIM MUSEUM

Gillermo
Zuaznabar

There is no world without a stage
and no one lives for not-appearing

Seeing of ears invites to speak
Knowing of eyes invites to show

Notice also, silence sounds
Listen to the voice of color

Semblance proves it can be truth
As every form has sense and meaning

—Josef Albers, *Poems and Drawings*[1]

WHAT COLOR DID FRANK LLOYD WRIGHT INTEND for the Solomon R. Guggenheim Museum? Fifty years on, with pictures of the inauguration to guide us, our immediate answer is white. Neither the question nor the reply poses any problems as long as we accept the color we think we see in those photos, and what we see is apparently white.

Yet seeing and saying "white" does pose a problem. The endeavor to recognize and define the color white is treacherous (as the American pioneers might have said) for ideas, architecture, and Wright's vision with regard to color and materials. "White,

FIG. 3 Monitor building under construction, ca. 1958

FIG. 4 Office workers in the Monitor building, ca. 1959

itself the loudest color of all, is the sum of all colors. If activated by strong light it is to color like a corpse," he said.[2] He viewed materials, the true ingredients of living architecture, as already possessing color and saw no point in applying more unless they need to take on color, texture, or form in order to achieve their definition. Concrete, for example, has to be finished, coated, or painted before offering a specific, "concrete" image: "If this material is to have either form, texture or color in itself, each must artificially be given to it, by human imagination" (figs. 3, 4).[3] Unlike most of Wright's projects, the Guggenheim was colored both inside and outside, precisely because it was built in concrete, a material he saw as having an indefinite nature.[4]

I. Interior Painting and Background

Solomon R. Guggenheim died in 1949, and Hilla Rebay left her position as the museum's director in 1952. Thereafter, Wright fought with James Johnson Sweeney, the new director, about how paintings should be exhibited at the still-unbuilt institution. Throughout the design and construction process, both Sweeney and Rebay had harbored doubts about the physical conditions in which the paintings were to be displayed, since Wright's walls were curved and slanted outwards. How were the canvases supposed to be hung on a curved wall? What type of fixtures would be used? How would the paintings be lit? What color paint would best serve the viewing of art?

Separating and differentiating the building from the artwork, Wright proposed a new frame for a new painting, a free ambience for a free painting.[5] In this new setting, the painting is inclined outward. Working in concert with the wall's curvature, this angling separates the wall and the canvas. The curved plane of the architecture and the flat plane of the painting are dissociated, producing a variable and immaterial depth between the work and the architecture. (Unfortunately this approach was for years left unimplemented; Sweeney insisted on hanging paintings on the vertical using projecting metal rods [fig. 5]. His successor, Thomas Messer, reverted to Wright's vision.) The background color fundamentally contributes to this phenomenon. Wright believed that the color of the bays on the ramps should act as a frame of light, "supporting" works meant to be perceived as suspended in the environment. Slightly tilted back to receive light from the skylight, the works were in a position reminiscent of a canvas on an easel. In Wright's words, "No fixation of the old square-set opus can compare with this new one where the opus is floated in the atmosphere of great architecture, Naturally lit!"[6]

The physical separation is also a move away from the display system developed at the Museum of Modern Art (MoMA), New York. In the thirties, MoMA established orthogonally arranged galleries and white walls as a seemingly neutral basis for showing new styles of art. Until then, the great museums—the Louvre, Paris; the Museo del Prado, Madrid; the State Hermitage Museum, Saint Petersburg; the Alte Pinakothek, Munich; the British Museum, London; and the Metropolitan Museum of Art, New York—had not used white. The difference between MoMA's way and the Guggenheim's was, for Wright, the difference between the deathliness of academia and the freedom of organic architecture.

What color did Wright imagine for the framing ambience? Light is never white. When we say "white," we refer by convention to a bright color or the concept of brightness. Therefore, for the Guggenheim, Wright resorted to chromatic scales that emphasize brightness. Over time he proposed many colors and materials, which are elements we should read as having equal rank: red marble; gold frame; aluminum; pale gold; no wooden frames for paintings; brass letters; warm ivory color on the exterior, light ivory on the interior;[7] roof-red gravel; gold carpet; and metallic gold. The list is senseless, even contradictory, if the materials are taken literally; however, each bears brightness. Red marble, gold frames, aluminum, brass, pale gold, and light or warm ivory carry light. Aluminum reflects it, mainly in bluish-grays. Gold and red are base colors that represent light itself.

II. Inside and Outside

Scientists maintain that, "as far as the earliest period of development can be followed, the sense of color is at first limited to the capacity to sense red."[8] At the origins of human perception, red and light are elements of equal value. And so they were in Wright's eyes when he designed the Guggenheim: "*Red is the color of Creation. It courses in even the veins of all of plant life: Green is the camouflage of red....Reds are as varied as the blue of sea and sky except that the sea is...a reflector of the rays of the Sun which, again, is red. The Sun is the soul of Red.*"[9]

The discussions on color became more intense when Wright had to define the building for his clients. In drawings made from 1944 to 1945, he envisioned a red marble exterior to give it a "honed" finish.[10] The marble was to be earth colored and striated so that it could be sandblasted or polished to hide the joints and ensure a monolithic appearance for the building.[11] The chosen color and character root the building in soil, earth, and stone. By 1952, he proposed finishing the spiral in shining white concrete and polished white-marble gravel, absorbing and reflecting the light in a look similar to alabaster, a treatment not unlike the one today in the paving of the museum. The compromise shows that what was sought with the white marble coating planned in 1952 was not a white building but a monolithic marble object capable of absorbing and reflecting light. The sun's reflections on the white marble would produce golden, ocher, and red sheens and tones. In the drawings from 1951 to 1952, the spiral is seen as white tinged with ocher and reddish tones, rather darker than—but still very close to—the architect's hallmark red. Finally, in 1958, when the marble coating was abandoned for paint, almost certainly for budgetary reasons, the color was changed to warm ivory on the exterior and light ivory on the interior. Wright strongly disapproved of the building being painted white:

> The building we have built was formed on the idea that an architectural environ-ment making the picture an individual thing in itself—emphasized like a signet in a ring (not placed as though painted on a flat wall)—would give relief and emphasis to the painting [to] an extent never yet known. Take that away and you have murdered the soul of a masterpiece. Whitewash would literally destroy the nobility of its conception. This I know you do not intend.
>
> The true relationship between inside and outside of a sculptural-building must be preserved. Great sculpture work seen half natural and half painted white invites derision. White—a devastating color under daylight—is the sum of all colors. Even used as a frame of reference for paintings (to say nothing of sculp-ture), it is a makeshift or a menace.
>
> Here by intention (and bequest) we have a great work of sculptural architec-ture calculated to set up a picture in the atmosphere of a harmonious series of daylighted-forms. This setting is new and may stimulate a new impulse in the art of painting whereas the old cliché of a white shroud for the painting seen by gaslight may in future well be called not only the "grave of modern art" but now the destruction of a great building.[12]

On July 24, 1958, William H. Short, the architect supervising construction, wrote to the Euclid Contracting Corporation, the firm in charge of painting the building, with the type of paint and the exact reference approved by Wright for the exterior: "The approved color for the cocoon vinyl plastic for the exterior of the Guggenheim Museum is color No. PV020-Buff, as shown on your Canadian Color Chart."[13] According to a July 28 letter, however, the sample applied to the building did not correspond to the cited number.[14] There is no written record of the paint's reference number. We have samples of the paint taken in 2007 as well as the photographs from the time, which appear to confirm an earlier description by Euclid, "various shades of ivory" (fig. 6). The exterior of the Guggenheim was finally painted in an ivory color of ocher tones, considerably darker than PV020-Buff.

FIG. 6 Color stratigraphy of paint layers removed during the museum's 2005–08 restoration

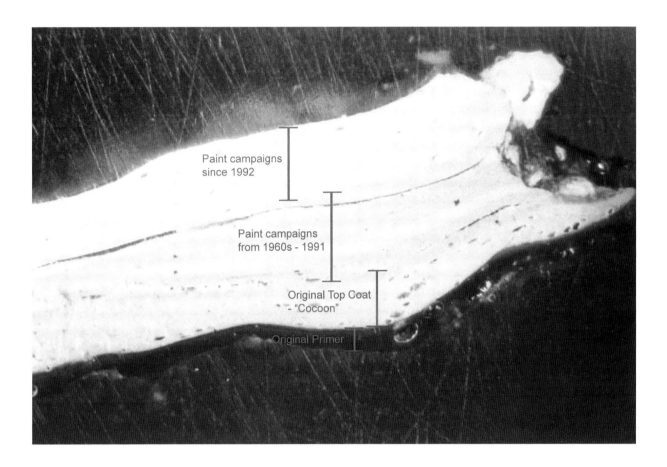

III. Form and Color

In a work of art, the expressive characters of form and color ought to be as though synchronized; in other words, the formal and chromatic effects should strengthen each other reciprocally.
—Johannes Itten, *Arte del colore*[15]

Form is also color. Without color there is no form. Form and color are one.
—Donald Judd, *Some Aspects of Color in General and Red and Black in Particular*[16]

In form, memory, and color, the Guggenheim alludes to a number of other projects, such as the Gordon Strong Automobile Objective and Planetarium (1924–25) at Sugarloaf Mountain, Maryland; the S. C. Johnson & Son, Inc. Administration Building (1936–39), Racine, Wisconsin; the V. C. Morris Gift Shop (1948–49), San Francisco; and the Max Hoffman Automobile Showroom (1954–55), New York.[17] All four turn their backs on the exterior in favor of the interior, whether through a spiral pattern (Strong and Hoffman); a baked clay screen (Johnson and Morris); or reflections, gleams, and glitters (Hoffman). As part of this strategy, the spiral, the color red, and a shimmery quality occur in all of them. As complementary groupings and in a full encounter with the desert landscape, red, glitters, and reflections are also found at Wright's temporary staff headquarters, Ocotillo Desert Camp (1928–29), Chandler, Arizona, and his home Taliesin West (1937–38), Scottsdale, Arizona. The outposts take refuge from the desert, while the commercial buildings hold "deserts" in their interiors. In Wright's work, gleams, glitters, and spirals might be seen as a translation of the landscape.[18]

To appreciate the color of the Guggenheim in conjunction with its form, we should neither search for it in the remains of its paint, now burnt by the sun, soiled by pollution, and concealed by human action, nor allow ourselves to be deceived by eyes and a mind that think they see white when perceiving brightness. To understand its color, we must visit the museum during its inauguration in 1959 with someone who has felt the form, light, and impression of architecture not visually but corporally. The body has a greater memory than the mind, and in this way, the Guggenheim can be understood in its correct correspondence between color and form. One exceptional visitor, a blind man who knew nothing of what has been said so far, clarifies:

[Jorge Luis] Borges: I think Frank Lloyd Wright was an admirable architect, a great inventor of spaces…. Many years ago now, I was at a museum in New York, which had recently been inaugurated.
Question: The Guggenheim Museum?
B: Yes, that's it. The architect was Frank Lloyd Wright, wasn't it?
Q: Indeed it was. And what do you remember of your visit?
B: By then I was nearly blind, but a blind man also sees.
Q: …!
B: Yes, I remember when I was in the desert. I felt the enormity of the vast stretches of sand, I felt the heat, the sun over my head, the dry air, the wind circulating without obstacles, the absence of sounds, all that…and I felt—how shall I put it?—a horizontal vertigo.
Q: And at the Guggenheim Museum?
B: I remember its circularity. I couldn't distinguish the objects, you see, but I could make out the light, and I noticed we were not moving in a straight line. With my mother, we were going down in circles, because the light was always to the right. Light was entering through a glass dome, they told me, and I perceived it over my head, as if we weren't inside a building but in the open air, and I wondered in anguish if it would all end abruptly in the void and I would fall over the edge.[19]

The color of the Guggenheim, in good correspondence with its form and memory, is and must be the color of the American desert it incarnates, Wright's landscape. Red, pink, gold, pale gold, ivory, warm ivory, light ivory, creamy soft gray. Never white.

Translated by Philip Sutton

Notes

1   Josef Albers, *Poems and Drawings* (New Haven, Conn.: Readymade Press, 1958), n.p.

2   Frank Lloyd Wright, "Concerning White White-Wash," June 1958, Solomon R. Guggenheim Museum Archives, New York (hereafter cited as SRGM Archives).

3   Wright, "In the Cause of Architecture VII: The Meaning of Materials—Concrete," in *Frank Lloyd Wright: Collected Writings*, vol. 1, *1894–1930*, ed. Bruce Brooks Pfeiffer (New York: Rizzoli, 1992), pp. 300–01.

4   According to Wright, his Unity Temple, Oak Park, Ill. (1905–08), was the first building to be designed by an architect in concrete: "Concrete was just then coming into use. Unity Temple at Oak Park became the first concrete monolith in the world." Wright, *An Autobiography* (1932), in *Frank Lloyd Wright: Collected Writings*, vol. 2, *1930–1932*, ed. Pfeiffer (New York: Rizzoli, 1992), p. 209. At Unity, unlike the Guggenheim, the exterior was finished with gravel from the concrete itself. Wright's description also explains the need for the finish to be of concrete: "What texture this concrete mass…? Why not its own gravel? How to bring the gravel clean on the surface?…Realism, the subgeometric, is however the abuse of this fine thing. Keep the straight lines clean and significant, the flat plane expressive and clean cut. But let texture of material come into them." Ibid., p. 215.

5   Wright's design followed the wishes of Solomon R. Guggenheim, who "[did] not want to leave [his] city just another museum." Wright "could see good reason for [Guggenheim's] point of view and eventually presented him with the controversial scheme of arrangement for showing free-painting, freely, in a free atmosphere." Wright, "Concerning the Solomon R. Guggenheim Museum," December 14, 1956, SRGM Archives.

6   Wright to Harry F. Guggenheim, May 10, 1958, SRGM Archives (Wright's emphasis).

7   Olgivanna Lloyd Wright, not her husband, notes the possibility of using "interior light ivory" in "Mrs. Frank Lloyd Wright Reports: N.Y. Controversy Rages on Interior Details of Museum," *Capital Times* (Madison, Wisc.), May 13, 1958.

8   Hugo Magnus, *Historia de la evolución del sentido de los colores*, ed. Francisco Álvarez (Madrid: Fortanet, 1884), p. 81. Quotation translated by Philip Sutton.

9   Wright to Hilla Rebay, February 6, 1944, SRGM Archives (Wright's emphasis).

10 Wright to Rebay, July 17, 1945, SRGM Archives.

11 Ibid.

12 Wright to Harry F. Guggenheim, March 17, 1958, SRGM Archives.

13 Office of Frank Lloyd Wright to Euclid Contracting Corp., July 24, 1958, SRGM Archives.

14 Office of Frank Lloyd Wright to Euclid Contracting Corp., July 28, 1958, SRGM Archives.

15 Johannes Itten, *Arte del colore* (1961; repr., Milan: Il Saggiatore, 1965), p. 120.

16 Donald Judd, *Some Aspects of Color in General and Red and Black in Particular* (Sassenheim, The Netherlands: Sikkens Foundation; Amsterdam: Stedelijk Museum, 1993), p. 21.

17 Jack Quinan also lists the Pittsburgh Point Park Civic Center (1946–47), Self Service Garage for Pittsburgh (1949), and the David Wright House (1950) in "Frank Lloyd Wright's Guggenheim Museum: A Historian's Report," *Journal of the Society of Architectural Historians* 52, no. 4 (December 1993), pp. 466–82.

18 Between ten and thirty years later, two artists who continued the tradition of the "aesthetic of the American desert" also read the landscape in terms of red and ocher spirals. In 1970, Robert Smithson built *Spiral Jetty* in red, black, and—today—white. In 1974, Judd designed his house in the El Rosario desert mountains in Baja California with a circular arrangement in adobe. In 1992, before his death, he was working on another great project in adobe at Marfa for the northern side of the Rio Grande border, also using an orthogonal spiral.

19 Cristina Grau, *Borges y la arquitectura* (Madrid: Cátedra, 1995), p. 82. Quotation translated by Philip Sutton.

FIG. 1 Study for the letter "N"
for Solomon R. Guggenheim Museum
signage, August 1959. Solomon R.
Guggenheim Museum Archives,
New York

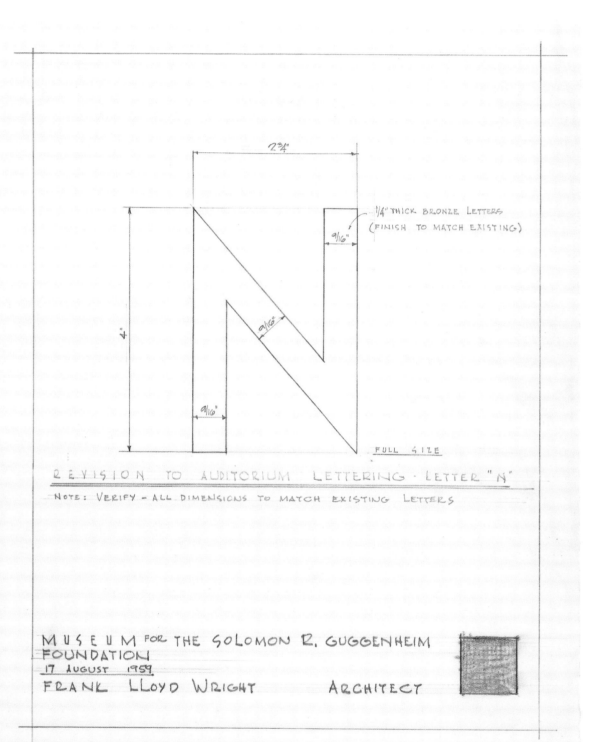

FURNITURE, PATTERNS, AND PERFECTION: THE SOLOMON R. GUGGENHEIM MUSEUM'S INTERIORS

Pat Kirkham and
Scott W. Perkins

Entering into the spirit of this interior, you will discover the best possible atmosphere in which to show fine paintings or listen to music. It is this atmosphere that seems to me the most lacking in our art galleries, museums, music halls, and theaters.

—Frank Lloyd Wright[1]

FRANK LLOYD WRIGHT SAW FURNITURE AND FURNISHINGS as integral parts of a unified interior that was, in turn, in unity with the building itself. He referred to this approach as "the integrity of each in all and all in each"[2] and applied this concept of *Gesamtkunstwerk* (total work of art) to domestic and nondomestic interiors alike for more than fifty years. Wright considered internal disorder in architecture and design akin to a disease and used modular schemes, usually based on geometric forms, to ensure an underlying rationality and order.[3] At the Guggenheim, circles predominate—encased in a grid—from the overall footprint of the building and the metal circles set into the sidewalk pavement to the bronze medallion in the vestibule and the circular tables and stools designed for the interior.

Vestibule

The entrance introduces the interior's visual vocabulary: circles, arcs, and a seedpod shape formed by two intersecting circles, known as a *mandorla* (Latin for "almond") or

FIG. 2 Lobby floor medallion. Cast bronze, diam: 136 cm

FIG. 3 Working drawing for lobby floor medallion. Graphite on tracing paper, 81 x 86 cm. Frank Lloyd Wright Foundation, Scottsdale, Arizona 4305.662

vesica piscis (fish bladder), a contour Wright often used when creating designs based on circles.[4] A circular cast-bronze floor medallion (figs. 2, 3), dedicated to the two driving forces behind this project, Wright and Solomon R. Guggenheim, greets visitors visually and through words. The imagery of the medallion speaks to the ambition of the enterprise: a phoenixlike creature rises over the earth's horizon with the sun in its beak. The motto "Let Each Man Exercise the Art He Knows," from Aristophanes, was the choice of Harry F. Guggenheim, who took the reins of the foundation after his uncle Solomon's death in 1949. Wright's widow Olgivanna (the architect died before the building was completed) had wanted "Respect the Masterpiece—It Is True Reverence to Man," a quotation from one of her husband's lectures.[5]

Main Gallery

When one steps into the main interior, the impact of the huge, sculptural spiraling ramp is so powerful that other elements of Wright's design are less apparent than in many of his other interiors. But they are there, quietly adding to the complexity and beauty of the whole. Created from the perspective of the first gallery level, Wright's presentation drawing of the ground floor "reception" area in the main rotunda depicts circles in a grid pattern on the terrazzo floors and shows the locations of oak furnishings, fixtures, and plants both potted and hanging. Wright envisaged a long, centrally positioned curved banquette upholstered in blue with similar banquettes around the

FIG. 4 View from above into main gallery (fountain covered, at right)

perimeter, as well as small circular occasional tables and stools that he called hassocks; a built-in information desk; and a spouting fountain with integral bench. Today, the fountain, information desk (and similar membership desk), and floor pattern remain, but the hassock seating has been relegated to the upper levels (fig. 4). The only resting places for visitors are those designed into the interior architecture, namely a curved low wall and the bench in the fountain's base.

Wright embedded the marble chips of the gallery's ivory terrazzo floor in light gray concrete. The museum's director, James Johnson Sweeney, preferred white concrete, but Wright thought it "too bright and disquieting."[6] The issue of color reared its head again vis-à-vis the interior walls, with Wright convinced that pure white—better termed "dead white" in his opinion—would "give the museum a flashy, cheap wallpaper effect."[7] Olgivanna recalled they were painted an ivory color which softened the daylight coming in from a skylight, a "crown webbed in metal and glass," thereby giving the space a more luminous appearance.[8]

The viewing experience Wright envisaged, along with his innovative means of hanging art, can be seen in his presentation artwork of 1958 known as "The Masterpiece" (see page 118, fig. 1). It illustrates his low, hassock-style seating—upholstered disks atop intersecting planes of stained oak—arranged to complement the terrazzo floor pattern of the gallery's sloping walkway. Another drawing from the same set, "The Watercolor Society—Top Ramp" (see page 125, fig. 8), offers

a view into the ways in which the bays of the top-floor gallery could be reorganized using moveable partition walls painted to match the concrete walls and trimmed with the same stained oak as the furniture. Slanted at the angle of a painter's easel, these partitions, which introduced a vertical angularity to an otherwise horizontal gallery, may have been offered by Wright as an alternative to exhibiting art on curved walls.

Irene R. Guggenheim Auditorium

Directly below the main gallery is the 281-seat auditorium dedicated to Irene R. Guggenheim, wife of Solomon and aunt of Harry.[9] Described by one critic as "the most delightful auditorium built anywhere in recent years,"[10] and often described as circular, it is actually an asymmetrical composition created out of overlapping arcs and tiered semicircular forms (fig. 5). The mandorla-shaped stage projects into the room more directly than more conventional, rectilinear stages, dictating the curved arrangement of the seating area.

As the opening date approached, Wright concentrated on completing the auditorium interior, describing its golden color scheme to Harry in late December 1958 but confessing that he still had not found the exact "true—metallic—gold, rich in color and in texture" that he wanted for the large stage curtain.[11] Other features were in place, including the pale gold upholstery of the silvered aluminum theater chairs Wright felt "quietly appropriate" to a "memorial-room" and the carpeting he described as "wearable stuff" in a similar gold hue. Having conceived the auditorium as a venue for imparting knowledge through lectures and films, Wright wanted a golden glow that can be read as a metaphor for the uplifting experience of knowledge and even for life itself, in a space dedicated to a life very dear to the client. Indeed, the visual warmth and the intimacy of the furnishings and finishes offers a contrast to the cooler-toned spaciousness of the spiral gallery above.

FIG. 6 Monitor building, section (presentation drawing). Graphite and colored pencil on tracing paper, 55.6 x 47.6 cm. Frank Lloyd Wright Foundation, Scottsdale, Arizona 4305.567

FIG. 7 Monitor building, plan for third story (presentation drawing, detail). Graphite and colored pencil on tracing paper, 89 x 102 cm. Frank Lloyd Wright Foundation, Scottsdale, Arizona 4305.565

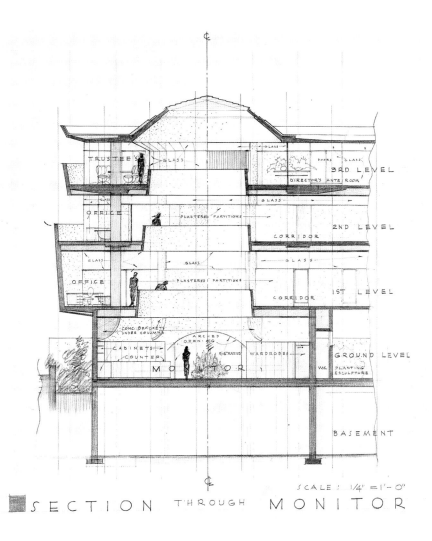

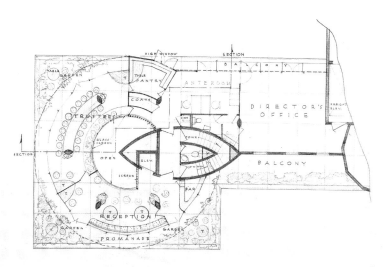

FIG. 8 Office workers in the Monitor building, as seen from the second floor, ca. 1959

The Monitor

The Monitor, the smaller of the two spiral buildings, also with a domed skylight, housed the museum's administrative and curatorial offices. Wright's design can be seen in the surviving presentation drawings (figs. 6 and 7), but photographs taken shortly before the opening of the building indicate that only part of what Wright presented to his clients was executed. Changes, such as eliminating an apartment for the museum director, were often the result of budget cuts, while other modifications accommodated the museum's growing collection, such as relocating the library to the museum's original cafeteria when exhibition and storage needs arose.

The furnishings for the upper floor that housed the trustees' conference room (fig. 7) included a conference table in the form of an arc and upholstered banquette seating for a reception area overlooking a landscaped promenade. Although the more sophisticated furniture for this executive floor was made to Wright's plans, he did not design the general office furnishings, as in some commissions. Instead, the Monitor offices used fairly new office furniture already belonging to the organization, leaving employees with the challenging task of positioning rectilinear furnishings such as desks, file cabinets, and bookshelves against curvilinear walls (fig. 8). For the museum, resolving the question of how to position flat artwork against the curving walls of the main gallery and furnishing the main gallery space were higher priority concerns.[12]

The expansion of the collection and increased numbers of staff soon necessitated the remodeling of certain spaces. Ongoing changes to the interiors of the main gallery and the Monitor building began as early as 1963, when Taliesin Associated Architects (a group Wright's former associates formed in 1959 following his death) refurbished the library in order to accommodate the Thannhauser Collection, a significant long-term loan to the Solomon R. Guggenheim Foundation that began that year (the works it comprises formally entered the museum's collection in 1976). At the same time, some of the offices located in the Monitor building were moved to an annex, freeing space for other uses, including exhibitions. In 1974, the driveway coursing between the Monitor building and main gallery was enclosed and new interiors created, including the new bookstore and restaurant. The task before the design team, the firm Donald Freed, was to change the structure and interior in the manner of Wright's overall aesthetic and specific design features. Using the same or similar materials that Wright had, these understated alterations achieved something close to a near-seamless connection between the 1950s fabric and the new. They were timely in that they allowed new generations to enjoy new types of facilities expected as part and parcel of museumgoing in the late twentieth and early twenty-first centuries, namely shopping and partaking of refreshments. For most visitors, however, the main joy of the interior continues to be the wonderful spiraling ramp that remains as it was designed by Wright.

Notes

We wish to thank Francine Snyder, Manager of Library and Archives, and Angela Starita, lead researcher and project manager, at the Solomon R. Guggenheim Museum for their assistance in our preparing this essay.

1 "Frank Lloyd Wright," *Architectural Forum* 88 (January 1948), p. 89.

2 Frank Lloyd Wright, "To the Young Man in Architecture," *Frank Lloyd Wright: Collected Writings,* vol. 2, *1930–1932,* ed. Bruce Brooks Pfeiffer (New York: Rizzoli, 1992), p. 92.

3 Ibid.

4 For examples of the mandorla motif in Wright's work, see David A. Hanks, *The Decorative Designs of Frank Lloyd Wright* (New York: E. P. Dutton, 1979), especially Plate 13 (dinnerware for the Imperial Hotel, 1916–22), Plate 17 (area rug for the David Wright House, 1952), and Plate 23 (textile design for F. Schumacher & Co., 1955).

5 Wright, "To the Young Man in Architecture," in *Two Lectures on Architecture* (Chicago: Art Institute of Chicago, 1931), p. 63. An undated letter from Olgivanna Lloyd Wright to Harry F. Guggenheim urged him to reconsider the medallion design already approved by the Guggenheim's Museum Committee. An unsigned reply of July 17, 1959, stated the committee felt the Aristophanes quotation "so apt." Sketches for three variations of the medallion were then sent from William Wesley Peters to Guggenheim. In a letter of August 10, 1959, Peters suggested that the name "Solomon R. Guggenheim" might not fit if the Aristophanes were used, while it would with Wright's quotation. He also expressed Mrs. Wright's "desirable solution" and their feeling that "in a building so eminently the product of American genius it still seems slightly irrelevant to insert classical Greece however pertinent the comment."

Guggenheim's response (through his secretary, George J. Fountaine, on August 18, 1959) gave the final decision—not the one Olgivanna favored. All letters from the Solomon R. Guggenheim Museum Archives, New York (hereafter cited as SRGM Archives).

6 Olgivanna Lloyd Wright, *Our House* (New York: Horizon Press, 1959), p. 300. Her husband's first choice for flooring had not been terrazzo, according to a letter to Harris H. Murdock, chairman of New York City's Board of Standards and Appeals, December 15, 1955. It states, "We have taken your advice in regard to the final covering of the ramps for the Guggenheim Museum, and have substituted abrasive ground terrazzo for the carpeting which we had previously intended to lay down." A January 20, 1956, letter from Wright to Harry F. Guggenheim noted the carpets were "a hang-over from the [Hilla] Rebay regime. For her, all had to be carpeted. I know of no museum in Europe that is carpeted. The 'honed-terrazzo' is right and less expensive." Guggenheim approved the final floor sample in a October 20, 1958, telegram to Wright. All documents from the SRGM Archives.

7 Olgivanna Lloyd Wright, "The Miracle on Fifth Avenue," in *Frank Lloyd Wright: His Life, His Work, His Words* (New York: Horizon, 1966), p. 164.

8 Ibid.

9 Today the auditorium is known as the Peter B. Lewis Theater, after the ex-chairman of the foundation's board whose 1995 gift funded the hall's restoration.

10 Peter Blake, "The Guggenheim: Museum or Monument?" *Architectural Forum* 111 (December 1959), p. 92.

11 Wright to Harry F. Guggenheim, December 19, 1958, SRGM Archives.

12 Clinton N. Hunt, SRGM business administrator, to Albert E. Thiele, vice president, July 1, 1958, SRGM Archives.

THE MASTERPIECE

7

SPACES FOR THE DISPLAY OF FINE ART

Bruce Brooks
Pfeiffer

IN 1914, FRANK LLOYD WRIGHT RECEIVED A COMMISSION TO DESIGN A GALLERY for the exhibition of Japanese woodblock prints, his first opportunity to create a space for the display of fine art.[1] The clients were the Spaulding brothers, William and John, Bostonians of considerable wealth. Both were enamored of that art form and wished to procure more for their collection. Learning of Wright's enthusiasm and expertise in acquiring prints, in 1912 they met with him to discuss the possibility of his acting as their agent to purchase more such works. Wright was about to make his second voyage to Japan, this time to secure the commission to design the New Imperial Hotel in Tokyo. His trip in 1913 was successful on both counts: the design of the hotel was up to him, and his work for the Spauldings would eventually amass them a collection of some 6,495 prints, now housed at the Museum of Fine Arts, Boston.

For the Spauldings' gallery (which was never built), Wright designed a square, two-story room in an existing building, presumably in Boston, although the location is not on record. Along the four walls were sloped easels integrated into storage cabinets; works removed from the drawers below could thus be elegantly set out for viewing. The entire room featured a relatively conventional form of lighting, a large overhead skylight (figs. 2 and 3).

Nearly thirty years later came a second request for Wright to design a building for the display of fine art: on June 1, 1943, he received a letter with the proposition of designing a building to house the collection of nonobjective paintings owned by the Solomon R. Guggenheim Foundation in New York. The letter, signed by Hilla Rebay,

FIG. 2 Spaulding Gallery (unbuilt), Boston, 1919. Section. Ink and ink wash on paper, 50.8 x 83.2 cm. Frank Lloyd Wright Foundation, Scottsdale, Arizona 1902.004

FIG. 3 Spaulding Gallery (unbuilt), Boston, 1919. Plan. Ink and ink wash on paper, 71.1 x 83.8 cm. Frank Lloyd Wright Foundation, Scottsdale, Arizona 1902.005

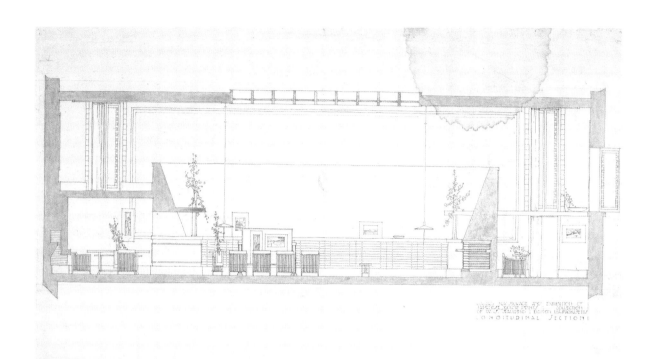

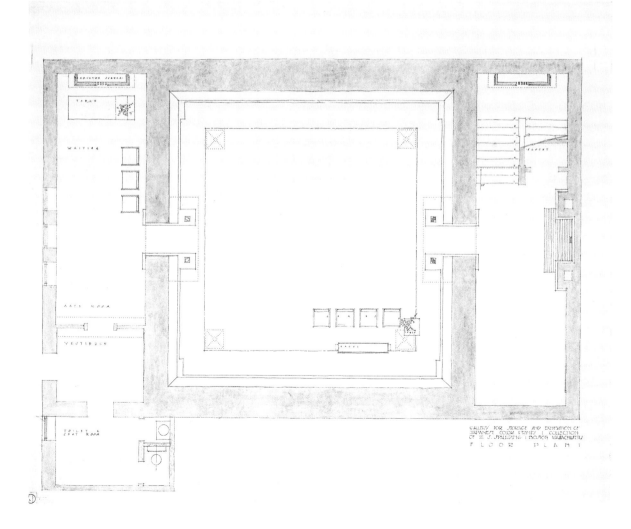

curator of the foundation's collection, stipulated her desire for a building that would be "a temple of spirit, a monument."[2] This time Wright's solution for such a space would prove to be far more radical.

Wright proposed a museum in the form of a circular spiral, a gentle ramp expanding as it rose six levels, creating a great open well in the center under a dome. Early sketches reveal that Wright was not only considering the ramp for exhibition purposes and the sloped wall as a site for hanging paintings; he was also concerned with the scale and the lighting of the interior. The ceilings were planned to be relatively low in comparison with other museums, so that the public could view the art in a more intimate environment.

Placing works of art in a more human-scale setting grew quite naturally out of his own experience with and preferences about the display of art. At Taliesin, his home in Spring Green, Wisconsin, which he had begun in 1911, Wright displayed his own Asian art collection—Japanese folding screens, prints, and *kakemono* (hanging scrolls); Chinese landscape paintings; and wood, bronze, iron, and stone sculptures from both Japan and China—as an integrated feature of the interior. The screens were set flat against the walls and bordered merely by a strip of cypress to match the other cypress woodwork throughout the residence. Kakemono were similarly hung flat against the walls or stone piers. Japanese prints were matted in soft, tan paper and placed on specially designed freestanding easels. The wood sculptures were carefully placed on shelves and decks around the interior, while bronze, iron, and stone sculptures were placed outdoors in the gardens and courts. Everywhere these works of art appeared in harmony with the architecture and were extremely sympathetic to the overall environment. Similarly, Wright's design for the Guggenheim strove to unify built form with the art that was to be exhibited. Even his early drawings of the museum's elevation show the manner of hanging pictures. The interior elevations with paintings on the walls have a distinctively different feature about them—their frames, or more specifically, their lack of frames. In Wright's drawings, paintings are displayed with no more than a narrow, almost imperceptible band around them.

An interesting event happened in Wright's life at just about this time. His friend Georgia O'Keeffe had decided to give him her painting *Pelvis with Shadows and the Moon* (1943) some time before, but sent it to him only after her husband, Alfred Stieglitz, died.[3] Wright had seen it and other works at Stieglitz's New York art gallery, An American Place, and was especially taken by the method of framing. Wright noted this in his acknowledgment of the gift: "The masterpiece arrived properly framed! That is to say *none* showing."[4] The painting was framed in thin metal bands, one-eighth of an inch wide by two inches deep.

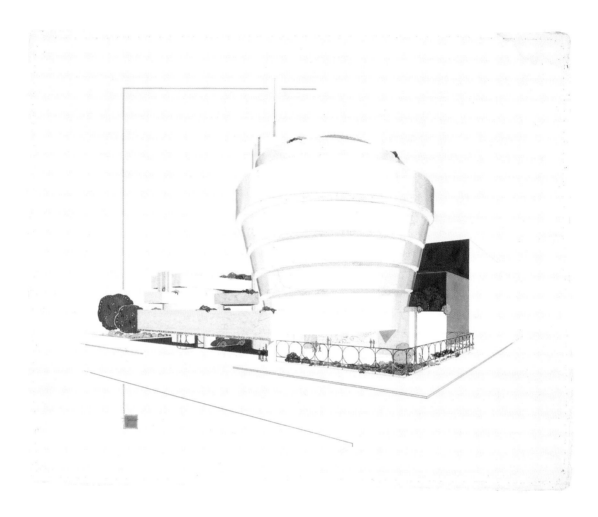

When Wright presented his design, Solomon R. Guggenheim was immensely pleased and authorized Wright to continue to develop the project. His one concern lay with the narrow skylights on the outer edge of the ramps above the exterior walls of the building. These skylights, also equipped with artificial lighting and moveable louvers, controlled the level of illumination on the artwork set against the walls. This was, indeed, a novel way of showing paintings (fig. 4). When visiting Wright at Taliesin, Guggenheim expressed his apprehensiveness about this lighting. Wright took him to the kitchen, where there was a small breakfast table set against the wall and, above it, a narrow skylight in just about the same circumstance as those Wright had designed for the ramps in the museum. From the studio's vault, he brought out some Japanese prints and placed them against the wall beneath the skylight. When Guggenheim saw how amply the prints were lit, he understood Wright's concept.[5]

From the beginning of the project, there was a constant stream of negative reactions about a spiral building being appropriate for the display of art. Adverse criticism centered on the sloping walls. Responding to this concern in 1958, the year before the building was completed, Wright explained, "Why do you think the walls of the Solomon R. Guggenheim Museum are gently sloping outward?…They gently slope because the donor and his architect believed that pictures placed against the walls slightly tilted backward would be seen in better perspective and be better lighted than if set bolt upright [fig. 5]. This is a chief characteristic of our building and was

FIG. 5 Solomon R. Guggenheim Museum, New York, 1943–59. Section, 1956. Graphite and colored pencil on tracing paper, 91.4 x 152.4 cm. Frank Lloyd Wright Foundation, Scottsdale, Arizona 4305.451

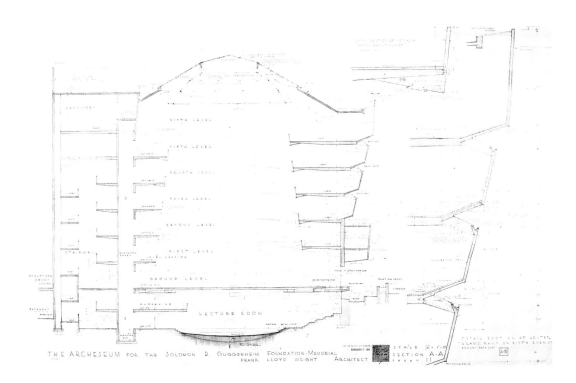

the hypothesis upon which the museum was fashioned. This idea is new but sound… [and] can create a precedent of great value."[6]

The criticism also suggested that the building's architectural impact would overpower the pictures themselves, to which Wright countered, "It is not to subjugate the paintings to the building that I conceived this plan. On the contrary, it was to make the building and the painting as an uninterrupted, beautiful symphony such as never existed in the world of Art before."[7] But constant worry, mainly on the part of Rebay, about the building dominating the paintings and about the lighting system hounded Wright year after year. He began to wonder why she had selected him as her architect in the first place. Although a model had been received enthusiastically in 1945, Wright increasingly began to doubt if Rebay really understood the building and its purpose. Guggenheim's faith in Wright, however, remained steadfast through the former's death in 1949.

The struggle over display methods continued after Rebay's 1952 departure. In 1956, after construction had begun, a group of twenty-one artists—among them Willem de Kooning, Philip Guston, Franz Kline, and Robert Motherwell—wrote to James Johnson Sweeney, Rebay's successor as director, and to the trustees voicing the same concerns.[8] Around that time, Wright realized that Sweeney had very strong, very conventional ideas about the exhibition of paintings. One thing that Sweeney definitely did not want was to place pictures on the sloped wall, as had been intended from the very start of the project in 1943.

In June 1958, with the form of the great ramp already visible along Fifth Avenue, Wright prepared a group of four interior perspectives to demonstrate further the various methods of exhibiting art in the museum. "The Watercolor Society—Top Ramp" (fig. 8), "Average—Sculpture and Painting" (fig. 6), "Middle of the Road" (fig. 7), and, finally, "The Masterpiece" (fig. 1) were drawn by his apprentices in graphite pencil

FIG. 6 Solomon R. Guggenheim Museum, New York, 1943–59. Interior view ("Average—Sculpture and Painting"), 1958. Graphite on tracing paper, 85.4 x 98.4 cm. Frank Lloyd Wright Foundation, Scottsdale, Arizona 4305.011

FIG. 7 Solomon R. Guggenheim Museum, New York, 1943–59. Interior view ("Middle of the Road"), 1958. Graphite on tracing paper, 89.2 x 102.9 cm. Frank Lloyd Wright Foundation, Scottsdale, Arizona 4305.012

AVERAGE SCULPTURE & PAINTING

MIDDLE of the ROAD

on tracing paper. "The Masterpiece" portrays a great color painting, possibly to represent a work by Vasily Kandinsky. The viewing public is both standing and seated, studying the canvas, while a little girl is turned toward the open well of the museum with her hands on the railing. When Wright came into the drafting room to sign the four drawings, without even sitting down, he took a pencil, leaned over the drawing, and drew a little yo-yo extending from the girl's hand. Turning to those in the room, he smiled and remarked, "Boys, in all this endeavor we must never lose sight of a sense of humor."[9]

Now, some fifty years after the museum's opening, the criticism and doubts have long since faded into oblivion. The idea of exhibiting fine art on a ramp, with a sloped wall, was novel and perhaps iconoclastic. But Wright's ability to design a space with flexible possibilities that would accommodate various exhibitions has fully proven itself.

Notes

1 In 1912, Wright designed the Mori Oriental Art Shop, located in the Fine Arts Building, Chicago. This space, however, was not so much for display as it was for the sale of fine art.

2 Hilla Rebay to Frank Lloyd Wright, June 1, 1943, in *Frank Lloyd Wright: The Guggenheim Correspondence*, ed. Bruce Brooks Pfeiffer (Fresno: The Press at California State University; Carbondale and Edwardsville: Southern Illinois University Press, 1986), p. 4.

3 Georgia O'Keeffe to Wright, May 1942, ficheid Oo2oBo3, Frank Lloyd Wright Foundation Archives, Scottsdale, Ariz. (hereafter cited as FLW Archives).

4 Wright to O'Keeffe, February 14, 1947, FLW Archives, ficheid Oo29Do5.

5 Wright in conversation with the author, circa 1957.

6 Wright to Harry F. Guggenheim, May 7, 1958, in Pfeiffer, *The Guggenheim Correspondence*, p. 266.

7 Wright to Harry F. Guggenheim, July 15, 1958, Solomon R. Guggenheim Museum Archives.

8 Various to James Johnson Sweeney, 1957, in Pfeiffer, *The Guggenheim Correspondence*, p. 242.

9 John Ottenheimer in conversation with the author, n.d.

MATTHEW BARNEY
THE CREMASTER CYCLE

Installation view of video screens
and flags by Matthew Barney for
the exhibition *Matthew Barney:
The Cremaster Cycle*, 2003

THE MUSEUM AS CATALYST

ARTIST INSTALLATIONS AT THE GUGGENHEIM

Nancy Spector

THOUGH INITIALLY DERIDED AS A SPACE UNINHABITABLE FOR ART, Frank Lloyd Wright's Guggenheim Museum has proven again and again the contrary to be true. It was originally conceived as a harmonious backdrop for modernist painting, which, for the most part, comprises canvases of modest scale. The fact that sculpture looks so remarkable in the building—silhouetted against the luminous, curving walls of the ramps—no doubt came as a surprise to the early custodians of the museum, since that medium was not part of the initial collecting purview of the institution.[1] As the scale and physical complexity of art has evolved since the middle of the last century, artists and curators have devised increasingly innovative methods to display work in all media in the building, often in ways Wright could never have imagined. His museum has served as a catalyst for invention for select contemporary artists who have responded uniquely to the particular challenges of its spiraling architecture.

The notion of site specificity gained traction during the late 1960s and early 1970s with the advent of Minimalist and Post-Minimalist art, the phenomenological dimensions of which directly implicated the viewing body and the spaces it inhabited. With this shift from the isolated, self-reflexive modernist object to one that engaged its context—often in a critical or analytical way—the museum itself became a subject to probe. The first expression of this impulse at the Guggenheim occurred during its 1971 *International Exhibition*, in which a roster of contemporary artists was invited to conceive work in direct relation to the building. Dan Flavin, whose sculptural medium was light itself, created an installation of fluorescent tubes that filled the ramps with volumetric color. Invited in 1992 to reprise this work on the occasion of an extensive renovation of the building, Flavin filled the entire rotunda with radiant color, the light-filled bays offset by a luminous pink tower stretching from floor to skylight.

The site-specific strategies of the 1970s extended beyond a focus on the physical confines of the museum to embrace a broader investigation into the discursive mechanisms that constitute the culture industry, including (but not limited to) art criticism, the art market, private patronage, and the exhibition model itself. Known as "institutional critique," this process often used the museum as a location for intervention and resistance. Daniel Buren's monumental striped curtain, which was removed from the center of the rotunda before the opening of the 1971 *International* at the request of the other exhibiting artists, was an early effort to deflect perception from the art object to the sociocultural codes defining its container. Nearly thirty-five years later, Buren presented an installation designed specifically for the Guggenheim's rotunda on the occasion of his solo exhibition *The Eye of the Storm* (2005). Manifested as an immense mirrored wedge situated in the center of the spiral, the work rendered the museum a dizzying, seemingly kinetic labyrinth. With a similar flair for the theatrical, Jenny Holzer transformed the rotunda in 1989 into an electronic arcade of circular LED signs that formed a veritable inventory of her writings to date. Known for her incisive, aphoristic texts, which first appeared guerilla style in urban spaces usually reserved for advertising, Holzer uses language both in and outside the museum to provoke questions about desire, identity, and representation. Lothar Baumgarten also deployed language as a structural device for his exhibition *America Invention* (1993), covering the rotunda walls with the names of tribes once native to the Americas. Written in a crisp

European font, these names were often those given by the conquerors and, in this context, called forth a vanishing history of vanquished peoples.

In more recent years, artists such as Nam June Paik, Matthew Barney, and Cai Guo-Qiang have orchestrated elaborate, technically virtuosic installations in the rotunda as part of their solo exhibitions. These site-specific constructions were epic in scale and unequivocally spectacular, as if deliberately courting current debates about art's (and the museum's) uneasy relationship to spectacle culture. Barney even went so far as to include the Guggenheim as a "character" in his feature film *Cremaster 3* (2002), which he shot in the museum and played on a five-screen "jumbotron" in the middle of the space as the literal centerpiece of his show, echoing the building's place at the heart of his five-part *Cremaster* cycle. For the recent group exhibition *theanyspacewhatever* (2008–09), which explored a postrepresentational, performative impulse in contemporary art, Philippe Parreno installed an illuminated movie marquee on the facade of the museum. Fabricated in white Plexiglas with neon and devoid of any text, the marquee invoked the theatrical dimensions of Wright's architecture and underscored its remarkable ability to inspire and provoke.

Note

1   The Guggenheim began aggressively collecting sculpture only after James Johnson Sweeney assumed its directorship subsequent to the 1952 resignation of Hilla Rebay, the museum's founding director. Rebay, who presided over the original Museum of Non-Objective Painting, before it was renamed the Solomon R. Guggenheim Museum, believed sculpture to be too corporeal and of the earth in relation to the spiritual aspirations of "non-objective" art.

Jenny Holzer, *Untitled* (Selections
from *Truisms, Inflammatory Essays,
The Living Series, The Survival Series,
Under a Rock, Laments,* and *Child Text*),
1989. Extended helical tricolor
LED electronic-display signboard.
Solomon R. Guggenheim Museum,
New York, Partial gift of the art-
ist, 1989; Gift, Jay Chiat, 1995; and

Purchased with funds contributed
by the International Director's
Council and Executive Members:
Eli Broad, Elaine Terner Cooper,
Ronnie Heyman, Dakis Joannou,
Peter Norton, Inge Rodenstock,
and Thomas Walther, 1996 89.3626,
95.4497, 96.4499. Installation views,
Jenny Holzer, 1989–90

The Guggenheim Museum and the Art of this Century

Dan Flavin, *untitled (to Tracy, to celebrate the love of a lifetime)*, 1992. Pink, green, blue, yellow, daylight, red, and ultraviolet fluorescent light. Solomon R. Guggenheim Museum, New York, 1992 92.4017. Includes at center *untitled (to Ward Jackson, an old friend and colleague who, during the Fall of 1957 when I finally returned to New York from Washington and joined him to work together in this museum, kindly communicated)*, 1971. Daylight, pink, yellow, green, and blue fluorescent light, 2- and 8-foot fixtures. Solomon R. Guggenheim Museum, New York, Partial gift of the artist in honor of Ward Jackson, 1972 72.1985. Installation view, *Dan Flavin*, 1992

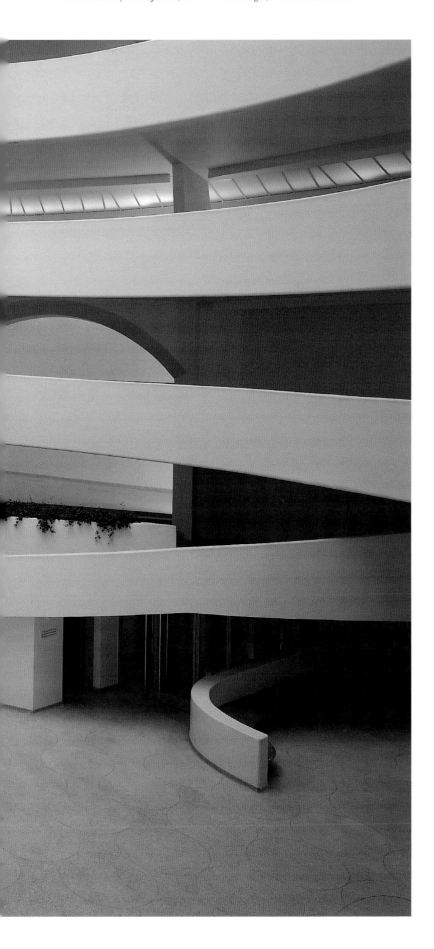

Lothar Baumgarten, *America Invention*, 1985 (realized 1993). Painted site-specific installation. Solomon R. Guggenheim Museum, New York, Gift of the Charles W. Engelhard Foundation, 1994 94.4257. Installation view, *Lothar Baumgarten: America Invention*, 1993

Installation view of *The Worlds of*
Nam June Paik, 2000

Installation views of metal-mesh
sculpture designed by Frank O.
Gehry & Associates for the Solomon R.
Guggenheim Museum for the
exhibition *Frank Gehry, Architect*, 2001

Daniel Buren, *Around the Corner*,
2000–05. Work in situ. Installation
view, *The Eye of the Storm: Works in
Situ by Daniel Buren*, 2005

Cai Guo-Qiang, *Inopportune: Stage One*, 2004. Nine cars and sequenced multichannel light tubes. Seattle Art Museum, Gift of Robert M. Arnold, in honor of the 75th Anniversary of the Seattle Art Museum, 2006. Exhibition copy installed as part of *Cai Guo-Qiang: I Want to Believe*, 2008

Philippe Parreno, *Marquee,
Guggenheim, NY*, 2008. Acrylic, steel,
LEDs, and incandescent, fluorescent,
and neon lights. Installation view,
theanyspacewhatever, 2008–09

Frank Lloyd Wright visting
Sixty Years of Living Architecture,
Solomon R. Guggenheim
Museum, New York, 1953

KEEPING FAITH WITH AN IDEA

A TIME LINE OF THE GUGGENHEIM MUSEUM, 1943–59

Angela Starita

THE DESIGN AND CONSTRUCTION OF THE GUGGENHEIM MUSEUM took place over a sixteen-year period. During that time, Frank Lloyd Wright's exceptional energy rarely flagged; while navigating the complicated and ever-changing challenges that the museum posed, Wright worked on dozens of other projects that defined the late period of his career. Besides being the museum's architect, he was its biggest booster—particularly when the project looked certain to go unrealized. In 1945, only two years after he had first taken the commission, Baroness Hilla von Rebay, the museum's first director and the prime mover behind the building, expressed her discouragement that construction was not underway. Wright urged her to persevere: "After all is it not finer to keep faith with an idea than it is to keep faith with one's sense of oneself." In this time line, we follow the intricate story that culminated in the construction of the museum and parallel developments in Wright's life and work.

'43

Unless otherwise noted, all correspondence, reproduced or quoted, is from the Solomon R. Guggenheim Museum Archives, New York. All correspondence from Hilla Rebay, reproduced or quoted, is from the Hilla von Rebay Foundation Archive, Solomon R. Guggenheim Museum Archives, New York.

BOTTOM LEFT Ralph Jester House (project), Palos Verdes, California, 1938–39. Plan and elevation. Graphite and colored pencil on paper, 34.9 x 53.3 cm. Frank Lloyd Wright Foundation, Scottsdale, Arizona 3807.002

TOP Installation view, *Masters of Four Arts: Wright, Maillol, Picasso, Strawinsky*, Fogg Art Museum, Harvard University, Cambridge, Massachusetts, 1943. Visual Resources Collection, File 1.252, Harvard Art Museum Archives, Cambridge, Massachusetts

BOTTOM RIGHT Roux Library, Florida Southern College, Lakeland, Florida, 1941–42. Interior

Though the design firmament of the 1920s had dismissed Frank Lloyd Wright's architecture as antiquated, by the early 1940s, the septuagenarian finds his star on the ascent as he works on a wide range of projects, from a college campus to a motor inn to the residential commissions that are a mainstay of his practice. At the same time, he begins to receive widespread recognition, including an exhibition mounted in 1940 by the Museum of Modern Art in New York in association with the Institute of Modern Art in Boston. The show surveys the many phases of Wright's extraordinarily long career and characterizes him as "the world's greatest living architect."

MAY 4–29
The Fogg Art Museum at Harvard University presents *Masters of Four Arts: Wright, Maillol, Picasso, Strawinsky*.

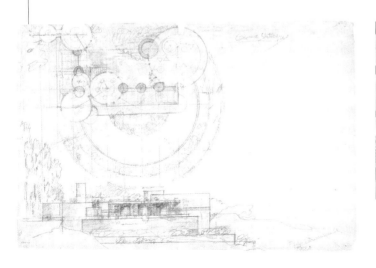

43

Letter (copy), Hilla Rebay to Frank
Lloyd Wright, June 1943

C O P Y

Mr. Frank Lloyd Wright,
Taliesin,
Spring Green, Wisconsin

Dear Mr. Wright:

Could you ever come to New York and discuss with me a building

for our collection of Non-objective paintings.   I feel that

each of these great masterpieces should be organized into space

and only you would test the possibilities to do so. It takes so

much thought and loving attention and the experience of an or-

iginator and his wisdom to be able to handle such a difficult

task.

In Berlin I once saw your exhibition which Mendelsohn arranged,

I believe - whose Einstein tower I witnessed.   His functional-

ism does not agree with Non-objectivity.   I met once your

sister in Westport.   She told me you would be interested in

our work.   I do not think these paintings are easel paintings.

They are order, creating order and are sensitive (and corrective

even) to space.   You feel the ground, the sky and the "Inbetween"

You will feel them too and find the way.   I need a fighter, a

lover of space, an originator, a tester and a wise man -

JUNE

Hilla Rebay, Solomon R.
Guggenheim's long-time art
advisor and the director of his
Museum of Non-Objective
Painting, writes to Wright asking
if he will build a new home
for Guggenheim's collection,
which is currently housed at
24 East Fifty-fourth Street in New
York. "To ennoble us all and to
demonstrate the evidence of
great men's call for the Real;
which is Art. This expression
in culmination is what I would
love to see come true," she tells
Wright in their early correspondence. Having never received
a Manhattan commission despite
fifty years of practicing architecture, he agrees to design the
proposed museum.

Mr. Wright - Cont'd P. 2

Your three books,which I am reading now,gave me the feeling that

no one else would do.

If you want to; and so I need your great advice if you could

come, to speak about it, and let me know the expense it would

cause.   I have never seen a building you made but photos, and

I feel them - while I never felt others work, as much lacking

in organic perfection and adapting to the task's originality.

I want a temple of spirit - a monument, and your help to make

it possible.

      May this wish be blessed.

          (Signed) Hilla Rebay

'43

JUNE 29
With the contract between Wright and the Guggenheim Foundation signed, the architect starts work on his design. Early on, he considers a hexagonal plan.

JULY 14
Wright asks Guggenheim to consider several potential sites, including one in the Bronx overlooking the Hudson River, another adjacent to the garden of the Museum of Modern Art on Fifty-fourth Street, and a third at Park Avenue between Sixty-ninth and Seventieth streets. He describes his new museum as providing "amply for both helicopters and cars," since he believes both forms of transportation will become ubiquitous after World War II ends.

JULY 26
Wright tells Guggenheim to contact Robert Moses, New York Commissioner of Parks and City Construction Coordinator, to help find a site for the museum. Moses, he writes, is a "splendid fellow and powerful."

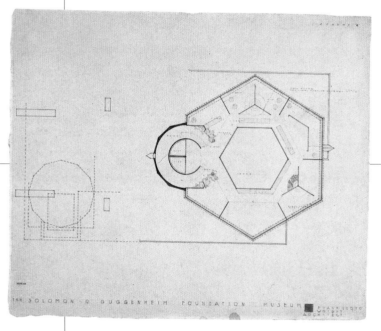

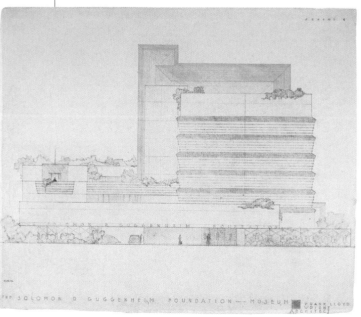

'43

TOP Frank Lloyd Wright's inscription to Hilla Rebay in her copy of Book Six of Wright's *An Autobiography* (Taliesin), 1943. Hilla von Rebay Foundation Archive, Solomon R. Guggenheim Museum Archives, New York

BOTTOM, CLOCKWISE FROM UPPER RIGHT Solomon R. Guggenheim Museum, New York, 1943–59. Perspective, September 1943. Ink and watercolor on art paper, 51 x 61 cm. Frank Lloyd Wright Foundation, Scottsdale, Arizona 4305.747

Solomon R. Guggenheim Museum, New York, 1943–59. Perspective, September 1943. Ink and watercolor on art paper, 51 x 61.1 cm. Frank Lloyd Wright Foundation, Scottsdale, Arizona 4305.745

Solomon R. Guggenheim Museum, New York, 1943–59. Perspective, September 1943. Ink and watercolor on art paper, 51 x 61.6 cm. Frank Lloyd Wright Foundation, Scottsdale, Arizona 4305.746

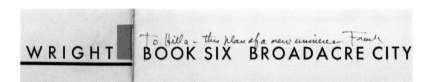

WRIGHT BOOK SIX BROADACRE CITY

SEPTEMBER

The architect produces a series of drawings depicting possible designs for the museum. His first ideas are for a marble exterior in any of a number of colors, including one of his favorites, red.

AUGUST

Albert Einstein, Archibald MacLeish, Robert Moses, Nelson Rockefeller, and sixty other notable figures sign a petition recommending that Wright's plan for decentralized towns, called Broadacre City, be supported by President Franklin Roosevelt. Wright sends Rebay an autographed copy of the section of his autobiography about the urban-planning proposal.

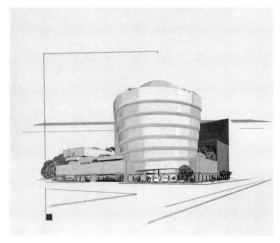

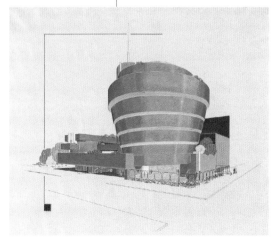

'43

DECEMBER 29
Rebay, concerned that Guggenheim may lose interest in the project, telegrams Wright.

DECEMBER 30
The architect responds immediately, hinting at a new line of approach.

OCTOBER 4
In a letter to Wright, Guggenheim agrees to employ Moses in the search for a site: "Mr. Moses is certainly a most intelligent man, and one who has the interests of the city at heart—he may prove to be very helpful to us."

CHARGE TO THE ACCOUNT OF

CHECK SERVICE DESIRED OTHERWISE MESSAGE WILL BE SENT AT FULL RATE

DOMESTIC	FOREIGN
FULL RATE	FULL RATE
DAY LETTER	CDE RATE
NIGHT LETTER	URGENT
SERIAL	DEFERRED
RESERVATION	NIGHT LETTER
TOUR-RATE	SHIP RADIO

CHARGE ACCOUNT NUMBER

CASH NO.   TOLLS

CHECK

TIME FILED   (STANDARD TIME)

Postal Telegraph
Mackay Radio   All America Cables
Commercial Cables   Canadian Pacific Telegraphs

Send the following message, subject to the Company's rules, regulations and rates set forth in its tariffs and on file with regulatory authorities   Form 2-C

December 29th, 1943

Mr. Frank Lloyd Wright,   Taliesin,   Spring Green,   Wisconsin,

IF YOU COULD COME FOR A DAY TO NEWYORK TO TELL MR. GUGGENHEIM SOME OF YOUR IDEAS FOR NEW MUSEUM MAYBE IT INSPIRES HIM AGAIN BEFORE HE LEAVES NEWYORK FOR SOUTH AFTER ILLNESS-STOP LOVE TO ALL.

Hilla

Charge to Guggenheim Foundation,   Carnegie Hall,
56th Street & 7th Avenue,
New York City.

WESTERN UNION   1201

CLASS OF SERVICE	SYMBOLS
This is a full-rate Telegram or Cablegram unless its deferred character is indicated by a suitable symbol above or preceding the ad⸺	DL=Day Letter
	NL=Night Letter
	LC=Deferred Cable
	NLT=Cable Night Letter

N. WILLIAMS
PRESIDENT

NEWCOMB CARLTON
CHAIRMAN OF THE BOARD

J. C. WILLEVER
FIRST VICE

(05) 1943 DEC 30 RM

The filing time shown ... ne on telegram and day letters is STANDARD TIME at point of origin. Time of receipt is STANDARD TIME at point of destination

NP225 42=SPRINGGREEN WIS 30 401P

BARONESS HILLA REBAY=

THE SOLOMON R GUGGENHEIM FOUNDATION CARNEGIE HALL

7 AVE AND 56 ST=

BELIEVE CHANGING IDEA OF BUILDING FROM HORIZONTAL
TO PERPENDICULAR WE CAN GO WHERE PLEASE WOULD LIKE TO
PRESENT THE IMPLICATIONS OF THIS CHANGE TO MR GUGGENHEIM
FOR SANCTION BEFORE HE LEAVES IF HE WILL AUTHORIZE TRIP
TO NEW YORK WILL COME IMMEDIATELY=

FRANK.

THE COMPANY WILL APPRECIATE SUGGESTIONS FROM ITS PATRONS CONCERNING ITS SERVICE

'44

TOP Letter (excerpt), Frank Lloyd Wright to Solomon R. Guggenheim, December 31, 1943

BOTTOM, CLOCKWISE FROM UPPER RIGHT Solomon R. Guggenheim Museum, New York, 1943–59. Section (conceptual drawing). Graphite on tracing paper, 53.3 x 91.4 cm. Frank Lloyd Wright Foundation, Scottsdale, Arizona 4305.069

Solomon R. Guggenheim Museum, New York, 1943–59. Ramp plan (conceptual drawing). Graphite on tracing paper, 46 x 69 cm. Frank Lloyd Wright Foundation, Scottsdale, Arizona 4305.067

Gordon Strong Automobile Objective and Planetarium (unbuilt), Sugarloaf Mountain, Maryland, 1924–25. Aerial perspective. Graphite on paper, 27.3 x 21.3 cm. Frank Lloyd Wright Foundation, Scottsdale, Arizona 2505.023

I can see a tall building of a new type perfectly appropriate to our purpose having monumental dignity and great beauty, requiring about half the ground area we have been looking for. Therefore I wish that you would authorize me to come to New York and spend some time with Douglas Gibbons looking for a site with this changed view in mind.

JANUARY

Wright's preliminary sketches are prepared. For the defining form of the building, he decides to use a spiral, a shape he previously used in the never-built Gordon Strong Automobile Objective and Planetarium (1924–25).

DECEMBER 31

Wright updates Guggenheim on his plans for the building. He tells him that the site will have to accommodate a building that is tall but also markedly different from the city's skyscrapers.

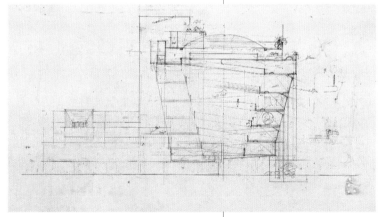

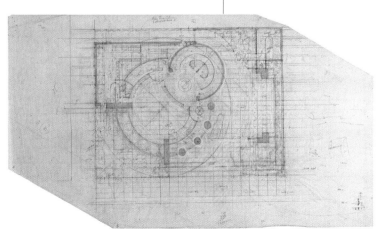

'44

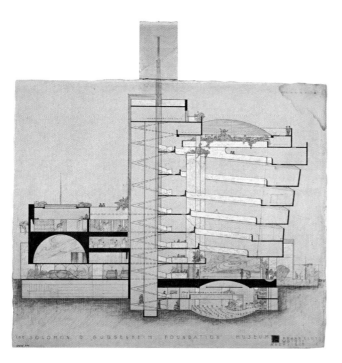 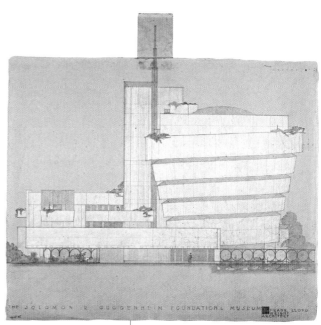

JANUARY

Letters early in the year show Wright articulating the central components of the museum's design. He writes Rebay about his ideas of what will suit the collection: "If non-objective painting is to have any great future it must be related to environment in due proportion as it pretty much is already, not to the high ceiling. And not to flat background of various tonalities suited to the paintings. The less texture in the background the better. A museum should have above all a clear atmosphere of light and sympathetic surface. Frames were always an expedient that segregated and marked the paintings off from environment to its own loss of relationship and proportion."

JANUARY 26

Though Wright's first sketches depict a spiral building with a wide base, he soon flips the structure so that it grows progressively wider as it travels upward. He writes to Rebay, "I find that the antique Ziggurat has great possibilities for our building. You will see. We can use it either top side down or down side top."

Solomon R. Guggenheim Museum,
New York, 1943–59. Elevation (pre-
sentation drawing). Graphite and
colored pencil on paper, 51 x 61 cm.
Frank Lloyd Wright Foundation,
Scottsdale, Arizona 4305.007

'44

FEBRUARY 6

Color is of particular interest to Rebay because in nonobjectivity it is a means of reaching the highest spiritual plane. In her correspondence with Wright, the two exchange ideas on the subject. In one offering, Wright defends his preference for red: "Red is the color of Creation. It courses in even the veins of all of plant life.... Reds are as varied as the blue of sea and sky except that the sea is a reflector. But so is the earth a reflector of the rays of the Sun, which again, is red. The Sun is the soul of Red." He allows, though, that, for the museum, his clients may choose any color "that appeals."

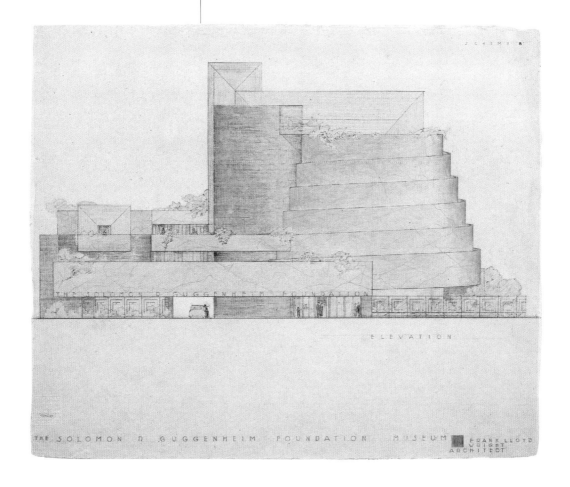

'44

Letter, Frank Lloyd Wright
to Solomon R. Guggenheim,
April 23, 1944

MARCH–APRIL

When the foundation signs a contract for the purchase of a plot of land on the southeast corner of Fifth Avenue and Eighty-ninth Street, Rebay announces the plans for a new museum to the press. Though she explains that the building has not yet been designed, she assures reporters that it will be of the most modern style, as befits the art collection it will house. Wright, meanwhile, congratulates Guggenheim on choosing a propitious site.

APRIL 5

Though she likes Wright's early sketches, Rebay demands that he consult with her before his plans become more detailed. "As paintings mean not much to you (or did you once go to our gallery while you were weeks in New York) you cannot so well feel as we do, who live it more than anything, even emptiness," she writes. "Of course, I have seen your plans only twice and for a short half hour I *got to study them*, you just got to let me ponder and think and feel our actual needs into what is to be done."

```
                                    File:Frank Lloyd Wright
                                         General Corresp.

MR. SOLOMON GUGGENHEIM: THE SOLOMON GUGGENHEIM FOUNDATION: CARNEGIE
HALL BUILDING: NEW YORK CITY


My dear Mr. Guggenheim:

I should, long ago, have written to say how much I appreciate the
site you have chosen for the memorial museum.

The more I think about it the wiser the choice seems.  The building
will be dignified by its surroundings not depreciated by them.
The park is New York's real center and will grow more so as the
place tightens up.

The Metropolitan helps us - we will benefit the Metropolitan.
Our building will stand by - in full view of all New York - where
anybody interested can easily reach it, not pushed around by
traffic.

After all a museum is not a mart in a big way?

Hilla keeps us posted concerning your health which we hope
continues as good as the best.



        Sincerely yours,
        FRANK LLOYD WRIGHT

        Taliesin West
        Scottsdale Arizona
        April 23  1944

                                                          9
```

MAY 24–OCTOBER 22

Elizabeth Mock, the director of the Department of Architecture and Design at the Museum of Modern Art, curates a show titled *Built in the USA: 1932–1944*. The exhibition aims to present the best of modern design since the museum's International Style show in 1932. In the catalogue, Mock, who was interested in residential architecture and had studied with Wright as a Taliesin Fellow, writes, "The new European architecture opened our eyes, stimulated our minds and finally *did* materialize as an important influence on the American scene, but in conjunction with two other factors: first, a strong new interest in Frank Lloyd Wright, encouraged by his renewed creative activity in the middle and latter 'thirties; and second, a revaluation of that very dark horse—traditional vernacular building."

Letter, Hilla Rebay to
Albert Thiele, December 6, 1944

44

DECEMBER 1
Guggenheim, on vacation at his home in South Carolina, writes to Albert Thiele, vice president of the foundation: "For a long time I have endeavored to have [Wright] push matters a bit more than he seems to, as I feel that the sooner we present our plans before the city authorities, the sooner we may receive our permit to go ahead with the construction of the building — which I am most anxious to see finished." Soon the roles will reverse, and Wright will be the one pressing a hesitant Guggenheim to begin construction.

DECEMBER 6
Wright, ever short on cash, asks for a $10,000 advance for his work. Rebay asks Thiele to approve the request.

JULY 5
Rebay has sent Wright several letters expressing her fear that his design will fail to serve the collection. She mentions the ideas of other artists, a serious affront to Wright. "[László] Moholy-Nagy has the nerve to suggest to us what a museum should be like? I never did respect him for his brains," he retorts.

JULY 27
Guggenheim, Rebay, and Wright meet to review building plans. Guggenheim concludes that "we are going to have something very beautiful and exceptional." The three agree that the architect will construct a model based on his drawings. Guggenheim, who finds the sketches "entirely satisfactory," sends Wright a check for $21,000.

File:Frank Lloyd Wright
Fees & Agreements

December 6, 1944

Dear Mr. Thiele:

Mr. Guggenheim and myself think it wise to send the requested $10,000 to Mr. Wright. The engineering job of the building due to its newness and originality must be a considerable one, and very evidently is of great importance and therefore cannot be rushed, and it seems wise not to give cause of any kind which might hinder *or rush* in the slightest way, the thoroughness and efficiency of this important matter, which time extension may involve expensive unavoidable outlay, which after all is to our best interest.

I have great confidence in the artistic and professional integrity and conscienciousness of Mr. Wright.

Sincerely yours,

HILLA REBAY

Mr. Albert Thiele
The Solomon R. Guggenheim Foundation
120 Broadway
New York City

'45

Adelman Laundry (unbuilt),
Milwaukee, Wisconsin, 1945.
Perspective. Sepia on tracing
paper, 59.7 x 92.7 cm. Frank Lloyd
Wright Foundation, Scottsdale,
Arizona 4507.002

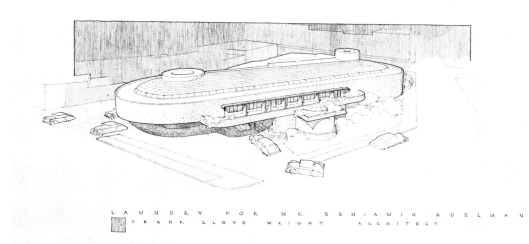

LAUNDRY FOR MR. BENJAMIN ADELMAN
FRANK LLOYD WRIGHT ARCHITECT

FEBRUARY 5

Rebay sends Wright a long
letter in which she again
expresses doubts about his
design. In a withering response,
he tells the museum director
that she is "neither intelligent nor
true." He hopes, though, that he
will one day teach her "that an
Organic building knows no division between Concept, Execution,
and Purpose. Conceived for a
purpose it definitely completes
the service of that purpose or
fails, ignominious. No details
(not even the smallest) can be
interjected or interfered with
without marring the peace and
quiet of the whole Concept,
Execution, and Purpose. You
could take this in, in a Painting.
Why then are you unable to
take this in, in Architecture—
the Mother-Art of which Painting
is but as a daughter?...Now
I am not 'humble'! But I
am competent."

MARCH 1

In another letter, Wright apolo-
gizes to Rebay and suggests that,
if it will assuage her fears, he
will gather a panel of "German
refugee-architects" including
Walter Curt Behrendt, Marcel
Breuer, Erich Mendelsohn,
Ludwig Mies van der Rohe, and
Walter Gropius to review his
plans. Despite some further
correspondence on the subject,
the review never takes place.

Benjamin Adelman, an admirer
and friend of Wright, asks the
architect to design a facility for his
industrial laundry business. To be
realized in reinforced concrete,
Wright's plan includes a driveway
for drop-off service, a dining
room for staff, and an immense
ceiling-roof to draw away steam
generated by the laundry. The
building is never built, but its
conception illustrates Wright's
predilection for fluid, circular
shapes in this period, whether
for residences, cultural and civic
centers, or industrial sites.

'45

Living City (unbuilt), 1958. Bird's-eye
perspective (presentation drawing).
Graphite on tracing paper, 71 x 91
cm. Frank Lloyd Wright Foundation,
Scottsdale, Arizona 5828.005

APRIL

Despite his client's doubts,
Wright grows more enthusiastic
about his design, marveling at
its intricacy and encouraging
Rebay and Guggenheim to travel
to Taliesin to see the complex
working drawings and model. He
continues to consider different
colors and textures for the museum's exterior. Options include
facing the building in red marble
and covering the surface with
an aggregate of ground marble,
a texture that would create what
he later calls a "noble monolith."

MAY 29

The Museum of Modern Art
mounts the exhibition *Tomorrow's
Small House: Models and Plans*,
which features furnished models
of houses that could be pre-
fabricated. It includes work by
Wright, Serge Chermayeff,
Philip Johnson, and others.

JUNE 19

Rebay objects to using red marble
for the museum's facade. "Dear
Frank," she writes. "Do you know
that in the dark, blood glows
with a yellow light? So the color
of blood is illusion also and its
life is its motion not its color.
Our building would be handi-
capped if such illusion gave a
reason for color. I do not like red
as it is of all colors the most
materialistic, and to me it ruins
the model. I wonder if we could
get yellow marble, and if not,
green." The color red disappears
from Wright's plans thereafter.

The University of Chicago
Press publishes Wright's *When
Democracy Builds*, which promul-
gates his vision for Broadacre
City. In the scheme, which he
first proposed in the 1930s,
citizens would live on one-acre
plots where they would erect
prefabricated houses and cultivate
the land. Wright returns to
Broadacre City repeatedly,
revising it as late as the year
before his death, in the form
of his Living City project. In later
versions, he incorporates some
of his more well known buildings,
such as the S. C. Johnson & Son,
Inc. Research Tower (1943–50;
below, at center right).

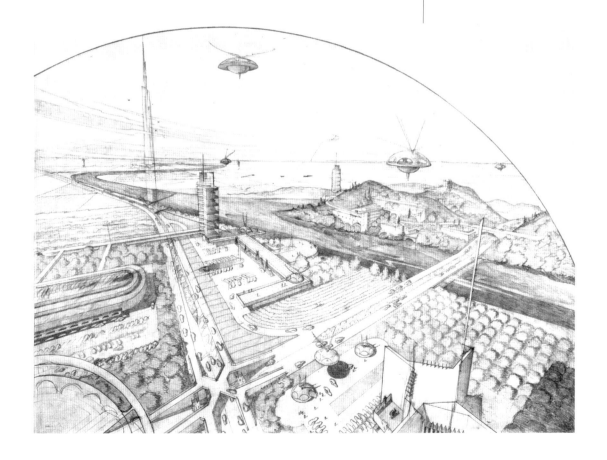

'45

TOP LEFT Solomon R. Guggenheim Museum, New York, 1943–59. Section (working drawing), 1945. Frank Lloyd Wright Foundation, Scottsdale, Arizona 4305.136

TOP RIGHT Headline from the *New York Times*, July 10, 1945

BOTTOM Letter, Frank Lloyd Wright to Solomon R. Guggenheim, July 27, 1945

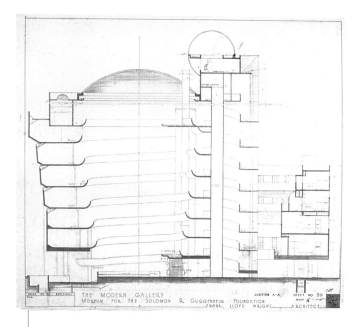

THE MODERN GALLERY
MUSEUM FOR THE SOLOMON R. GUGGENHEIM FOUNDATION
FRANK LLOYD WRIGHT ARCHITECT

MUSEUM BUILDING TO RISE AS SPIRAL

New Guggenheim Structure Designed by F. L. Wright Is Called First of Kind

JULY 27

Wright urges Guggenheim to buy a second piece of land, just south of the plot already purchased.

JULY 9

At a luncheon at the Plaza Hotel, the press is shown sketches of the proposed museum. It will be what Wright calls a "true logarithmic spiral" and, according to one article, "was designed in conformity with the human figure, a principle to which [Wright] referred as 'one of the secrets of organic architecture.'" The main gallery will sit on the north end of the property, and a smaller adjacent building called the Monitor (a term of Wright's invention) will serve as a residence for Rebay. At the event, Wright also announces that a vacuum mechanism will be installed at the front door so that patrons will be dust-free before viewing the art, since the paintings themselves will not be exhibited in frames or behind glass.

File:
Frank Lloyd Wright
Fees & Agreements

7/27/45

My dear Mr. Guggenheim: I have yours of the 23rd. But since the acquisition of the next door piece of land so greatly benefits our project in so many vital ways -- adding to the value of what we have already done - that I take the liberty to suggest that you at least take an option on the piece . . . option to be acted upon within - say sixty days. Would you kindly call Mr. Gibbons directly and ask him to get this for you?   The cost would be negligible as he has already had the benefit of your patronage.

Were we to sit down together with the plans I could show you how much we would gain in general proportion and light in the interior court by the additional Fifth Avenue frontage. That frontage was always <u>tight</u>.   To change the plans now would only cost me hundreds whereas after they are completed the change would cost me thousands.   But I shall gladly assume the burden for the sake of the great improvement in quality of the whole "Affair-Guggenheim".

I have not mentioned this to Hilla because I believed she would hesitate (as circumstances are) to ask more of you than you have already given for the project and I didn't want to push her into the initiative. So I took it upon myself to present it directly to you which may offend her - however. So I wrote her that I had sent an important letter to you, asking her "to make sure that you got the letter about the ground".

I hope you are all having a good rest and the weather is at its best.   I've been knocked out a few days by excessive heat - 96° in the shade.

To Mrs. Guggenheim our best and thanks to her for The Razor's Edge. We will be glad to read it.

Faithfully,
Frank Lloyd Wright   July 27th, 1945

28

45

TOP Frank Lloyd Wright, Hilla Rebay, and Solomon R. Guggenheim at the unveiling of the museum model, Plaza Hotel, New York, September 20, 1945

BOTTOM Solomon R. Guggenheim Museum, New York, 1943–59. Model, 1945

OCTOBER 8

Life magazine runs a story on the museum with photographs of the model. The photos are later put on display at the Museum of Non-Objective Painting.

AUGUST 11

Rebay, who despite her doubts has remained a fervent advocate for the museum, reassures Wright that it will be built: "I am often ready to go into seclusion; but it is funny to see how I continue whether I like it or not; as who would—if there had been or would be a who, I certainly would have long ago run away. But God did not for one moment fail the end in sight and so how could I, and you know you never do. I wanted the very darned least evidence of distinguished enemies' objections licked all through, and I hope we will."

AUGUST 28

Wright informs Guggenheim that the model of the museum— what he calls "a great beauty"— is being sent to New York.

SEPTEMBER 20

Another press luncheon is held at the Plaza, this time for the unveiling of the model. Wright takes the opportunity to explain that the museum's form has been inspired by ancient ziggurats but that he has turned the shape upside down to express expansive possibility: the spiral could theoretically go on infinitely toward the sky. "This is pure optimism," he tells the crowd. *Time* observes, "To some of the newsmen, impressed by Architect Wright but irreverent by nature, the model looked something like a big, white ice cream freezer."

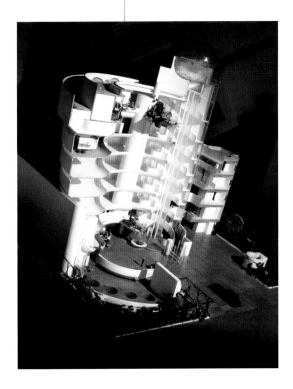

'46

Ayn Rand House (unbuilt), Los Angeles, California, 1946. Perspective (presentation drawing). Graphite, colored pencil, and ink on tracing paper, 61.6 x 92.1 cm. Frank Lloyd Wright Foundation, Scottsdale, Arizona 4717.001

JANUARY

Architectural Forum counters the criticisms leveled at the museum design: "If this building is 'strange,' so is the chambered nautilus, the structure of a leaf, the wing of a bird." The article includes a description of Wright's use of glass tubing for the central skylight as well as his plans to keep motorized wheelchairs available for visitors who want to sit through their visit. In the same article, Wright predicts his design's longevity: "When the first atomic bomb lands on New York [the museum] will not be destroyed. It may be blown a few miles up into the air, but *when it comes down it will bounce!*"

In 1943, Ayn Rand published *The Fountainhead*, a novel about an architect who defiantly adheres to his aesthetic vision in spite of pressures to compromise. Rand based her protagonist on Wright, but the architect saw little of himself in the character and was largely unimpressed with Rand. Nonetheless she asks the architect to design a "cottage" for her. The house is never built.

JULY

Despite Wright's urging (in one letter to his client he writes, "Hope long deferred maketh the heart sick"), Guggenheim decides to suspend further action on the museum, feeling that the postwar climate is too uncertain to make any definite building plans. The architect, discouraged by what has already been a three-year discussion with no immediate plans for construction, tells Guggenheim that he has stopped working on the museum for the time being and that he hopes the public will not think the announcements made over the years were a mere publicity stunt.

COTTAGE STUDIO
FOR AYN RAND
FRANK LLOYD WRIGHT

'46

Letter (excerpt), Frank
Lloyd Wright to Solomon R.
Guggenheim, August 14, 1946

File: Frank Lloyd Wright
General Correspondence
folder #4

8/14/46

My dear Mr. Guggenheim: I shall be very
happy to make any model, or illustrations
either, that might serve to clear up any
troublesome doubts that you entertain as to
the advantages to non-objective art natural
to their display in an environment such as
is characteristic of my work and which we
are planning for your new museum.

The fact is, Hilla has brought the matter
up before several times in different ways
and I have done my best to answer. But every
so often the matter comes up again to show
me I haven't really succeeded in showing
her anything. She now writes that "I dis-
like paintings anyway - have none in my houses"

2

etc, etc, - which renders me still "suspect"
in this important matter rather than giving
her the confidence she should have felt long
ago.

Well, to put the exact truth on record:
the old representational picture does not
enhance the interiors of my buildings. So I
don't use many (if any) by my own choice. But
abstractions do harmonize and so for that
reason does the noblest of old Chinese art
and that of the great Momoyama period of Japan.
You will find all these great works on the
walls of most of my buildings. Non-Objective
Paintings (for much the same reason) are well
suited to my interiors and were they available
we would have them constantly on view in the he
houses I build which are rapidly becoming the

3

pattern for the civilized world.   So I don't
know on what the assumption that I do not like
paintings and do not use them in my houses
could rest except idle uninformed gossip.

Surely, at my own house, Taliesin, you
saw a house with beautiful pictures, noble
screens and one of the finest (and largest)
collections of antique prints in existence?

.   .   .   .   .

AUGUST

In Wright's conception of the
museum, the paintings are to
be bathed in natural light from
the great central dome and the
peripheral skylights just above
the museum's spiraling walls.
In addition, artificial lighting
will be installed, and the walls
will have a slight outward incline.
Rebay and Guggenheim voice
doubts about this arrangement
and ask the architect to make a
model wall to show how the
paintings will be mounted and
lit. Wright agrees but tells Rebay
that he can't understand why
she should feel that the building will upstage the collection.
To Guggenheim, meanwhile,
he defends himself against
the charge that he does not
like painting, citing his love of
Japanese prints. His collection,
started in the 1890s, was valuable
enough that he often used it as
collateral when trying to leverage
his ever-unstable finances.

'46

John Lloyd Wright, the architect's second son and the inventor of Lincoln Logs, publishes a memoir, *My Father Who Is on Earth*. It is later republished with the pair's marginalia: the elder Wright's comments and John's responses.

AUGUST

Wright's request for the land adjacent to the initial museum site is met: the foundation purchases the property at 1071 Fifth Avenue, home of the Gardner School for Girls. Wright's goal is to obtain the entire Fifth Avenue blockfront between Eighty-eighth and Eighty-ninth streets for his building. When construction of the museum is delayed, however, the Gardner School townhouse will be remodeled to make a temporary home for Guggenheim's collection, replacing the Museum of Non-Objective Painting's Fifty-fourth Street location from 1948 to 1956.

Walt Whitman, Kandinsky, Louis Sullivan, or Laotze are no more entitled to claim originality than a casual stevedore on the docks? So what? Simply that there is only the one Idea. Agreed. We both happen to represent the great ego as they did. You with a brush. I with a hod of mortar, some bricks and an industrial-system. But just the same I'll take Whitman over the stevedore!

And I do not conceive that whom you call God would like me any better if I were what you call "humble". Most "humble" people are hypocrites like those who think and speak we instead of I: the Fascists instead of the Democrats.

SEPTEMBER 19

After Rebay chastises Wright for his arrogance, he defends his position as a democratic one.

Telegram, Frank Lloyd Wright
to Solomon R. Guggenheim,
September 23, 1947

'47

WESTERN UNION

CLASS OF SERVICE		SYMBOLS
This is a full-rate Telegram or Cablegram unless its deferred character is indicated by a suitable symbol above or preceding the address.	JOSEPH L. EGAN PRESIDENT	DL=Day Letter
		NL=Night Letter
		LC=Deferred Cable
		NLT=Cable Night Letter

(00)

1947 SEP 23 PM 5

The filing time shown in the date line on telegrams and day letters is STANDARD TIME at point of origin. Time of receipt is STANDARD TIME at point of destination

N388 DL PD=PRINGGREN WIS 23 157P

SOLOMON R GUGGENHEIM=

    BOX 190 PORTWASHINGTON NY=

ENTIRE MODEL NOW COMPLETED MOST EXCITING HARMONIOUSLY
BEAUTIFUL USEFUL THING ON EARTH ANNEX ADDS GREATLY TO
THE EFFECTIVENESS OF THE WHOLE=
    FRANK LLOYD WRIGHT.

File: Gardner School
Folder: 1071 5th Ave.(Gardner)
    Frank Lloyd Wright

THE COMPANY WILL APPRECIATE SUGGESTIONS FROM ITS PATRONS CONCERNING ITS SERVICE

MARCH 6

Moses and Wright speak at
Princeton University's Conference
on Planning Man's Physical
Environment. Wright declares
that the existence of the atom
bomb is proof that our "educational, economic and political
systems" had failed. As a result,
he suggests that all higher education should be abolished for
ten years, adding that soldiers
returning from World War II
should not be sent to school but
rather given land, "where they
can get in touch with and be
touched by their own birthright—the good ground."

APRIL

The model of the museum is
shipped back to Taliesin and
is badly damaged in transit.
Wright, however, believes that
the model would have to have
been redone in any case, since
the plans had changed so
extensively to accommodate the
newly purchased plot. It is a
time-consuming and expensive
revision, "but the result is so
happy in every way that I don't
mind," he writes to Rebay. "The
money it costs me is well spent.
But the greatest time-killer of
all, I find, is the change from the
field construction of reinforced
concrete to steel—pre-fabricated
in the shop to save S.R.G. time
and money."

SEPTEMBER

Eager to build, Wright suggests
to Guggenheim that they begin
with a newly conceived annex,
which would hold gallery space,
a lecture hall, offices, and storage
space until the full museum is
ready; at that point, the annex,
which Wright says can be completed within four months, would
become home to the museum's
administration. Exhorting his
patron, the architect writes:
"We would make a good start
on the ultimate Museum and in
dignified fashion." He and his
apprentices build a second model
that includes the new addition.

'47

TOP Brochure for Usonia Homes Cooperative, Pleasantville, New York, 1947. Douglas Steiner Collection, Edmonds, Washington

BOTTOM Letter (copy), Albert Thiele to Frank Lloyd Wright, November 12, 1947

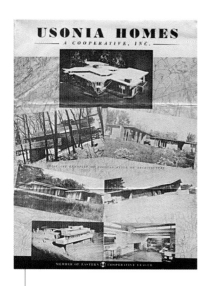

OCTOBER–NOVEMBER

Guggenheim, Rebay, and Thiele travel to Wisconsin to visit Wright and his wife, Olgivanna, at Taliesin. At this meeting, Guggenheim makes clear that he does not want to proceed with building either the annex or the museum at this time. Instead, he has decided to remodel the Gardner School townhouse as a temporary museum and proposes exhibiting the second model of the building there.

A group of New Yorkers organized by David Henken, a former apprentice at Taliesin, buy ninety-five acres of land in Pleasantville, New York, where they plan to build a cooperative community based on Wright's ideas about organic architecture and decentralized cities. In addition to designing three of the forty-seven houses eventually built, Wright devises the site plan, which is made up of circular one-acre plots. The group calls the community Usonia, derived from the name Wright had given to his model for an affordable house first built in Madison, Wisconsin, in 1936 for Katherine and Herbert Jacobs.

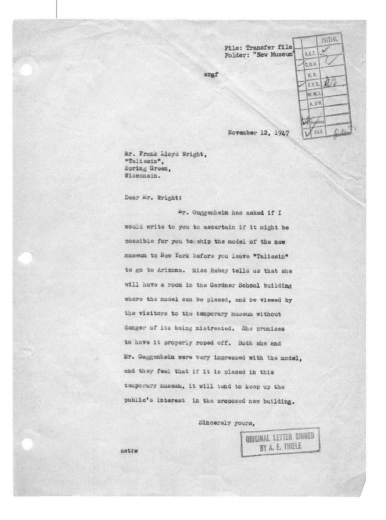

LEFT Letter, Solomon R. Guggenheim to Frank Lloyd Wright, November 21, 1947

RIGHT Frank Lloyd Wright, Hilla Rebay, and Olgivanna Lloyd Wright at Taliesin West, Scottsdale, Arizona, 1947. Hilla von Rebay Foundation Archive, Solomon R. Guggenheim Museum Archives, New York

'47

NOVEMBER

Wright tells Guggenheim that, at the very least, the foundation should apply for a building permit. Guggenheim remains unconvinced. In the post-war economy, building costs have become inflated, and Guggenheim believes that his interests would be better served by waiting.

November 21, 1947

Mr. Frank Lloyd Wright,
Taliesin,
Spring Green, Wisconsin.

Dear Mr. Wright:

I was pleased to hear from you by your letter of November 15th in regard to the proposed application for a building permit for the rear or annex-feature, as you call it, of the museum.

I think I understand your position and, needless to say, I am most anxious not to do anything which would hamper you in any possible way.

My concern is that since the local building situation and the foreign picture both now are so unsettled, it might be a pointless thing to take a step in relation to the museum which later might turn out to have been unnecessary or not the best thing to have done. I would suppose future developments might make it necessary for you to revise your ideas as to materials and construction techniques. If that is so, would it not be unwise to have Holden, McLaughlin & Associates devote time and effort to getting plans approved which might become obsolete?

This is my feeling about it, for your consideration.

With best personal regards,

Sincerely yours,

S. R. G.

DECEMBER

Rebay goes to Arizona to visit the Wrights at Taliesin West, their home and studio near Scottsdale.

'48

TOP View of permanent-collection exhibition, Museum of Non-Objective Painting, New York, 1950. From left: Vasily Kandinsky, *Painting with White Border*, 1913; Vasily Kandinsky, *Composition 8*, 1923; Vasily Kandinsky, *Blue Circle*, 1922 (above); Vasily Kandinsky, *Dominant Curve*, 1936 (below). In passageway: Rudolf Bauer, *Light Fugue*, 1937

BOTTOM V. C. Morris Gift Shop, San Francisco, 1948–49. Longitudinal section (presentation drawing). Graphite, colored pencil, and ink on tracing paper, 75 x 91 cm. Frank Lloyd Wright Foundation, Scottsdale, Arizona 4824.009

OCTOBER 26

Shortly before the presidential election of 1948, Wright informs Rebay that he plans to vote for Henry A. Wallace, the Progressive Party's candidate, who is running on an antiwar platform. "[Thomas] Dewey will be elected," the architect incorrectly predicts. "But if there is a loud shout from the people for peace he will take it as a warning. That's all there is to my vote for Wallace—a vote for peace not by appeasement but by reason, in time! Surely S.R.G. would not blame me for that. Do we all have to see politics alike to be friends?"

JANUARY 31

The Museum of Non-Objective Painting opens its doors at its new location, 1071 Fifth Avenue.

Wright renovates the V. C. Morris Gift Shop (1948–49) in San Francisco, which features an interior ramp.

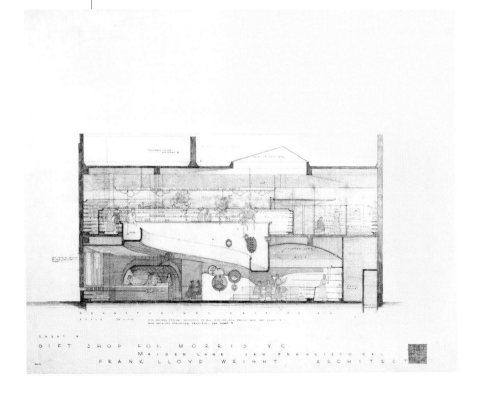

'49

MUSEUM FOR THE SOLOMON R. GUGGENHEIM FOUNDATION
FRANK LLOYD WRIGHT ARCHITECT

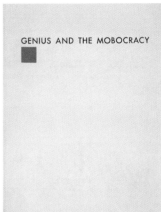

GENIUS AND THE MOBOCRACY

Wright revises the plans to encompass the second plot of land. His new drawings include one fewer ramp.

In 1943, Katherine and Herbert Jacobs solicited the architect's services for a second time, just as he began working on his drawings for the Guggenheim. The resultant second house, called the Solar Hemicycle and completed this year, sits on a farm outside Madison and warms and cools itself in part with passive solar energy.

Genius and the Mobocracy, Wright's biography of Louis Sullivan, is published. Wright, who worked for Sullivan from 1888 to 1893, argues that his teacher's work has been unjustly ignored because of the conformity and mediocrity that Wright believes characterizes much of American culture.

'49

Article from the *New York Times*,
May 26, 1949

MAY 26

Anthony Leviero, a Pulitzer
Prize–winning reporter for the
New York Times, covers a visit
Wright makes to President Harry
Truman to suggest the United
States' capital be moved west
of the Mississippi.

FEBRUARY 28

In a letter to Rebay, Wright
bemoans the fact that
Guggenheim has not yet given
approval for construction to
begin: "For five years we have
been wanting to get the building cheaper. We will all be gone
before as adequate a home for
the S.R.G. collection and your
work can be done at the figure
he hopes to pay for it. Let's stay
level and keep hoping he will
see the light and realize his
dream before he passes away."

Frank Lloyd Wright Wants Capital To Move to Functional Old Prairies

By ANTHONY LEVIERO
Special to THE NEW YORK TIMES.

WASHINGTON, May 26—Frank Lloyd Wright, titular head of American architects, as he styled himself, visited that plain Democrat, President Truman, today, and what a shellacking he delivered to American ideas and ideals.

Mr. Wright is nothing if not modern. And he's probably the most iconoclastic person who has ever entered that degenerate old renaissance mansion in which this barbaric republic compels its Presidents to live. (That last sentence is written the way Mr. Wright talks.)

Epigrammatic thunderbolts began to crash the moment that reporters massed across Mr. Wright's path. Here is the sequence of the intellectual encounter:

"I came to see if he [Mr. Truman] would join me in my design and plea to move the capital out West, west of the Mississippi," Mr. Wright said casually. "The President quite agreed with the project."

That sounded quite interesting, but after a measured pause, Mr. Wright added: "But he didn't promise his support."

Approves That Balcony

What did he think of the balcony Mr. Truman put on the White House?

"I haven't seen it, but if the President wants it, I think he ought to have it," said Mr. Wright. (He likes things to be functional.)

"Where out West would you move the capital?"

"I think out on the great rolling prairies," opined the architect, "or around Des Moines or in northern Missouri. Or it might be placed near the center of population, near Denver or Colorado Springs."

"Where are your investments, Mr. Wright?" This question was meant to be devastating.

"Right here under my vest," fenced Mr. Wright. "I think that's where you boys ought to keep yours for the next ten years."

The conversation got scrambled at this point, but it got back to the subject of moving the capital. Mr. Wright thought we ought to make a new start, plan it anew along modern lines—presumably the way Mr. Wright would plan it.

"You see, democracy never built anything," Mr. Wright declared. "All we have here is monarchic and militaristic."

Civilized? Perish Thought

A reporter said something about our having been busy building civilization.

"I deny it's civilization," replied Mr. Wright. "I think the Frenchman had it right when he said we were the only great nation on record which had proceeded from barbarism to degeneracy with no civilization in between." (Mr. Wright did not specify which Frenchman.)

One of the older reporters remarked with some asperity that that wasn't very smart, and where did he get the stuff.

"From what I see looking around," said Mr. Wright, looking around. "Look at you, standing there, wearing a series of bags that were invented by the British."

This exchange invited an inspection of Mr. Wright's personal architecture. A man soon to be 80 years old, he looked more like the Chrysler Building—tall, streamlined and erect—than, say, the Imperial Hotel at Toyko, a groundhugging structure which Mr. Wright designed and won him fame.

On his roof Mr. Wright was wearing a tan hat, pork-pie design. The hat was conventional enough, but Mr. Wright did to it what he would do to a neo-colonial house: squash it down into a rambler or one-story affair.

And With a Cane

As for a series of bags, Mr. Wright was wearing one more than the reporter. He had a vest and the reporter didn't. Mr. Wright's three-piece, pepper-and-salt tweed could have been British, too. His cane, with a curved handle, seemed old-fashioned.

"All we have is a state of mind, not a civilization," continued Mr. Wright.

"You mean there is nothing you like in this city designed by that great Democrat, Thomas Jefferson?"

"Jefferson," retorted Mr. Wright, "was like a country gentleman, an English gentleman. He had a culture and an education and it made him what he was when he came here, but it didn't change his mind and heart."

"Well, is there any architecture in Washington that you do like?"

"There is nothing here that isn't derivative, or sentimentally gone to seed," Mr. Wright said. "I don't think there is a noble building in Washington. No, we haven't awakened, we haven't been born, really, but our time is coming. I think what we need more than anything else in life is a good licking. I think we are the most arrogant, self-satisfied, inconsequential, insignificant people * * *"

The reporter wearing the bags cut in to say that Mr. Wright seemed to have prospered in this degenerate country. Mr. Wright replied that he would have eaten in any event.

With so much swept away, nobody expected a good opinion about the man from Missouri, but this is what the architect said:

"I think the President has some very sound and promising views of what constitutes a Democrat and this I was delighted to see because I had some doubts—but not now."

Mr. Wright went off to deliver a lecture at the Institute of Contemporary Arts, leaving the cosmos about where it was.

'49

LEFT Edgar J. Kaufmann Self-Service Garage (unbuilt), Pittsburgh, 1949. Perspective (presentation drawing). Colored pencil and sepia on tracing paper, 91 x 119 cm. Frank Lloyd Wright Foundation, Scottsdale, Arizona 4923.054

RIGHT Solomon R. Guggenheim, n.d. Solomon R. Guggenheim Museum Archives, New York

AUGUST

Fearing the devaluation of American currency, Guggenheim elects to continue waiting before proceeding with the building of the museum. In the meantime, Wright makes revisions to the museum and adds two apartments to the annex, one for the museum's caretaker and another for Guggenheim.

OCTOBER 24

Rebay, concerned that the museum will overpower the artworks, again asks for changes to be made to the plans. Now six years into the project, Wright has little patience for her request: "It depresses us all to learn from your hasty, nasty, unsigned note that you can read plans not at all and have formed an entirely erroneous idea of the plans already made and accepted by you and S.R.G. Plans are not Paintings, unfortunately, so we had better not waste more time and stop work on them."

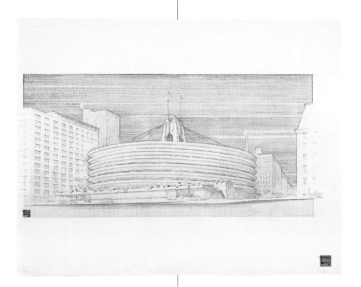

NOVEMBER 3

Solomon R. Guggenheim dies at the age of eighty-eight. He leaves $8 million to the foundation, of which $2 million is earmarked for construction of the museum.

SEPTEMBER

Wright designs a self-service garage for his long-time client Edgar Kaufmann, the department-store magnate for whom Wright built one of his best-known buildings, Fallingwater (1934–37). Meant to serve a downtown shopping district of Pittsburgh, the garage is to be formed by spiraling concrete ramps with a central open court. The structure is never built.

'50

LEFT Larkin Company Administration Building (destroyed), Buffalo, New York, 1902–06. Frank Lloyd Wright Foundation, Scottsdale, Arizona 0403.0030

RIGHT Lord Arthur Castle Stewart with Olgivanna Lloyd Wright, ca. 1959

With Guggenheim no longer guiding the project, rumors abound that the foundation plans to abandon the new museum, so Wright goes on the offensive. In a letter to be read to the trustees, the architect writes, "The fact is Mr. Guggenheim employed me and trusted me. The trustees are not my employers and of course I do not regard them so. This is all post-mortem I think. Were it not for my promise to Mr. Guggenheim several weeks before he died that I would build this building for him — exclusive of architect's fees and minor furnishings — for two million dollars I would be quite content to withdraw and leave the matter to the trustees. But I do have a conscience in this matter whether they have any or not, above the money matter." Wright will invoke his promise to Guggenheim in much of his correspondence in the years to come.

Lord Arthur Castle Stewart, a former member of the British Parliament, is appointed second president of the Solomon R. Guggenheim Foundation. In 1920, Castle Stewart had married Eleanor Guggenheim, a daughter of Solomon. Harry F. Guggenheim, Solomon's nephew, becomes chairman of the board of trustees.

JANUARY 26

The Larkin Company Administration Building (1902–06), designed by Wright for a mail-order company, is sold by the city of Buffalo for $5,000 with the proviso that it must be destroyed by July 1951. The building had included many innovations that became standard in office buildings. Wright said of it, "I think I first consciously began to try to beat the box in the Larkin building. I found a natural opening to the liberation I sought when I finally pushed the staircase towers out from the corners of the main building, made them into freestanding, individual features."

When designing houses, Wright was careful to consider siting, making sure that a home was integrated with the landscape. Yet he also designed buildings that turned their backs on the street and instead had an inward focus. This was true of the Larkin building as well as the Guggenheim.

After demolition, the building is replaced by a warehouse and truck garage.

'50

TOP Headline from the *New York Times*, June 9, 1950

CENTER David Wright House, Phoenix, Arizona, 1950–52. Aerial view

BOTTOM David Wright House, Phoenix, Arizona, 1950–52. Elevation. Graphite and colored pencil on tracing paper, 35.6 x 91.4 cm. Frank Lloyd Wright Foundation, Scottsdale, Arizona 5030.003

JUNE 8

Because of his fame as an architect, Wright's opinions about world events are frequently covered by the press. After World War II, he often comments on the dangers of atomic energy. On his eighty-third birthday, Wright tells reporters that the United States should outlaw the atomic bomb even if Russia does not: "We have nothing to fear in abandoning the atom arms race. Russia wants peace just as much as we do."

FEBRUARY 28

Wright contacts Arthur Cort Holden, the New York architect from Holden, McLaughlin & Associates whom he's retained to apply for the museum's building permit since Wright does not hold a New York license. He tells Holden that he is working to keep Rebay director of the museum, though he rightly suspects that the foundation would like her to step down.

Frank Lloyd Wright Bars Bombs

Wright designs a house in Phoenix for his son David. Made of concrete, the design is based on an article Wright wrote two years before, "How to Live in the Southwest." The spiral-shaped dwelling is lifted off the ground to catch breezes and escape the heat of the desert floor.

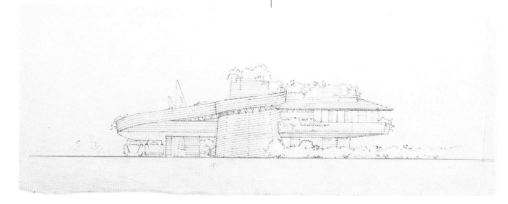

'50

Letter (excerpt), Frank Lloyd
Wright to Harry F. Guggenheim,
September 19, 1950

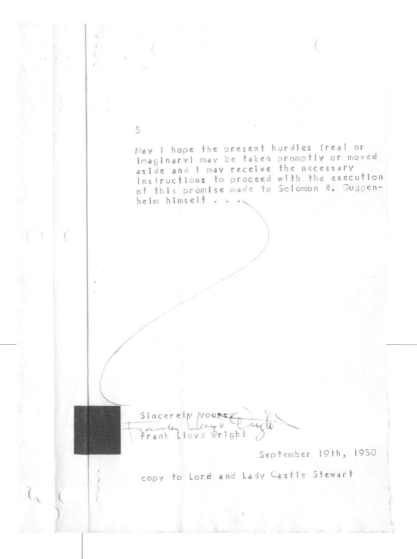

5

May I hope the present hurdles (real or
imaginary) may be taken promptly or moved
aside and I may receive the necessary
instructions to proceed with the execution
of this promise made to Solomon R. Guggenheim himself . . . .

Sincerely yours,
Frank Lloyd Wright

September 19th, 1950

copy to Lord and Lady Castle Stewart

JULY 14

Frank and Olgivanna Lloyd
Wright travel to London to visit
the Castle Stewarts to enlist their
support for the museum. The day
after they lunch together, Lord
Castle Stewart writes to Harry
Guggenheim: " [Eleanor] feels
that his method of presenting
the paintings on the walls will be
not only novel but highly suitable
to the types of paintings which
have to be shown. On the whole,
therefore, Eleanor and I both feel
confident that provided the financial situation warrants it, the time
has now come when we might go
very thoroughly into the question
of getting the Museum erected as
soon as possible."

SEPTEMBER 19

In a letter to Harry F. Guggenheim,
Wright urges the foundation
to purchase a parcel of land at
the corner of Fifth Avenue and
Eighty-eighth Street, the third and
final piece needed to acquire the
entire frontage between Eighty-
eighth and Eighty-ninth streets.
Reminding him of their mutual
obligation to Harry's late uncle,
Wright writes, "It would seem there
should be no further delay in starting to execute this will of his so far
as this building which he desired
is concerned. But manifestly until
I have the ground to build upon I
can do nothing."

'50

TOP LEFT S. C. Johnson & Son, Inc. Research Tower, Racine, Wisconsin, 1943–50. Historic American Buildings Survey, Prints and Photographs Division, Library of Congress, Washington, D.C.

BOTTOM LEFT S. C. Johnson & Son, Inc. Administration Building, Racine, Wisconsin, 1936–39. Interior. Historic American Buildings Survey, Prints and Photographs Division, Library of Congress, Washington, D.C.

RIGHT Letter, Frank Lloyd Wright to Hilla Rebay, October 23, 1950

Wright's S. C. Johnson & Son, Inc. Research Tower is completed. The building is faced in glass so that the alternating circular and chamfered floors may be seen from the exterior. Eleven years earlier, Wright built the company's administration building, which features funnel-shaped columns. Wright places a service core at the center of the tower with floors cantilevered outward, a technique he uses in a modified form in the Guggenheim design.

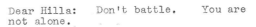

Dear Hilla: Don't battle.   You are not alone.

Disregard the talk and all suspicion.

You have been wrong about me, But, never mind - we will do best now by letting the Foundation, such as it is, do the worrying.   Neither of us has been unfaithful to the will and wish of S. R. G.   If there is to be treachery let it be theirs.

Faithfully,

Frank Lloyd Wright

October 23
1 9 5 0

N. B.   Your relatives are much like those generally where gratitude is concerned. Why look for that?

. . . will send pictures of the Johnson Building as soon as they are made - working on them now   . .

OCTOBER 23
During the early 1950s, Rebay and Wright fear that the building will not survive Guggenheim's death. Nonetheless, the museum director continues to remind Wright that his design must be well suited to the collection and the goals of nonobjectivity. Though he often expresses frustration with Rebay, in this letter Wright tries to reassure her.

'51

JANUARY
A retrospective of Wright's work called *Sixty Years of Living Architecture* opens in Philadelphia. The show consists of original drawings, models, photographs, and furniture as well as a section of one of Wright's Usonian houses. His Guggenheim model is also on display. The show next travels to the Palazzo Strozzi in Florence. It will go on to Switzerland, France, Germany, the Netherlands, and Mexico before coming to New York in 1953.

FEBRUARY 10
Talbot Hamlin reviews the exhibition for the *Nation:* "It is good to know that in these days when hate is considered a virtue and destruction an admirable way of life, in these days of McCarran acts and McCarthyism and hysteria in the newspapers, America is at last to be represented abroad by such an eloquent voice to tell Europe that American exports are not limited to cannon. For the Wright show is the record of a life devoted to art and love, not to killing and hate."

THE SOVEREIGNTY OF THE INDIVIDUAL

IN THE CAUSE OF ARCHITECTURE   FRANK LLOYD WRIGHT

PREFACE TO AUSGEFUHRTE BAUTEN UND ENTWURFE PUBLISHED BY WASMUTH BERLIN 1910 REPRINTED AS INTRODUCTION TO EXHIBITION PALAZZO STROZZI FLORENCE ITALY 1951

MARCH 9
Before leaving for a business trip to South America, Harry Guggenheim informs Wright that negotiations have been completed for the purchase of the land at the corner of Eighty-eighth Street and Fifth Avenue—what Wright has referred to as "the old hang-nail at the corner of the lot."

TOP LEFT Telegram, Frank Lloyd Wright to Harry F. Guggenheim, March 15, 1951

BOTTOM LEFT Telegram, Albert Thiele to Frank Lloyd Wright, March 29, 1951

RIGHT Manhattan Transfers column, *New York Times*, May 1, 1951

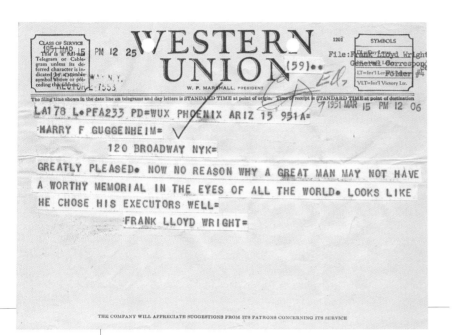

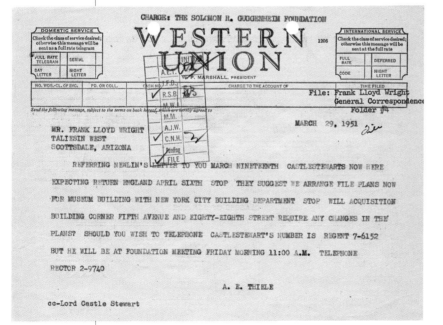

MANHATTAN TRANSFERS

56th St. 60 E. 22x100.5: Jen-Bur Holding Corp (Harry Ackerman, v pres) to Pader Realty Corp, 295 Madison Ave ($58.85).
Same property: Pader Realty Corp (Paul Englander, pres) to Oleg Cassini Inc, 60 E 56th St: mtg $66,663; p m mtg $50,000.
52d St. 55-61 E. 55.3x100.5: 7545 Realty Corp (Frederick Brown, pres) to 57 East 52d Street Realty Corp, 565 5th Ave ($236.50).
7th Ave. 2217-2243, n/e/cor 131st St, 199.10 to 132d St (168-170 W)x125: Murrain Realty Corp (John Murrain, pres) to Williams Institutional Colored Methodist Episcopal Church, 220 W 130th St ($235.40).
Horatio St. 6, 16.8x87.6: Samuel Robinson, heir of Mary A. Taggart, to Robert Taggart. East Orange, N. J.
137th St. 43-45 W. 50x99.11: Essex Properties Inc (Seymour M. Tannenbaum, pres) to Elwood Brown, 32-37 99th St, Corona, Queens; mtg $40.500; p m mtg $8,000 ($15.40).
121st St. 326 E. 18.9x100.10; E. Mario De Nicolais to Eddie Lopez, 188 E 109th St.
110th St. 309 E, 25x100.11; 309 East 110th Street Inc (Simon Kahan, pres) to Shirley Jacobs, 1270 Croes Ave, the Bronx; mtg $15,250 (55c).
147th St. 630, 18x99.11: Errol A. Thompson to Leslie F. Thompson, 630 W 147th St (55c).
166th St. 458 W. 25x113.8x irreg: Mary Newman to 460 West 166th Street Corp, 52 Wall St: mtg $24.132 ($15.40).
3d Ave. 1391-1403, n/e/cor 74th St, 164.4x85.2x irreg: Dudley W. Hayward to Hoguet Real Estate Corp, 415 Lexington Ave.
Same property: Hoguet Real Estate Corp (Robert L. Hoguet, pres) to Dudley W. Hayward, 168 West Islip Rd, Babylon, L. I.
Lexington Ave. 641, 25x100: Catholic Young Women's Club Inc (Constance Armstrong, pres) to Archbishopric of New York, 451 Madison Ave ($134.75).
Madison Ave. 1943, 17x82: Barnad Corp (Philip H. Seaman, pres) to Nada H. Seaman, 17 Vine St, Bronxville, N. Y.
Greenwich St. 275. 24.11x79x irreg: 275 Greenwich Street Corp (C. W. Carneval, v pres) to Frank Perri, 374 E 2d St, Brooklyn ($19.25).
Lenox Ave. 65, 25x100: E. C. Realty Co Inc Archebold Orler, pres) to Harriet Rabinovitz, 2406 Ave R. Brooklyn; mtg $10,000; p m
2d Ave. 991, 24.11x100x irreg: Rosaria Perniciaro to Shoholla Realty Corp, 307 E 50th St; mtg $12,841 ($33).
112th St. 314-316 E. 40x100.10: Sophie Garrow to Vinglo Realty Corp, 1537 Madison Ave; p m mtg $18,000 ($1.10).
46th St. 10 E, 24.4x100.5: Miramar Forty-Six Inc (Charles Goldner, pres) to Dezso Goldner, 200 Cabrini Blvd (55c).
93d St. 137 W, 18.9x95.6x irreg: Catherine Dewald to Sophie B. Kimels, 127 W 93d St; mtg $5,860; p m mtg $5,640 ($15.40).
Chambers St. 195. 20x34.2x irreg: Joseph R. Nayvin to The Bellaire Automotive Corp, 55 W 42d St; mtg $5,000 ($5.50).
Rutgers Pl. 21, 26x110: Rose Wildorf to David Simon, 14 Clinton St & ano: mtg $7,340 ($7.10).
134th St. 315 W. 24.10x99.11: Tadeush Thomashefsky to David S. Chassen, 37-21 65th St, Woodside, Queens: mtg $6,100 ($13.20).
Manhattan Ave. 374, 36.3x87: 504 West 126th Street Realty Corp (Solomon Siegel, pres) to Harlynn Realty Corp, 2188 5th Ave; p m mtg $16,200 ($25.30).
48th St. 315 W. 18x100.5: Antoine Rey to 315 West 48th Street Realty. Corp, 315 W 48th St (55c).
5th Ave. 1070, n/e/cor 88th St. 25.8x102.8: William Zezendorf to The Solomon R. Guggenheim Foundation, 120 Broadway ($187).
4th Ave. 390-396, 86x85: The Gerry Estates Inc (Edward H. Gerry, v pres) to Fourth Avenue Retail Corp, 1107 Broadway ($198).
Fulton St. 29-31, 43.3x41.9x irreg: Abraham Ellis to Mitchell Kay, 350 W 57th St & ano; mtg $9,657: quit claim deed ($13.20)
109th St. 121-123 E. 50x100.11: Dansker Realty & Securities Corp (Jerome Dansker, pres) to Wadsworth Realty Corp, 1754 Lexington Ave; mtg $24.475 ($12.65).
[Amounts in parentheses show revenue stamps on deeds, each $1.10 indicating $1,000 grantor's equity above mortgages.]

MARCH–APRIL

With the foundation now in possession of a full blockfront , Wright enthusiastically begins to reconceive his plans for a third time. He returns the central gallery to the southern end of the site and includes the proposed annex for offices and apartments. This building is meant to serve as a backdrop for the rotunda but is never built since the project runs considerably over budget.

'51

AUGUST 4

Harry Guggenheim announces that the museum will add "objective" modern painting to its collection, but the following day Louchheim writes another article in which she declares his statement insufficient. In particular, she worries that the museum will keep its "present fanatic devotion" to nonobjective art if Rebay, who goes unnamed in the article, continues as director.

APRIL 22

Aline Louchheim, associate art editor and critic at the *New York Times*, argues that the Museum of Non-Objective Painting has no right to tax-exempt status as an educational institution since it gives full artistic control to its director. Louchheim says Rebay has a "doctrinaire attitude" and traffics in "mystic-double-talk" when discussing the superiority of nonobjective art. The critic also objects to the exclusion of paintings that include recognizable figures: "Though these 'paintings with an object' are of far greater importance than most of those now on view, they are at present in storage. Presumably they cannot be shown together lest the representational art contaminate the other!"

MUSEUM CHANGING EXHIBITION POLICY

Guggenheim Foundation Will Show Old Masters as Well as Non-Objective Works

By the beginning of next year the Museum of Non-Objective Painting, at present housed in a small building at 1071 Fifth Avenue, will be exhibiting not only the kind of art from which it takes its name but also, for the first time, old masters and "objective" modern work.

The new exhibition policy, part of a general program of broadened activities, was announced yesterday by Harry F. Guggenheim, chairman of the board of the Solomon R. Guggenheim Foundation, which operates the museum. The foundation was organized and received its charter as an educational institution in 1937. Its founder, a philanthropist and mining executive who died in 1949, gave the foundation more than $3,000,000 in his lifetime and left it by bequest $2,000,000 for a new museum building and $6,000,000 as an endowment fund.

The museum's revised exhibition policy will be implemented in greatly expanded quarters. These will include the present building and an apartment house at 1 East Eighty-eighth Street, which the foundation recently acquired. Eventually the two buildings will be demolished and the apartment house, which soon will undergo alterations to make it usable as a museum, will make way to complete a plan that will occupy an area from Eighty-eighth to Eighty-ninth Street.

The first construction of the block-long building will be on the northeast corner of Eighty-ninth Street, on the site of the present museum building. Plans for the larger museum, drawn by Frank Lloyd Wright, have been in existence for some time and are now under revision to include the incorporation of the apartment site.

Mr. Wright has designed a cylindrical, eight-story building enclosing a three-quarter-mile-long ramp rising in a spiral. The paintings will hang on the continuous outside wall of the ramp.

In the museum's collection are more than 1,400 paintings, most of them non-objective. Artists represented include Kandinsky, Robert Delaunay, Franc Marc, Rudolf Bauer and Baroness Hilla Rebay, the museum's director. Besides these and others of the non-objective school the foundation owns American and Barbizon School landscapes and paintings by Luini, Bellini, Perreal, van Cleef and other old masters.

Mr. Guggenheim said that the foundation's board of trustees had given much consideration to ideas for the foundation's activities as advanced by artists, critics and others concerned with art. He also disclosed that the board was considering the award of scholarships and acquisitions of paintings. Since the foundation was organized, $500,000 has been spent for paintings under the supervision of the Baroness Hilla Rebay, who has been the director from the outset.

52

LEFT Hilla Rebay and Solomon R. Guggenheim, 1946. Hilla von Rebay Foundation Archive, Solomon R. Guggenheim Museum Archives, New York

RIGHT Letter (excerpt), Frank Lloyd Wright to Arthur Cort Holden, March 4, 1952

MARCH

Nine years into the project, the foundation finally requests a permit to begin construction from the New York City Department of Buildings (DOB). Wright tells reporters that current building codes won't be suitable for the museum. "In such new buildings," he says, "we are laying the basis for the codes of the future." Privately, he anticipates a struggle with the DOB, and writes to Holden in preparation for upcoming permitting meetings.

MARCH 29

Hilla Rebay, who has been the museum's director since its inception in 1939, resigns. Though officially she leaves due to poor health, her resignation is more the result of pressure from the foundation, whose trustees found her intransigence damaging to the mission of the museum.

```
page two

At the moment I am sending you a complete set of plans to
file with the building department together with a letter
from me authorizing you to do so as my representative.
After the preliminary skirmish in which you can answer many
questions that may arise and present the case pro and con,
I expect to come on myself and take care personally of
any necessary appeal. I suppose as is usual - unless the
Commission is extraordinarily intelligent - an appeal
will be necessary.

But we are giving the city so very much on this site
unusual in every way and desirable that petty or minor
rules made in other times for other circumstances, if they
conflict, should be traded in for the advantages our scheme
offers the City of New York like, say, the opening wide
of the street corners from the Avenue to the side streets
by curves; the landscape parking of the lot as a whole on
Fifth Avenue and return on side streets; the lowness and
simplicity of the whole structure; its dignified purposes of
of adult education; finally its temple rather than
commercial character. Finally the benevolent purpose
should have consideration over a selfish private project.
All of which you, no doubt, can present as well or better
than I could myself.

I have held up the plans for ten days or so to simplify
various details of construction. Some of them occured to
me while showing the plans to the Trustees. I've saved
at least $150,000.00 and improved the building. This we
have to show for the minor delay.

Affection as always,                    March 4th, 1952

Frank Lloyd Wright
```

'52

R. Buckminster Fuller with model of geodesic dome, ca. 1949. The Estate of R. Buckminster Fuller, Santa Barbara, California

APRIL 3
Philip Johnson, MoMA's architecture and design chief, invites Wright to exhibit his Guggenheim plans: "The Museum of Modern Art would like very much to formalize our greeting to your museum by giving a one-person show to your design." Though the exhibition never occurs, the proposal is a vindication for Wright: in 1932, when Johnson and Henry-Russell Hitchcock organized MoMA's *Modern Architecture: International Exhibition*, they chose to include Wright's work only as a predecessor to modern architecture.

APRIL
Architectural Forum runs a long article about the museum's design, calling it Wright's masterwork.

MARCH
Wright, who has never before built in New York, boasts of the addition the museum will make to the city's architecture: "The building for the Solomon R. Guggenheim Museum on Fifth Avenue will mark the first advance in the direction of organic architecture which the great city of New York has to show…. Unity of purpose [in the design] is everywhere present and, naturally enough, the over-all simplicity of form and construction ensure a longer life by centuries than could be sustained by the skyscraper construction usual in New York City."

MAY 14
In a letter to Harry Guggenheim, Wright says, "Other millionaires cuddled up to the Past for their memorial when they died. Not so Solomon R. Guggenheim. No. He died facing the way he had lived—forward."

AUGUST
The Museum of Modern Art shows R. Buckminster Fuller's Geodesic Dome House as part of an exhibition called *House of Tomorrow*. Aline Louchheim finds Fuller's design, a sphere made of aluminum tubing that is light but extremely strong, a defensive kind of architecture: "The organic architecture of Frank Lloyd Wright seeks, it seems to me, to find a way in which man can come to terms with nature. The Fuller scheme suggests that man must control nature and withdraw from it spiritually as well as physically."

'52

SEPTEMBER

At a hearing, the DOB rejects Wright's first proposal for the museum, citing fifteen code violations. For the project to proceed, the foundation must appear before the city Board of Standards and Appeals (BSA). Wright decides that next time he himself, rather than Holden, will appear.

OCTOBER 15

James Johnson Sweeney is chosen as the museum's new director. He formerly headed the department of painting and sculpture at the Museum of Modern Art. Twelve days later, the Museum of Non-Objective Painting officially changes its name to the Solomon R. Guggenheim Museum.

NOVEMBER

The foundation gives Wright permission to ask contractors to submit bids for construction of the building.

SRG FDN

File:Frank Lloyd Wright
General Correspondence
Folder #4

October 27, 1952

Mr. Frank Lloyd Wright
Taliesin
Spring Green, Wisconsin

Dear Frank Lloyd Wright:

Mr. James Johnson Sweeney, recently appointed Director of the Museum, is anxious to pay his respects to you at Taliesin, and get first hand from you a description of the new Museum. I am especially anxious that he discuss with you your proposals for framing and attaching paintings to the exhibition walls. This is especially important at this time because we are in the process of reframing certain pictures, and so it would be to great advantage to frame them at this time in an appropriate manner for use in the new Museum. If you would extend Mr. Sweeney an invitation to come out to meet you, I am sure it would be most appreciated by him, and it certainly would be by me. Or, if you expect to be in New York in the near future and prefer to see him here, of course we will await your arrival.

In the meantime, warm regards for you all.

I must add my "delenda Carthago est". When do we get going?

Very sincerely,

HFG:mks

cc:JJS
Lord & Lady Castle Stewart

'53

TOP LEFT Frank Lloyd Wright demonstrates a principle of organic architecture in his suite at the Plaza Hotel, New York, 1953

CENTER *The Future of Architecture* (Horizon Press), 1953. Douglas Steiner Collection, Edmonds, Washington

BOTTOM Masieri Memorial, Student Library and Dwelling (unbuilt; detail), Venice, 1953. Perspective. Graphite and colored pencil on paper, 63.5 x 48.9 cm. Frank Lloyd Wright Foundation, Scottsdale, Arizona 5306.002

JANUARY

While working on the Guggenheim, Wright also makes drawings for a proposed dormitory and architectural library on the Grand Canal in Venice, a tribute to Angelo Masieri, an Italian architect who died in a car accident after visiting Wright at Taliesin. It is to be constructed of dark-veined white marble and blue Murano glass at its corners. Though the building is never built, it causes a sensation in the Italian press when the following year *Corriere della Sera* reports Ernest Hemingway's reaction: "Should it be built? If it should be built, then it should burn!"

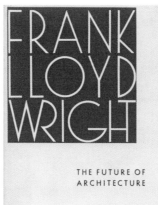

FRANK LLOYD WRIGHT

THE FUTURE OF ARCHITECTURE

Wright publishes a set of essays and interviews entitled *The Future of Architecture*. One reviewer writes of the book: "Carried to its logical conclusion, a sense of unity…implies that every house Mr. Wright builds is his own house and the people who live in them are not his clients but his guests." The book includes twelve photographs by Pedro Guerrero showing Wright explaining the tenets of organic architecture through a series of hand gestures.

JANUARY 20–MARCH 15

The Museum of Modern Art presents *Built in USA: Post-War Architecture*, curated by Henry-Russell Hitchcock and Arthur Drexler, with work by Alvar Aalto, Charles Eames, Raphael Soriano, Wright, and others.

'53

Preface of Appeal by the Solomon R.
Guggenheim Foundation to the Court
of Appeals of the City of New York,
February 14, 1953

```
P r e f a c e    o f    A p p e a l    by The Solomon R. Guggenheim
                                        Foundation
                                        to The Court of Appeals of
                                        The City of New York

      Architecture, may it please the court, is the welding of
imagination and common sense into a restraint upon specialists,
codes and fools.  Also it is an enlargement of their imaginations.
Architecture therefore should make it easier to conceive the
infinite variety of specific instances which lie unrealized by
man in the heart of Nature.


      It is an Architect's responsibility to take the whole
evidence of Nature into account as the only way to safety against
the fickle tides of opinion and fashion.  Freshness of being must
evaporate under compelled repetition.  Life refuses to be em-
balmed alive".  Either advance or decay.  These are the only
choices offered to us when we build as men should build today.


      The late Alfred North Whitehead, great philosopher at
Harvard said, as I remember, "The art of free society must
consist, first in maintaining a civil code; second in fear-
lessness of revision in order  to secure that the code satisfies
the enlightened reason of progress.  Any society failing to
combine reverence  for their codes with freedom of revision must
decay either from anarchy or the slow atrophy of a life stifled
by useless shadows!
      Those small traditions that only obscure the great Tradition
which codes should be intended to uphold.

F r a n k   L l o y d   W r i g h t  .  Taliesin West
                                        February 14th, 1953
```

MARCH
Wright comes to New York to
speed up the permitting process.
He alters his design even as he
dismisses the city's requests that
he do so as "mostly red tape by
the fire department and all silly."

FEBRUARY 14
Wright's revisions to the museum progress, but he fails to change certain key elements of the design that had troubled the DOB, including the glass oculus, the glass elevators, and the second floor's 2 ½-foot extension over the Fifth Avenue sidewalk. At the same time, he girds for battle with the BSA. For his variance application, he drafts a statement to the Court of Appeals of the City of New York, sending the preface to Harry Guggenheim for approval. Guggenheim makes only one revision, in the first paragraph, noted by Wright in a letter sent the following month: "Dear H. G.: 'Fools' is out."

'53

Letter, Frank Lloyd Wright to Hilla
Rebay, March 9, 1953

3/9/1953

Dear Hilla: In reply to your specially contrived insults, my first impulse was to give you as bad as you send. But what good. I am sorry you feel as you do. What I could say would make no difference, so why say it.   You seem obsessed by some idea that the Museum made my architectural reputation whereas most all the architectural profession of the world feels the opposite is true and I don't think you can change it no matter how loud you talk .

But leave that . . . I carried the financial burden of making repeated plans for the museum of seven years, revising and revising, meeting only postponement, waiting. Waiting to take advantage of a depression that never came.   So our dear old patron never saw his beloved ideal. He might well have seen it while alive. But you got your place on Fifth Avenue fitted out extravagantly your own way, and at expense to the main scheme. The museum might be standing there now with you in it but for your ambition in that instance.

Why did you not get (what I supposed you had) an agreement with S.R.G. concerning that bequest. You did not get it because (as I know from him) he was plainly worried about leaving you in business charge of his adventure. He worried for your own sake. He wished you to be free to exercise your artistry in which he had faith. He felt you would mess up with your temperamental ego the task of management.

Now, I have had nothing whatever to do with what his trustees have done except to insist that the building he approved and admired, for what his admiration was worth it was his,

T A L I E S I N   W E S T

2

be kept as he wished to see it built, though I had to leave you out of residence. I could not obtain that. As for Bauer, you played him so hard that Fiske Kimball said to me, "Frank, when is your Bauer House going to be built?"   Bauer does not qualify (with the artist's public) with Kandinsky yet. If he ever does it is not likely to be our life time. I do not think you can manage it.

So - too much Bauer ruined our enterprize and is, I suspect (coupled with too much Rebay) what antagonized the present trustees of the museum and brought on a crisis.

I had nothing whatever to say concerning Sweeney . . . his selection or his selections. I am only the Architect. However, I have warned Harry G. and the trustees that it was precisely not S.R.G.'s idea to have another museum such as already existed but it was his idea to create (building) an atmsphere in which the more advanced painting of our time could be seen for what it was worth and not be intruded upon nor intrude into any environment that did not belong to it or with it. That atmosphere I have provided. He felt it. So did you in your more lucid moments. I insisted on a place for your work in it and have provided a little special gallery for the purpose. I asked no one's permission to do this.

It is a pity that you seem to know so little of Architecture as the great mother Art. I suppose you never did know much about it. But I did not see it. Another misfortune was your obsession with God in place of Non. I do not believe painting is the ne-plus-ultra of the E-pluribus-unum of Art. And God as a negative force in the world of Art is too personal a disintegration of all the values I know to be looked upon as other than an idiosyncrasy. That

T A L I E S I N   W E S T

3

term I never believed in and tried to find another term more truly expressive of the values we all seek now in a new reality of experience. Painting is only one means and not the most humane as a basis for a Cutlure.

As for Bach. Well, he was among the greatest. You understand him better than I do, I know. Vivaldi as well or better.

Now, why cry and try to lap up spilled milk.

Let's see what can be saved out of the wreck of your own museum-fortunes. The memorial to S. R. G. which he wished to stand in his beloved city of New York is not helped any by this personal bickering, jealousy, and fearsome frustration.

So good better health and may good sense come to you, wherever you are or this catches up with you . . .

T A L I E S I N   W E S T    Frank Lloyd Wright   March 9th
                                                                        1 9 5 3

MARCH 9
Relations between Wright and Rebay grow strained as she accuses him of having backed her replacement, Sweeney. Wright responds with vitriol, cataloging the troubles that led to her ouster and to the many delays in building the museum, including her consultation about the project with Rudolf Bauer.

TOP Solomon R. Guggenheim
Museum, New York, 1943–59. Plan
(presentation drawing). Graphite,
colored pencil, and sepia on tracing
paper, 99 x 107 cm. Frank Lloyd
Wright Foundation, Scottsdale,
Arizona 4305.049

BOTTOM Letter (copy), Frank Lloyd
Wright to Harry F. Guggenheim,
April 9, 1953

'53

APRIL

Elizabeth Gordon, editor of
House Beautiful, writes an incen-
diary article called "The Threat
to the Next America" in which
she decries International Style
architects: "They are promot-
ing unlivability, stripped-down
emptiness, lack of storage space
and therefore lack of posses-
sions." Gordon holds up Wright
as an example of good modern
design, which she defines as
architecture that "combines the
best technological knowledge
with sensitive understanding of
people's requirements."

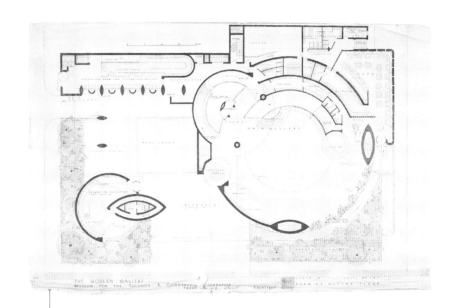

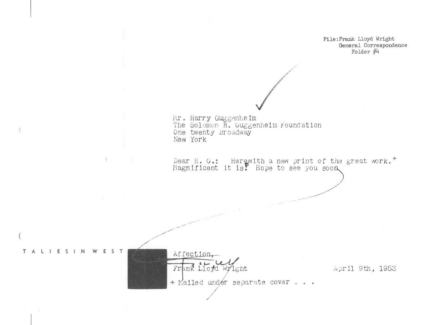

APRIL 9

Wright's meeting with the BSA
will occur in July. He redraws the
plans for the museum, eliminating a terrace garden and
walkway at the base of the dome.
In addition, he adds a photography department and widens
the ramps. In a letter to Harry
Guggenheim, Wright pronounces
the revised design an unequivocal
success.

'53

TOP Solomon R. Guggenheim Museum, New York, 1943–59. Night rendering (presentation drawing), 1953. Tempera on black illustration board, 69 x 102 cm. Frank Lloyd Wright Foundation, Scottsdale, Arizona 4305.062

BOTTOM H. C. Price Company Tower, Bartlesville, Oklahoma, 1952–56. Floor plan (presentation drawing). Ink on tracing paper, 64.8 x 91.4 cm. Frank Lloyd Wright Foundation, Scottsdale, Arizona 5215.016

One of Wright's draftsmen, Allen Lape Davison, creates a thrilling rendering of the Guggenheim Museum at night that shows the proposed annex behind the rotunda. The drawing illustrates the distinctive "Wright style," which in fact was developed over the course of decades by the many talented apprentices who worked for the architect throughout his career. His first draftsman, Marion Mahony Griffin, joined the office in 1895 and lay the groundwork for the visual elements that came to be identified with Wright's renderings: lush natural settings, dramatic perspectives, and buildings clearly defined in ink, set off with color washes or pencil.

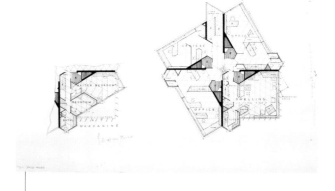

MAY 27

The National Institute of the American Academy of Arts and Letters awards Wright a gold medal and exhibits what Louchheim calls "a random selection of the work and writings that reveal the originality, the freshness and the imaginative inventiveness that have been [Wright's] distinctive marks since the early Nineteen Hundreds." The show includes Wright's drawing for H. C. Price Company Tower (1952–56), a concrete skyscraper in Bartlesville, Oklahoma, begun the year before. The building follows his "taproot" scheme—a service core at the center with floors cantilevered outward—and in plan, has a pinwheel form. "Instead of the old stacked stories and the old post-and-lintel, here is movement going up and around," Wright tells Louchheim. The building will be covered with gold-colored glass and include louvers to protect workers from the sun.

53

TOP Robert Llewellyn Wright House, Bethesda, Maryland, 1953. Ground-floor plan. Graphite and colored pencil on tracing paper, 51 x 91 cm. Frank Lloyd Wright Foundation, Scottsdale, Arizona 5312.07

BOTTOM Letter (copy), Harry F. Guggenheim to Frank Lloyd Wright, July 24, 1953

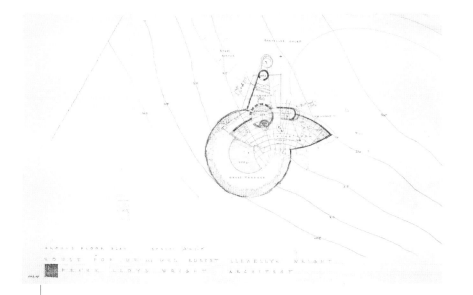

JULY 24

The Guggenheim Foundation decides to host *Sixty Years of Living Architecture*, the exhibition of Wright's work that has been touring the world. The show will be housed in a temporary pavilion designed by Wright on the site of the future museum. Though the architect is pre-occupied with his appearance before the Board of Standards and Appeals in just a few days, Harry Guggenheim is anxious for *Sixty Years* to be mounted.

JULY

Wright designs a house to be built in Bethesda, Maryland, for his son Robert Llewellyn Wright. The elder Wright's scheme reveals his continued fascination with overlapping circles and a shape he refers to as a "seedpod."

'53

Newspaper clippings, July 1953

TOP *New York Post*, July 28, 1953

Rocky Mountain (Denver, Colo.) News, July 28, 1953

BOTTOM, CLOCKWISE FROM TOP
New York Newsday, July 28, 1953

New York World-Telegram and Sun, July 27, 1953

Flint (Mich.) Journal, July 26, 1953

Brooklyn Daily Eagle, July 28, 1953

Wright Battles For His 'Washtub' Art Museum

Bad Boy of Architecture
Frank Lloyd Wright In Battle With NYC
Code Called One for Fools

JULY 27

During the last week of July, Wright's battle with the BSA becomes a matter of public record, with newspapers around the country running a United Press story that refers to Wright as the "84-year-old bad boy of architecture." The *New York World-Telegram and Sun* runs a particularly critical article, comparing Wright's design for the Guggenheim to a "horrible Hollywood avacadoburger [sic] stand." In a letter to the newspaper, however, one reader argues that the editors "succeeded in showing only your complete unfamiliarity with Mr. Wright's work.... Why not give Mr. Wright a fair chance to show what he can do?"

City May Shatter Glass Dream

Ultra Modern Art Museum Under Attack

Odd Building Is Puzzler
N. Y. May Disapprove Round Art Gallery

No, No, Not That.

Frank Lloyd Wright, the architectural iconoclast who is forever designing buildings that look like old pizza curled up in the hot sun, is at it again. Now he has, er, designed a building which—unless somebody does something about it—is going to house the proposed Solomon R. Guggenheim Memorial Museum. It will occupy a site on Fifth Ave. from 88th to 89th St.

Mr. Wright's plan calls for a building which looks like a particularly horrible Hollywood avacadoburger stand. We trust that the city's Board of Standards and Appeals and the Building and Housing Department will do something to dissuade Mr. Wright before it is too late.

Article from the *New York World-Telegram and Sun*, July 24, 1953

'53

JULY 28
Wright appears at a hearing of the Board of Standards and Appeals. Dismissing his arguments, the board tells him to withdraw his plans, revise them to fall in line with New York building codes, and resubmit them that autumn. Wright agrees but tells the committee, "We are anxious to build.... But since this will be a benefaction to the city we had thought the city would be anxious to do something for us. If it embarrasses this court to make this concession, it's up to us to concede." The chairman of the board, Harris H. Murdock, informs Wright that he is not embarrassed "one particle." Besides adjusting the building overhang, Wright must add fire stairs and change the material of the dome.

JULY 30
Writing about the hearing for the *New York Post*, columnist Murray Kempton addresses the 84-year-old architect: "You got a long way to go, Wright, but the first thing you got to understand is that the engineer is the one that counts. But good luck, kid; the best of it."

Frank Lloyd Wright's House Of Glass Worries City Dads

Guggenheim Art Home Unusual

By SALLY MacDOUGALL,
Staff Writer.

When an architect designs a huge glass-domed building shaped like an orange on plans that let the middle bulge of the orange extend as an overhead high above the sidewalk, and with no inside provision for fire prevention, city authorities have to decide whether that building will be a safe place for crowds inside and out.

That question will come up at a July 28 meeting of the city's Board of Standards and Appeals and the Building and Housing Department, along with a representative of the architect, Frank Lloyd Wright.

The controversial building is the proposed $2,000,000 Solomon R. Guggenheim Memorial Museum on a block-long Fifth Ave. front, 88th to 89th St., facing Central Park, to house the world's largest collection of non-objective and abstract paintings and other forms of modern art.

2 Million Marked for Building.

When Solomon R. Guggenheim died four years ago he left $8,000,000 of his copper mining fortune to the Solomon R. Guggenheim Foundation "for art education and the promotion and encouragement of art," of which $2,000,000 was marked for a memorial museum to house his vast modern art collection and to be free for all-time to the public.

He also left the wish that the building would be designed by Frank Lloyd Wright, famed as the world's least traditional architect.

"We'll break ground just as soon as we get clearance from the building commission," said Harry F. Guggenheim, nephew of the donor and chairman of the board of the Solomon R. Guggenheim Foundation. He and other heirs and directors welcomed the change in the title from Museum of Non-Objective Painting to the donor's name in memorial form, thus leaving the museum free to broaden its scope while enlarging its collection.

"Most important of all is that the gallery should be a memorial to my uncle," Mr. Guggenheim stated.

The former ambassador to Cuba,

This picture of the proposed glass-domed art museum was taken in 1945 with Architect Frank Lloyd Wright looking on. The building would be called the Solomon R. Guggenheim Memorial Museum and would house one of the world's richest art collections.

owner of the Derby winner, Dark Star, copublisher with his wife, Alicia Patterson, of a Long Island newspaper, Newsday, and head of the Guggenheim Foundation in a big mahogany-paneled office at 120 Broadway, explained why he, a mere nephew of the donor, came to be head of the museum board and why his cousin-in-law, Lord Castlestewart, of Surrey, England, is president.

That came about because Solomon R. Guggenheim, one of seven sons of Meyer Guggenheim, founder of the family fortune, had no son. The Earl of Castlestewart came into the family by marrying his eldest daughter.

"My uncle went through all phases of art collecting for 40 years," he said. "He was attracted to the modern school. Abstract art was the nucleus of the collection.

Continued on Page Two

HARRY F. GUGGENHEIM.

'53

TOP *Sixty Years of Living Architecture* Exhibition Building (demolished), New York, 1953. Perspective (presentation drawing). Graphite and ink on tracing paper, 91 x 196 cm. Frank Lloyd Wright Foundation, Scottsdale, Arizona 5314.001

CENTER Program (back and front cover) for *Sixty Years of Living Architecture*, Solomon R. Guggenheim Museum, New York, October 22–December 13, 1953. Solomon R. Guggenheim Museum Archives, New York

BOTTOM Invitation to opening of *Sixty Years of Living Architecture*, Solomon R. Guggenheim Museum, New York, October 22–December 13, 1953. Solomon R. Guggenheim Museum Archives, New York

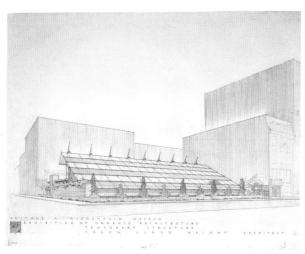

OCTOBER 22–DECEMBER 13
Sixty Years of Living Architecture opens in New York on Fifth Avenue where the museum will eventually be built. The temporary exhibition structure, the first Wright building in New York City, is made of glass, fiberboard, and pipe columns. Visitors may also enter a life-size model of a Usonian house that is demolished after the exhibition closes.

'53

From the start, the exhibition draws large crowds, and reviews are overwhelmingly positive. Though slated to close on November 29, the museum decides to extend the show through December 13.

THRONGS INSPECT WRIGHT'S EXHIBIT

Visitors Marvel at Architect's Display of Work in House Near Guggenheim Museum

Interest ran high yesterday at the opening of the Frank Lloyd Wright exhibition—a fully furnished house and a pavilion displaying much of the architect's work on land adjoining the Solomon R. Guggenheim Museum, Fifth Avenue and Eighty-ninth Street.

Behind a closed door workmen were still finishing one of the two bedrooms in the house, but the absence of one small part made little difference to the day-long stream of visitors.

Women came wheeling their babies in buggies; invalids came in wheel chairs. A class of students in architecture at Princeton University, luncheon guests of Mr. Wright, minutely inspected the house. But the scope of the exhibit of models, plans and drawings could be assimilated only in part:

Some spent hours poring over the material. One visitor said: "It's wonderful, but it's too much. You can't take it all in." And James Johnson Sweeney, curator of the museum, said it was only a fraction from the master architect's work.

In the large and gracious living room, visitors made themselves at home on comfortable furniture, looking like guests at a housewarming. Others filtered through the house taking note of the built-in kitchen range and other fixtures, the piano hinges on cabinet doors, the lighting like baby spot lights in the plywood ceilings.

Behind the scenes, the talented group of a dozen apprentices from the Wright Foundation at Taliesin, Spring Green, Wis., still labored during the day to bring the exhibition to perfection.

In the evening they were the guests of honor of Mr. Wright at a party in the pavilion. A concert grand piano set at rest any doubts about the pavilion's acoustical rightness. The pavilion's skeleton is of metal pipes and its roof is partly of corrugated glass.

The museum is open free to all, as usual. The Wright exhibition, which is reached through the museum, is at 50 cents admission. It will remain until Nov. 29. Hours are Wednesdays and Saturdays, 10 A. M. to 10 P. M.; Sundays, noon to 6 P. M. and other days, 10 A. M. to 6 P. M.

Museumgoers show particular interest in the Usonian house, which they enter through a garden on the north end of the site that is landscaped with potted shrubs, yews, and hemlocks. Wright tells a journalist that the Usonian "is characteristic of the so-called 'Prairie House' of sixty years ago with its modern, human scale, its open-plan and flowing space, its corner windows and sense of indoors and outdoors." One critic singles out for praise the open kitchen, which frees "the housewife from the isolated drudgery of the kitchen and permit[s] her to be a gracious hostess instead of a kitchen mechanic."

'53

TOP Frank Lloyd Wright visiting *Sixty Years of Living Architecture,* Solomon R. Guggenheim Museum, New York, 1953

BOTTOM Article from the *New Yorker,* November 7, 1953

NOVEMBER

The *New Yorker* covers *Sixty Years of Living Architecture* on several occasions in its Talk of the Town section, frequently capturing Wright's flamboyant persona and provocative declarations. In one column, speaking of a talk he's recently given, Wright tells the reporter, "Americans like to take a beating. I like to administer a beating. You can't talk to people who agree with you, can you? I get deflated if people agree with me."

Visitors to *Sixty Years* see building models, floor plans, drawings, and photographs covering the architect's long career. New Yorkers' great interest in Wright's work supports a *New York Times* editorial advocating that the city buildings department make exceptions for Wright's unconventional design for the Guggenheim. "Will New York continue to be rigid in its refusal to give [Wright] a chance to demonstrate his genius in our town?" the article asks.

NOVEMBER

House and Home and *Architectural Record* run stories about the exhibition and publish the plan of Wright's Usonian house. *Architectural Record*'s headline declares, "Wright Makes New York!"

Mr. Wrong

WE'D just promised ourself to let a week go by without mentioning Frank Lloyd Wright in these pages when in came our upper Fifth Avenue man with a flash that made us decide the week better be *next* week. Two special policemen were standing guard in the living room of Wright's Usonian House up at the Guggenheim Museum's pavilion when one of them, on his first day of Usonian duty, spotted an elderly, white-maned visitor sitting in an easy chair and puffing a forbidden cigarette. The guard walked over and sternly told the old fellow he'd have to leave the premises. This the malefactor did, without a murmur. "Nice work," the cop's companion told him a moment later. "You just threw out Mr. Wright."

TOP Le Corbusier, Oscar Niemeyer, et al. with Wallace Harrison and Max Abramovitz, United Nations Headquarters, New York, 1947–53

BOTTOM Telegram (excerpt), Frank Lloyd Wright to Harry F. Guggenheim, December 8, 1953

NOVEMBER 28

Lewis Mumford reviews the exhibition for the *New Yorker*, referring to Wright as an innovator who "more than any other architect, has helped bring about…a change in our attitude toward American art, a change from colonial dependence upon European models to faith in our native abilities, from worship of the partly historic to confidence in the living present, from formality and urbane gentility in our style of life to breezy openness and rustic relaxation." In particular, he praises Wright for being responsive to materials. Yet Wright's arrogance, he argues, has at times kept him from doing his best work: "Each building by Wright stands in self-imposed isolation—a monument to his own greatness, towering defiantly above the works of his contemporaries. Though it dazzles us by its brilliance, it sometimes fails to invite our love, because it offers no halfway place between rejection and abject surrender."

NOVEMBER 14

In an essay that runs in the *Saturday Review of Literature*, Wright calls the United Nations complex, completed just three years before, "a great slab in a great graveyard…. I believe that any individual who loves his country can't feel anything but dismay by what is called the power of his nation. It's not a real power. It's not exuberance in the sense of Blake. It is excess along artificial lines. We are now in for the consequences of excess, not the fruits of exuberance."

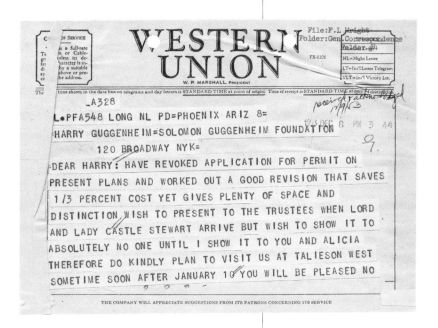

DECEMBER 8

Wright decides to abandon his attempt to receive a variance from the BSA and instead offer up a fresh set of drawings to the DOB—provided that the foundation trustees approve.

'54

APRIL
Max Hoffman, the owner of a Jaguar car dealership, leases a building at 430 Park Avenue to house a new showroom to be designed by Wright. The plan features a rotating showroom floor and a ramp that allows the cars to be seen from above.

JANUARY 12
The previous December, Wright told Hilla Rebay that she should drop the term *non-objective art*. "Semantics is not a negligible science," he wrote. "Non is negative. God is positive or he does not exist for humanity." In response, Rebay writes a twenty-five-page letter defending the term: "In this world everything is based on the principle of duality: in and out, day and night, male and female, mortality and immortality, static and rhythmic, weak and strong, light and dark, finite and infinite. But there is only one God, and this God is spirit, and this spirit is the 'non.' It is the climax of all—invisible, intangible, unreachable—found in evidence by the deepest thinkers, and contained in everything and all."

MARCH
In his new drawings, Wright meets fire-safety regulations by replacing the original oculus of glass decorated with brass circles. The U-shaped supports of the new dome are the culmination of the web walls that punctuate each of the museum's ramps.

'54

TOP LEFT Sitting Room, Plaza
Hotel Suite (destroyed), New York,
1954. Interior elevations (conceptual
drawing). Graphite on reproductive
print, 55 x 77 cm. Frank Lloyd Wright
Foundation, Scottsdale, Arizona
5532.009

TOP RIGHT Frank Lloyd Wright's suite
at the Plaza Hotel, New York, ca. 1954

BOTTOM Letter (excerpt), Frank Lloyd
Wright to Harry F. Guggenheim,
April 10, 1954

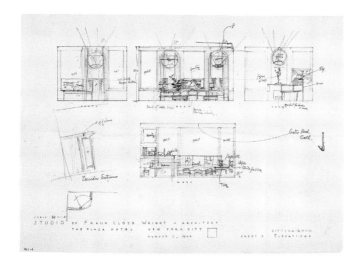

APRIL 10

After Harry and Alicia Patterson Guggenheim visit Taliesin West, Wright sends several letters in which he thanks them for supporting the design that had been approved by "Uncle Sol." Yet he expresses grave doubts about Sweeney's vision of the museum after Sweeney sends him requests for more floor space. "Harry!" he writes. "How can anyone say intelligently how much space, here and there, is required for any reasonable reasons until the way those spaces are arranged in relationship to each other is known and carefully considered." He goes on to compare the Guggenheims to the Medici, incorrectly assuming that they were the patrons of Michelangelo's *David*.

AUGUST

Wright moves into the Plaza Hotel to accelerate the beginning of construction. (Despite his efforts, groundbreaking will not occur for another two years.) He completely redesigns his suite, which had been decorated five years earlier by Christian Dior. He writes a press release, never published, announcing his new home and office: "He has always worked where he ate and slept and is doing so now with the air of magnificence and expense one associates with the Plaza."

Isn't it really for the Solomon R. Guggenheim unique
gallery something like the deMedicis sending in to
Michelangelo commissioned to do his David, required
circumference of biceps, area of belly, number of inches
around diameter of calf? Etc., etc.

page two

I make this ridiculous simile because a great, good
building is an organism -- all of it proportioned to
facilitate the kind of museum the donor wanted to
buy - one he approved and provided money to pay for
before he passed away. By experienced adaptation of
space to purpose this was done to his extreme satisfaction.
Now many changes have been made to meet altered
circumstances. I am willing to go on making them but
I am only interested in building S.R.G.'s memorial
museum as near as he desired it as his money will go --
making all reasonable changes to meet changed conditions
where inevitable.

'54

TOP Letter (excerpt), Frank Lloyd Wright to James Johnson Sweeney, October 13, 1954

BOTTOM Beth Sholom Synagogue, Elkins Park, Pennsylvania, 1954–59

File: Frank Lloyd Wright
General Correspond-
ence Folder #4

Mr. James Johnson Sweeney
The Solomon R. Guggenheim Museum
1071 Fifth Avenue
New York

Dear James: S. O. S. !

It is now apparent that we cannot build Solomon R. Guggenheim's
Memorial and at the same time build whole big buildings for
carpentry, photography, storage, conservation, etc., etc.

We can manage them all including all of the etc., etc. But it
seems to us your experts want about the entire area of the
Guggenheim lot or about 23,000 sq.ft., excluding any building
for exhibition purposes whatever, and allowing only a reasonable
amount for the corridors, circulation, etc. In short, with
no galleries at all for exhibition, they want the entire lot-
area for such manufacture. The several elevators and various
mechanical equipment are all beside this.

Something, James, is radically wrong (not to say "rotten
in Denmark".)

NOVEMBER 12

The Wisconsin Supreme Court rules that Wright's apprentice-ship for architects, the Taliesin Fellowship, does not deserve tax-exempt status, claiming that it is a business rather than a nonprofit entity. Wright composes a long response in which he refers to the court's judgment as "the kind of legality destined to reduce our Democracy to its lowest common denominator—Mobocracy." He threatens to leave his home state and never return.

AUGUST 8

The critic Aline Saarinen (formerly Louchheim, now married to Eero Saarinen) visits Wright at Taliesin, where she takes note of the architect's large collection of ancient Asian art. He tells her, "People often ask why I, a modern architect, have so many old things around. Why not? I, too, belong to tradi-tion—back to the oldest American architecture, that of the Mayans, and to the Japanese and others. All of them are brought into now."

OCTOBER

Sweeney and Wright cannot agree on the dimensions of the museum, with Sweeney request-ing much more space for storage, offices, and conservation than Wright has allotted.

NOVEMBER 15

Ground is broken for Wright's Beth Sholom Synagogue in Elkins Park, Pennsylvania, a hexagonally shaped tower meant to symbolize Mount Sinai. It is completed in 1959.

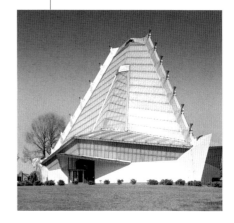

54

TOP Letter (copy), Frank Lloyd Wright to Robert Moses, November 23, 1954

BOTTOM Letter (copy), Robert Moses to Frank Lloyd Wright, November 29, 1954

COPY

THE PLAZA

Fifth Avenue at Fifty Ninth Street

New York 19, N.Y.

Dear Bob - the MOSES!

We seem to be slated for the old Weber and Fields act (privately good friends, publicly enemies) that makes amusing effects?

Anyhow, dear Bob and Mary, it is "mit luff" Olgivanna and I think of you always - we value your friendship as we do the Lindbergs - (Charles was fired from Wisconsin U - I walked out 3 months before I would have had a degree as an engineer) and look forward always to a meeting with you.

But Olgivanna has savage attacks of her old malady while here - we are at the Plaza for a year (in the old Presidential Suite) to get the museum built - we hope you can't stop it) and we go now to Arizona - Phoenix where we would be overjoyed to welcome you both for a visit this winter. Do you both good.

Affection, Frank and Olgivanna -

New York - Plaza - November 23, 1954

NOVEMBER
Wright and Robert Moses exchange jocular letters acknowledging their differing views of the museum. Wright compares them to a vaudeville comedy team popular at the turn of the century.

Babylon, N.Y.

November 29, 1954

Mr. Frank Lloyd Wright
Taliesin West
Phoenix, Arizona

Dear Frank:

Don't be absurd. We are friends in all respects and at all times, however much we may disagree on occasion. So, for that matter, were Webber and Fields.

To be honest about it, even with Mary's local knowledge and my own basic sympathy, I don't comprehend your Taliesin Wisconsin litigation. The laws, the decisions, the slant of judges, the sympathies of the public, personalities are so different in different states. At the offset there are articles of incorporation, declarations of purpose, etc., which are also interpreted in the light of local standards.

Probably you have stepped on a lot of sensitive toes over the years, and there are those who are much more concerned over their tender tootsies than about a special dispensation for the only man in Iowa County the big world has ever heard of and recognized.

What do you care about the tax collectors and judges around Spring Green? Suppose they turf you out. The reflection is on them. You will find a hearty welcome elsewhere.

As to the Guggenheim Museum, you know my benighted point of view. I can't grasp the idea of the building and am horrified by what will be hung inside. Nevertheless, you are entitled to it. I mean you have earned the right to be conspicuously represented here. I only wish it could have been the horizontal hillside structures we planned at Spuyten Duyvil which were frowned on by the departed Baroness. That would have been something for the ages. I'm a conservative. You represent youth.

Our love to you both, and tell Olgivanna to get well fast.

Cordially,

RM:MR

'55

TOP V. C. Morris House ("Seacliff"), version #2 (unbuilt), San Francisco, 1955, Perspective (presentation drawing). Graphite and colored pencil on tracing paper, 56 x 89 cm. Frank Lloyd Wright Foundation, Scottsdale, Arizona 5312.005

BOTTOM Skidmore, Owings & Merrill (Gordon Bunshaft), Lever House, New York, 1951–52

SEACLIFF

MAY 21
In an essay for the *Saturday Review*, Frank Lloyd Wright calls for decentralization of cities, saying they are unnecessary, degenerate, and unsafe in the age of the atomic bomb, when large concentrations of people could be annihilated in moments. Glass skyscrapers like Lever House (1951–52), which Wright refers to as a "very dangerous mirror used as a poster for soap," represent sterility and a deadening equalitarianism.

In 1945, Mr. and Mrs. V. C. Morris, the owners of an eponymous gift shop in San Francisco, hired Wright to design a home on their property near the Golden Gate Bridge on a cliff overlooking San Francisco Bay. Wright created a dramatic extension of the cliff by stacking the house's floors, which were made of reinforced concrete and steel. They were connected to each other by ramps in an open well where plants were to be hung from the uppermost level. When the Morrises hired Wright to redesign their store as well, the house plans were suspended and eventually abandoned. In 1955, Wright designs a second version of the house that will also go unrealized.

55

TOP Letter (excerpt), Frank Lloyd Wright to Harry F. Guggenheim, September 3, 1955

BOTTOM *An American Architecture* (Horizon Press), 1955. Douglas Steiner Collection, Edmonds, Washington

T A L I E S I N

Personally, I've"done my damdest" to get you a four or five
million dollar building for two and a half. "Angels can't do no
more". Yet, everything is well designed and definitely covered
by complete detail drawings and specifications -- all well done.
The long years of study andpreparation expended upon it will not
all be wasted. The Guggenheim fortune here finds a glorious
memorial, if Solomon R. picked the right trustees.

I will be coming to New York again. Whenever you are ready to
say "go", send for me. There isn't much time left, Lieber
Harry. I am almost as old as Uncle Sol was when he had to give
up and none of us are any younger - except in the spirit of youth.

Faithfully with affection,

Frank Lloyd Wright, Architect   September 3rd, 1955

JULY 7
Wright testifies before the Subcommittee on the Department of the Air Force Appropriations of the House of Representatives, severely denigrating all the architects working on the design of the new Air Force Academy, among them Pietro Belluschi, Eero Saarinen, and the firm Skidmore, Owings & Merrill. A few months later, John Knox Shear, editor of *Architectural Record*, writes an editorial criticizing Wright for summary dismissal of their work.

SEPTEMBER 3
Wright asks Harry Guggenheim to accept the high costs of building the museum, which exceed the $2 million amount that Solomon had set aside for it. The architect reminds Harry that had his uncle acted with greater alacrity, he might have lived to see the museum built.

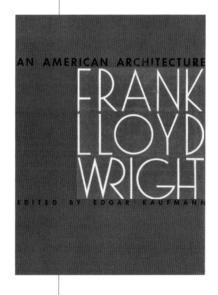

FALL
Wright publishes *An American Architecture*. Edited by Edgar Kaufmann Jr., the book presents the architect's philosophy and oeuvre and is illustrated with dozens of photographs and drawings.

'55

Letter (copy), Robert Moses to Harry F.
Guggenheim, October 20, 1955

OCTOBER

After reviewing the correspondence
between Robert Moses and Frank
Lloyd Wright, Harry Guggenheim
writes to the former: "I see that
you two geniuses can only agree
on one thing, i.e. — how to spend
the Solomon R. Guggenheim
Foundation's money." Moses's
response reveals his feelings
about Wright's design and the
Guggenheim collection.

```
C
O                                        File:  Robert Moses
P
Y
                ROBERT MOSES
             One Gracie Square
             New York 28, N. Y.


             October 20, 1955


        Mr. Harry F. Guggenheim
        120 Broadway
        New York, N. Y.

        Dear Harry:

                Thanks for your jolly note.  You are wrong
        about only one thing.  I'm not in the least interested
        in spending the Guggenheim Foundation's money for the
        Museum.  I don't personally like either the Museum or
        what's going into it, and it's no part of my official
        duties to do anything about it.  I have simply tried at
        their request to help some good friends in a dubious enter-
        prise because they are friends and for no other reason.
        If the Courts would let you divert the money to the Metro-
        politan Museum or to an indoor recreation center, I would
        be positively enthusiastic.

                        Cordially,


                        /s/  Robert Moses


        RM:VW:W
```

OCTOBER 5

Sweeney wants the museum to
be lit by artificial light rather than
the skylights on the outer edge
of the ramp, but Wright finds the
suggestion opposed to what he
calls the "modern thesis" of the
museum. He deems artificial
lighting dishonest, arguing that
the museum as he designed it will
"supplant the phony museum.
A humanist must believe that any
picture in a fixed light is only a
'fixed' picture! If this fixation be
ideal then see death as the ideal
state for man. The morgue!"

'55

TOP *House Beautiful*, November 1955.
Pictured: Living-dining room,
Taliesin, Spring Green, Wisconsin,
1925. Douglas Steiner Collection,
Edmonds, Washington

BOTTOM Letter, Frank Lloyd Wright to
Harry F. Guggenheim, January 27, 1956

DECEMBER 15

In a letter to the BSA's Harris Murdock, Wright guarantees that no more than 350 people will be allowed into the building at once. Guggenheim flatly rejects Wright's proposal: "Your limitation of three hundred and fifty people at one time to visit the great work for which the world has waited for ten years is unthinkable. Merry Xmas. Nuts to the squirrels of Wisconsin. Harry." In his next letter to Guggenheim, however, Wright, sticks to this number.

NOVEMBER

House Beautiful dedicates an issue to Wright's work. The magazine includes an essay by architectural historian James Marston Fitch praising the model house in *Sixty Years of Living Architecture.*

Lieber Harry: Thanks for your brotherly sentiments which
I fully share. I am only anxious that you see my point concerning quality instead of being at the mercy of quantity
and would like to lay my case before the trustees -- so
since Wes (nor anyone else) cannot dot an i or cross a t on
the museum plans without sanction, I will come down to your
giant city and do what I can to keep things right side up. . .
for the integrity of the opus.

I wanted you to scan the plans I sent which would seem to
indicate a pretty full house at 350 simultaneous visitors
which would mean about 3,500 a day, etc., etc.

I will be at the Plaza about February 15th hoping to see you
well and happy - if not amenable to reason, which I hope I
am myself - also

Affection,

Frank Lloyd Wright

January 27th, 1956

N. B. " Trifles make perfection but perfection is no trifle "
and nonetheless than perfect shall be our museum? Too many
cooks always did upset perfection.

TALIESIN WEST

'56

BOTTOM H. C. Price Company Tower, Bartlesville, Oklahoma, 1952–56. Price Tower Arts Center, Bartlesville, Oklahoma

TOP Press release (copy, excerpt) announcing the start of construction on the Solomon R. Guggenheim Museum, May 4, 1956

THE SOLOMON R. GUGGENHEIM FOUNDATION
120 Broadway
New York 5, N.Y.
REctor 2-9740

Released for Publication in Newspapers
of Monday, May 7, 1956

May 4, 1956

Harry F. Guggenheim, Chairman of the Board of The Solomon R. Guggenheim Foundation, announced today the start of construction of the Foundation's new Museum, designed by Frank Lloyd Wright, at Fifth Avenue between 88th and 89th Streets. This is the first Frank Lloyd Wright building to be constructed in New York City.

"The hope of the Trustees is that the new building will in time be the home of the finest art that the world may produce," Mr. Guggenheim said. "Paintings and sculpture will be exhibited in a novel manner which we believe will be under the most favorable conditions for the enjoyment of the public."

The Price Tower, often referred to as the Prairie Skyscraper, is completed. It is the only skyscraper designed by Wright that is erected.

MARCH 9

Tensions between Wright and Sweeney escalate when the museum's director makes a number of suggestions about how to display art. Wright believes Sweeney's ideas are a betrayal of the spirit of the museum and asks if the director intends to sabotage plans for the museum. "Jim! Tell me—did you expect to destroy the idea of the Guggenheim Museum at the last and psychological moment as so often reported, or are you as insensitive to the character of the whole affair as this last suggestion of yours would indicate?"

MAY 4

Harry Guggenheim announces the beginning of construction for the new museum. The press release quotes Wright: "Solomon R. Guggenheim, of the House of Guggenheim, among America's most illustrious benefactors, said to me, his Architect, that he did not want to give his beloved City of New York 'just another museum.'... When I presented the design of the edifice [to Guggenheim]...tears were in his eyes as he said: 'Mr. Wright, this is it! I knew you would do it.'"

'56

SEPTEMBER

Architect William H. Short is named Clerk of the Works, essentially acting as project manager for the building of the Guggenheim Museum. In addition to overseeing almost every aspect of the construction, Short photographs the museum as it begins to take form. His photographs prove to be an important part of the institution's archives. Short also appears on local television to explain how the building will be constructed.

MAY 7

In interviews and drawings, Wright refers to the Guggenheim as the "archeseum," a word he coined meaning "to see the highest." Harry Guggenheim objects, but Wright continues to use the term. Finally Guggenheim writes to his architect to bring an end to its use: "Please lay off for all time this 'Archeseum' stuff."

AUGUST 14

Ground is broken for the new museum. Work on the site occurs steadily, but the edifice itself will not begin to rise until next summer. In the meantime, the Museum of Non-Objective Painting is closed and the collection moved temporarily to a townhouse at 7 East Seventy-second Street. It will reopen as the Solomon R. Guggenheim Museum the next year.

'56

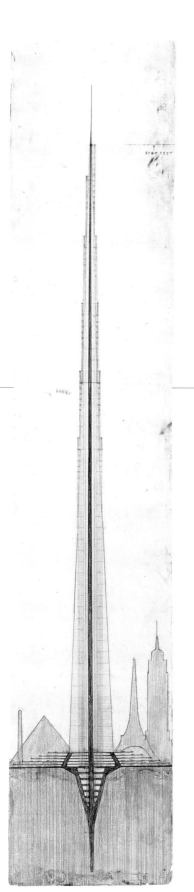

FALL

Construction of Brasília, Brazil's new capital, begins. The city, which will take four years to complete, is planned by Lucio Costa with architecture by Oscar Niemeyer. Like the Guggenheim, Niemeyer's sculptural buildings show the formal potential of concrete. Two years later, and two years before Brasília is completed, Costa tours the Guggenheim as it is being built.

OCTOBER 17

Chicago's Mayor Richard J. Daley has declared October 17, 1956, Frank Lloyd Wright Day. To celebrate, the architect unveils a 26-foot drawing for the "Illinois," popularly known as the Mile High Building, a skyscraper a mile tall with 528 floors to hold one hundred thousand people at a time. According to Wright, it would make large numbers of skyscrapers obsolete: with just a few Mile High towers, cities could have large concentrations of people while also conserving acres of green space. The design depends on cantilevered floors and suspension cables to make a relatively lightweight construction. When an interviewer later asks Wright what holds his buildings up, he replies, "They hold themselves up. Take my Mile-High building. It has a spine with ribs growing out from it. In the Guggenheim Museum the spine is coiled and the ribs or, if you want, the floors grow only inward. The outer wall is the spine or support and the floor is cantilevered from it."

'56

TOP Telegram, Frank Lloyd Wright to James Johnson Sweeney, December 14, 1956

BOTTOM Letter, Frank Lloyd Wright to Harry F. Guggenheim, ca. December 1956

DECEMBER 14

Enraged by the artists' letter, Wright fires off a telegram to Sweeney, asserting that the museum director encouraged the artists to make their objections known. He remains secure in Harry Guggenheim's support for his design, however.

DECEMBER 12

The *New York Times* reports that a group of twenty-one artists has written to Sweeney and the museum's trustees to ask that Wright's design not be executed. The letter, signed by Milton Avery, William de Kooning, Philip Guston, Robert Motherwell, and others, argues that a nautilus-shaped museum will detract from the artworks: "The basic concept of curvilinear slope for presentation of painting and sculpture indicates a callous disregard for the fundamental rectilinear frame of reference necessary for the adequate visual contemplation of works of art."

'57

TOP Greater Baghdad Master Plan (unbuilt), 1957. Opera house with entrance story and main story (plan). Graphite, colored pencil, and ink on tracing paper, 109 x 91 cm. Frank Lloyd Wright Foundation, Scottsdale, Arizona 5733.028

BOTTOM Jorn Utzon, Sydney Opera House, Sydney, 1957–73

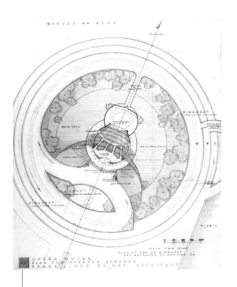

JANUARY 19

Jorn Utzon wins the competition for the Sydney Opera House, a plan that calls for several concert halls to be unified under a set of concrete shells. Like Wright in Baghdad, Utzon creates an expressionistic design meant to formally suggest the hall's connection to its use and environment.

FEBRUARY 19

In a prescient letter, Wright tells Harry Guggenheim that the museum's construction should be documented: "There is sure to be a demand for a comprehensive record of the building of a record-breaking building such as our museum."

JANUARY

King Faisal II of Iraq invites renowned Western architects, including Alvar Aalto, Le Corbusier, and Walter Gropius to design important civic structures in Baghdad. Wright, who has been asked to build an opera house, travels to Iraq in May and begins working on the project the following month. Having convinced Faisal that the opera house should be built on an island in the Tigris River, Wright designs a structure that draws on Mesopotamian architecture, Islamic culture, and *A Thousand and One Nights.* Circular in shape, the opera house sits on top of a three-tiered spiral ramp for automobiles, and its proscenium arch—what Wright names the Crescent Rainbow—extends to the building's exterior and into a pool of water.

'57

LEFT Workers lay the foundation of the main gallery, Solomon R. Guggenheim Museum, New York, ca. 1957

RIGHT Workers at the Solomon R. Guggenheim Museum construction site, New York, ca. 1957

MAY 18

George N. Cohen, president of the contracting company hired to build the museum, talks to the *New Yorker* about the building's construction: "The concrete becomes the finished structure. That's unusual. Most public buildings have facades of marble, limestone, or aluminum. Here's a fine, old-fashioned homely material—concrete—that Mr. Wright is putting on Fifth Avenue and making beautiful." Cohen, whose company also worked on the Tappan Zee Bridge and parts of the Brooklyn-Queens Expressway, says, "There's nothing I like better than a reinforced-concrete job of an unusual nature, and that's certainly what this is."

AUGUST 10

The *New Yorker's* Talk of the Town asks the construction workers their views on the building. One man says: "The way I figure it is that this is the screwiest project I ever got tied up in. The whole joint goes round and round and round and where it comes out nobody knows." Another says that his coworkers "talk about [Wright] as much as they do about women. How many buildings do you think I've been on without ever knowing who the hell the architect was? Hundreds, I'll bet. But this joker has the knack of attracting attention."

'57

TOP Envelope from contractor and paint swatch (verso and recto) chosen for elevator interior, Solomon R. Guggenheim Museum, New York, March 5, 1958. Douglas Steiner Collection, Edmonds, Washington

BOTTOM Construction of terrazzo floor, Solomon R. Guggenheim Museum, New York, ca. 1957

OCTOBER 17

Short meets with Wright and William Wesley Peters, an architect who is Wright's son-in-law and frequent representative in New York, at the Plaza Hotel to work out job details as minute as the interiors of elevator cabs, the dinette set in the caretaker's apartment, and bathroom wainscoting. Short's notes of the session, excerpted below, reveal the pressures of working for the demanding, sometimes impulsive Wright.

General Discussion of Colors: Mr. Wright at this meeting stated he wanted a light buff color for the building and he wanted the terrazzo floors to be the same color. The total impression being one of smooth continuous space. (This is in conflict to ideas he has had before about the floor color. WHS has heard him state that he wants grey or gold, on the floor, on different occasions.)

Round Skylights: WWP and WHS decided to OK this themselves.

Design of sidewalk: Mr. Wright would like to have the Module lines carried out to the curb as a sidewalk pattern. The joints should be "V" shaped in section as shown for those at the entrance loggia. He does not want trees along the sidewalk.

Message of [Jorn] Utzon: Mr. Wright was not impressed with Mr. Utzon's message.

SEPTEMBER 22

In an interview, Wright says that organic architecture is "the principle I've always worked toward. But this eleventh-hour building [the Guggenheim Museum] is a thoroughbred." He criticizes Lever House and the Manufacturers Hanover and Seagram buildings while defending his museum design from its detractors: "What we wanted to do was to create an atmosphere suitable to the paintings. Each one would exist in the whole space, the whole atmosphere, not within its rectilinear frame in a rectilinear room. The whole atmosphere and spaciousness will be the frame. And once he stops having to think in terms of rectangles, the painter will be free to paint on any shape he chooses—even to curve his canvas if he wants." Later in the article, he mentions that he also included a "grand gallery," a more traditional room for viewing art.

'57

TOP *A Testament* (Horizon Press), 1957.
Douglas Steiner Collection, Edmonds,
Washington

BOTTOM Sculpture made by
workers at the Solomon R.
Guggenheim Museum construction
site, New York, 1957

A TESTAMENT
BY
FRANK LLOYD WRIGHT

NOVEMBER 4
Wright is interviewed on the
museum site for *The Today Show*.
Two months earlier, he had
appeared on *The Mike Wallace
Interview*; viewers requested
Wright return to the show for
a second time.

DECEMBER
Construction workers make
a sculpture that parodies the
modern art that will be installed
inside the museum.

FALL
Horizon Books issues
A Testament, an overview of
Wright's long, remarkably varied
career that includes never-before-
published drawings. The book
prompts architectural historian
Henry-Russell Hitchcock to write,
"Whether one likes this or that
among the successive periods of
Wright's work is as irrelevant as
whether one prefers this or that
period of Picasso."

'58

LEFT Letter, James Johnson
Sweeney to Frank Lloyd Wright,
February 18, 1958

TOP RIGHT Letter, Frank Lloyd
Wright to James Johnson Sweeney,
February 14, 1958

BOTTOM RIGHT Letter, Frank Lloyd
Wright to Harry F. Guggenheim,
May 7, 1958

FEBRUARY

Though well into the construction phase, Sweeney and Wright revive their battle for control of the museum's design. Sweeney argues that the building does not provide enough space for administrative offices, and more important, doesn't serve the needs of the art to be shown there because of the slope of the floors and walls. As a result, he demands that the Monitor building be expanded and the art be mounted on poles extending from the walls so that they sit at a perpendicular angle to the floor. In addition, he wants the art to be artificially lit and Wright's peripheral skylights blocked, and the entire museum, inside and out, to be painted white. Wright again offers to build an annex for administrative purposes, this one only two stories tall, but he will not compromise on the other points: for example, paintings must be mounted directly on the walls. Seeing himself as the guardian of Solomon Guggenheim's vision for the museum, Wright asserts a long-held tenet of his career: the architect must design *all* aspects of a building. He passionately argues his case in many letters to Sweeney, and later to Harry Guggenheim, who finds himself caught between the two strong-willed men.

Jim, I want to keep your "business" (so far as I can) out of the amenities of the Monitor as designed for the Memorial Museum, so with what ingenuity I have, I have designed an additional office-wing -- two stories high directly connected to both Museum and amenities Monitor. A very practical solution of

page two

the Museum seen as a business. This I will try to get the Trustees to do for you and do you do likewise. Our meeting at the Plaza has made clear to me what now the trouble really is. The sub-basement you requested years ago would have been like adding another hold below the keel of an ocean liner. We were getting into water already. I now see the hopeless schism between "the museum-as-a-business competing-with-other-museums" that it is your ambition to run and the amenities of the memorial-museum Mr. Guggenheim made his bequest to build and himself went through with his architect step by step. The main museum and its monitor for the amenities of the artistry engaged in conducting the museum itself he did desire and himself approve.

We now have the frame only of the edifice which he intended to express this feeling. Oh yes, Jim, he had intense feeling of his own about it all. The Baroness Hilla Rebay was only the spark-plug, so to speak, and while she scouted for him, he always decided. He was a collector of two Bauers in Paris a year or more before he came to know her or she to work with him. Where are those two Bauers now and the others he loved?

Well, all this means to you is only "the dead hand over the living" as you said to me. But if what that hand (the Past)

page three

has in beneficence saved and presented to the Present is not a living part of our Present, then we have no great Future,

To cut a long story short, Jim, this change in character and purpose of the memorial-building - the change you now represent-he would have hated in his guts and not a cent would be available to build the kind of museum you want or to pay your salary to conduct it.

COPY FOR MR. HARRY F. GUGGENHEIM.

February 18, 1958

Dear Mr. Wright:

I had been heartened by your assurance last week, when I lunched with you at the Plaza, that you would expand the passage offices in the Administration Building on the floor below the Director's office by extending the glass walls to absorb three feet of the exterior terrace.

Your letter from Taliesin West this morning was a distinct disappointment to me, as I do not feel it reasonable to propose such an additional construction as your letter describes - badly needed as is work-space in the current project.

Sincerely yours,

James Johnson Sweeney

Mr. Frank Lloyd Wright
Taliesin West
Scottsdale
Arizona

JJS/w

THE PLAZA   FILE:: HFG OFFIC
FIFTH AVENUE AT 59TH STREET   1958 File
NEW YORK

MEMO:
Dear Harry - I find that
in order to use our precious
VIOLIN - we have a man
who can only play the
PIANO!
Sic -
F.Ll.W.

'58

Marin County Civic Center, San Raphael, California, 1957. Aerial perspective. Colored pencil and ink on paper, 87.6 x 188.9 cm. Frank Lloyd Wright Foundation, Scottsdale, Arizona 5746.001

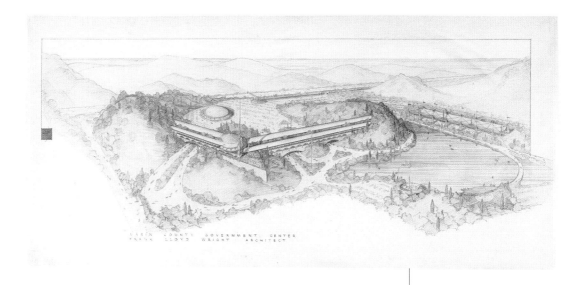

FEBRUARY 4
Though estranged from the Guggenheim Foundation, Hilla Rebay visits the museum construction site accompanied by William Wesley Peters. Two weeks later she sends Wright a letter, exclaiming, "How beautiful is the building in its harmony and reposeful interflow, expressing the Spiritual Realm in which Art lives. To see a dream come true, and to such magnificence, is an experience indeed." When the museum opens, however, she will not be present.

MARCH 6
Harry Guggenheim writes to Sweeney that, as the museum's director, he has the "duty and right to present the works of art as [he sees] fit." Yet, he says, Sweeney must recognize that the museum itself is a work of art, one that will have an impact all over the country.

MARCH 25
Wright travels to California to present his plans for a new civic center in Marin County, just north of San Francisco. The focal point of the center is a circular administration building with two wings attached that comprise several levels of arches, reminiscent of a Roman aqueduct. Though Wright is ninety years old, the center shows him still experimenting with the ways form can create unity in a building, or in this case, a set of buildings.

'58

On many occasions, Wright writes to Guggenheim defending his vision. The architect requests an opportunity to present his ideas about displaying art to the foundation trustees. To that end, he creates perspective drawings of the museum's gallery, which he distributes with an explanatory essay called "The Solomon R. Guggenheim Museum: An Experiment in the Third Dimension." He sends them to the foundation as well as to architecture publications in the United States and Europe.

SPRING

The Seagram Building, designed by Mies van der Rohe with Philip Johnson, opens. Constructed of glass, steel, and bronze, the building's exterior is faced with vertical I beams; though not actually structural, the beams evince Mies's rejection of added facades and the high value he puts on showing how a building stands. Wright, though on good terms with Mies, claims to have little use for the architects he refers to as "the glass-box boys."

physics that can create a precedent of great value. "A natural." Is it fair to the donor and his architect to relentlessly, without trial, destroy an essential feature of the building's character? On what basis c could this honorably be done?

 Friends — affection

N.B. The battle to be fought here has been on the way since organic architecture appeared instead of "academic disaster."

copy sent to members of museum Committee 5/8/58 mcl

THE PLAZA
FIFTH AVENUE AT 59TH STREET
NEW YORK

File: F.LW.
CORRES.

May 7th, 1958

Harry--Lieber!

Why do you think the walls of the Solomon R. Guggenheim Museum are gently sloping outward? . . - . .

They gently slope because the donor and his architect believed that pictures placed against the walls slightly tilted backward would be seen in better perspective and be better lighted than if set bolt upright. This is a chief characteristic of our building and was the hypothesis upon which the museum was fashioned. This idea is new but sound

LEFT Storage space on Ramp 6, Solomon R. Guggenheim Museum, New York, ca. 1959

RIGHT, TOP TO BOTTOM Four letters (excerpts), Frank Lloyd Wright to Harry F. Guggenheim, March 17, 1958; June 24, 1958; July 31, 1958; and (bottom two) August 25, 1958

Wright realizes that Guggenheim does not support his ideas about art display or the color of the walls, so he scrambles to make his case heard. Throughout the spring and summer, his dispatches grow increasingly urgent.

Lieber Harry: Lend me your ears!

Dear Harry: When you told me to start my fight for the integrity of the Solomon R. Guggenheim Memorial Museum. I soon began to realize that even if I wanted to "fight" a Guggenheim I could only lose.

Lieber Harry!   You are not only dead white, you are dead wrong!   You see me in the Times article? Well, I am not guilty!   *piece*

Dear Harry!   Wes brings word of an authority - over-wrought — and no wonder!

I wish I could do something substantial to make your job at the museum easier but the situation there is such that I have to destroy the building, so far as I am concerned, to do it. How I hope you will see this!

Affection! Nevertheless. I have seen your good side, Harry, and would like to be alongside to stay - if I could, honorably...
The Will is not dead!
Frank Lloyd Wright   August 25th, 1958
N.B.   The building of this great building should have been a great joy to us all . . .

MAY 8

Harry Guggenheim grants Wright's request for a meeting in New York where the architect may demonstrate his methods for lighting and exhibiting paintings. On the same day, Guggenheim asks Sweeney to write a memo describing *his* ideas about exhibiting art works. Sweeney replies that in addition to needing "a flat wall parallel to the vertical of the observer," the top ramps closest to the dome should be used for conservation, storage, a library, and the registrar's department.

'58

Letter (excerpt), Harry F. Guggenheim
to Frank Lloyd Wright, July 8, 1958

The present director of the Museum, James Johnson Sweeney, is recognized throughout the art world, at home and abroad, as a master "par excellence" in arranging and presenting exhibitions. This has been demonstrated to the great satisfaction of our Trustees, the art world and the public since Sweeney's directorship.

We all want to make progress in the presentation of art, and those most concerned in the improvement of our shows are Sweeney and the Museum Committee. Let us see what you propose and how we can make use of your proposals to enhance our exhibitions.

Whether or not the Committee accepts your method, your basic design of the building remains intact, perhaps to present art in your way, is not now, sometime in the future when others have reached that point of perception that you believe you have achieved now.

And now finally let me lay, once and for all, my Uncle's ghost that you exorcise when all else fails. In your letter of May 7, you said:

"......They gently slope because the donor and his architect believed that pictures placed against the walls slightly tilted backward would be seen in better perspective and be better lighted than if set bolt upright....."

On May 8, I replied as follows:

"......We have no evidence that the donor had such a belief, and even if we had it would not be appropriate for the Trustees of the Museum to accept his view if it were not in the best interests of the Museum....."

Since then, I have had an examination made of correspondence between my Uncle and your good self in which I find evidence that is completely contrary to your assertions. Your last one is in your letter to the Trustees of June 24, in which you say: ".....I shall have done my best to preserve what Solomon R. Guggenheim himself approved and left provision to build as his memorial....." There is not one shred of evidence to support your reiterated appeal to the memory of, to paraphrase you, that good man our benefactor who must not be betrayed. On the contrary, let me refresh your memory of the fear that was always with him about his architect's method of presenting his cherished paintings.

On August 10, 1946, he wrote you the following:

"For some time I have been trying to visualize how our paintings are going to look in the new museum—being installed right in the walls, and without frames. I have asked Hilla to explain to

---

JULY 8

Harry Guggenheim fears that the argument between architect and director will damage the reputation of the foundation. He tells Wright: "Our opening can be and must be, thanks to your beautiful and grand building, an event of dignity and importance. We don't propose to have it marred by bickering, and we don't want it turned into a burlesque show by jabbering controversy of a highly theoretical nature as a publicity stunt." In the same letter, Guggenheim explains that he has looked up correspondence between his uncle and Wright proving that Solomon himself had doubts about the exhibition methods.

The Solomon R. Guggenheim Foundation
July 8, 1958
Page 3

"me how this could be done so as to give each painting the individual emphasis it deserves, and she has suggested that you might be able to product a small model, using a few of our color prints as illustrations, in order to convince me of the merit of this arrangement. Will you please be good enough to let me know about this at your earliest convenience?"

You never did let him know. There is voluminous correspondence from you on the subject, soothing, persuasive, poetically phrased, but only generalities, and no satisfactory reply to his request. The correspondence shows reiterated fears expressed by our good benefactor, to quote him, that "the building must, and should, enhance the paintings but on the other hand, the paintings should be in no danger of being overwhelmed by the building... the paintings must not be subjected to the building."

Now, Querido Francisco, cease your diabolical manoeuvres because your building is for the angels. Stop causing everyone, including yourself, quite unnecessary bile and labour. Let us finish this job that your cussedness would have killed aborning without our help, and help us dedicate in harmony your beautiful and ingenious pile to an eager world.

    With affection,

        As ever,

        Harry F. Guggenheim

Mr. Frank Lloyd Wright
Taliesin
Spring Green
Wisconsin

hfg:mks

William H. Short's photographs of
the Solomon R. Guggenheim
Museum under construction,
New York, 1957–59

'58

JULY 15

Wright, sounding bleak and ener-
vated, scolds Guggenheim for
not being more supportive of his
architect's vision. In a postscript
to the letter, Wright mourns the
assassination of King Faisal and
Crown Prince 'Abd al-Ilah of Iraq,
implying that their deaths (and
the subsequent demise of the
Baghdad opera house project)
have made it difficult for him
to respond to Harry's last letter:
"When I am a little more full
of piss and vinegar than I am
now I'll comment on the points
you raise."

Short photographs the job site,
taking portraits of the museum
and the men building it. In
October, the *New York Times*
notes that "among the laborers
and craftsmen working [on the
site], comradeship and respect
for the 'old boy' who created the
museum abound. On a recent
Sunday, when all was quiet,

the Italian-speaking watchman
walked around with his grand-
children, explaining Mr. Wright's
building in proud but broken
English. What he said could not
be heard, but the watchman's
married son remarked, 'Pop
worries about this building as
if it was his own.'"

'58

TOP *The Living City* (Horizon Press), 1958. Douglas Steiner Collection, Edmonds, Washington

BOTTOM LEFT Olgivanna and Frank Lloyd Wright at the Solomon R. Guggenheim Museum construction site, New York, ca. 1958. Amanda Short Collection, New York

BOTTOM RIGHT William H. Short showing Wright the state of construction, Solomon R. Guggenheim Museum, New York, ca. 1958. Amanda Short Collection, New York

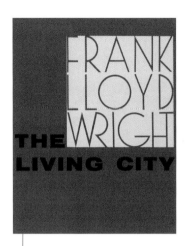

Wright publishes *The Living City*, which expands on the ideas—including the Broadacre City plan—that he first introduced in *The Disappearing City* (1932) and *Democracy Builds* (1945).

Wright approves a color called Buff No. PV020 for the building's exterior, which will be covered in a a kind of sealant known as cocoon. The architect wants a warm ivory for the interior, but Sweeney favors white.

NOVEMBER 7
The Wrights visit the site as work progresses. In recent months, the building has been toured by a host of renowned figures, including Alexander Calder, Henry Moore, I. M. Pei, Alfonso Reidy, Saarinen, and Utzon.

Telegram, Olgivanna and
Frank Lloyd Wright to William H.
Short, December 26, 1958. Amanda
Short Collection, New York

'58

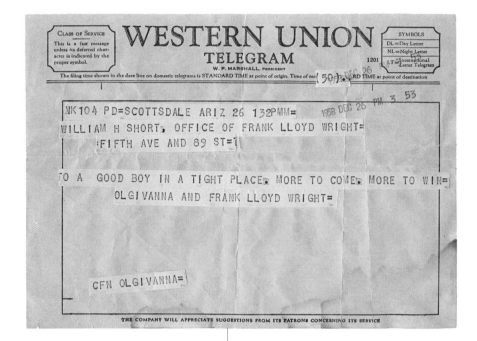

DECEMBER 4

William Wesley Peters presents
Wright's ideas about lighting,
color, and the exhibition of art to
Guggenheim and the foundation
trustees. The architect feels too
weak to return to New York from
Taliesin West.

DECEMBER 19

The trustees decide in favor of
Sweeney's methods for exhibiting
the collection, but Wright passionately
maintains that only the architect
can make the right decisions for
his building. Guggenheim again
tries to lay the argument to rest.
"My dear Frank, we have had so
very much correspondence about
all these things," he writes. "I have
tried so patiently to explain our
needs and requirements, and
responsibilities as public trustees
of a great Foundation, but it has
become so much an emotional
matter that I am afraid my explana-
tions are completely unsatisfying
to you. I feel confident that all these
matters will be straightened out,
and that your beautiful basic architecture will remain unimpaired, both
for the present and for future
administrations of the Foundation."

DECEMBER 26

Over the three years that
Short has been working on
the construction of the museum,
he has often found himself
caught between Wright and
the Guggenheim Foundation.
With the year drawing to a close,
Wright acknowledges Short's
finesse in a trying situation.

'59

JANUARY
Wright visits the Guggenheim site for the last time.

APRIL 9
Frank Lloyd Wright dies in Arizona at the age of ninety-one after a brief illness. Four days later, a funeral cortege is held at Spring Green, Wisconsin, with Wright's body carried by horse-drawn carriage to the grave site where his mother and her family are buried. Years later, his ashes are moved to Taliesin West, where he is buried next to Olgivanna.

'59

TOP LEFT Invitation to the Solomon R. Guggenheim Museum's opening ceremonies on October 21, 1959. Amanda Short Collection, New York

BOTTOM LEFT Cover (front and back) of opening-day program, Solomon R. Guggenheim Museum, October 21, 1959. Solomon R. Guggenheim Museum Archives, New York

RIGHT Press release announcing the opening of thc Solomon R. Guggenheim Museum, October 21, 1959. Solomon R. Guggenheim Museum Archives, New York

OCTOBER 21

Sixteen years after it was first conceived by Guggenheim, Rebay, and Wright, the Solomon R. Guggenheim Museum opens to the public.

Though not in attendance, President Dwight D. Eisenhower sends a congratulatory message to be read during the opening ceremonies. The presentation of his notice is followed by a roster of notable speakers, including New York City Mayor Robert F. Wagner and Henry Cabot Lodge, U.S. Ambassador to the United Nations.

The President and the Trustees
of
The Solomon R. Guggenheim Foundation
cordially invite you to the
Formal Opening
of
The Solomon R. Guggenheim Museum
1071 Fifth Avenue, New York City
on
Wednesday, the twenty-first of October
at noon

Kindly respond by enclosed card

This invitation admits two

PRESS RELEASE

from The Solomon R. Guggenheim Foundation · 120 Broadway, New York 5, N. Y. · REctor 2-9770

> **For Release**
> Noon, EDT, Wednesday
> October 21, 1959

The new Solomon R. Guggenheim Museum designed by Frank Lloyd Wright was opened today (Wednesday, October 21, 1959).

Dedication ceremonies began at noon in the Auditorium of the Fifth Avenue structure, Mr. Wright's only major work in New York City. As soon as they were completed, Mayor Robert F. Wagner cut the ribbon at the Fifth Avenue entrance and the doors were opened to the public.

Arthur S. Flemming, Secretary of Health, Education and Welfare, delivered the principal address at the dedication. Other speakers included Mayor Wagner; Henry Cabot Lodge, United States Ambassador to the United Nations; Commissioner Robert Moses; the Countess Castle Stewart, daughter of the founder, and the founder's nephew, Harry F. Guggenheim, President of the Board of Trustees of The Solomon R. Guggenheim Foundation.

The Solomon R. Guggenheim Museum
1959

The Solomon R. Guggenheim Museum
1959

'59

OCTOBER 21

At the dedication ceremonies, Moses says of Wright, "With all his pretended extravagant contempt for New York, Cousin Frank was convinced in his heart that the big city could not survive without at least one major building designed by him."

Magazine and newspaper headlines herald the opening with colorful headlines: "The Guggenheim: Museum or Monument?" "Mighty Tower & Babel of Discord," "Nautilus at 88th Street."

The inaugural exhibition includes work by Jean Arp, Constantin Brancusi, Marc Chagall, Stuart Davis, Max Ernst, Paul Klee, and Vasily Kandinsky. Ironically, several of the artists who three years before had protested the design of the building were also represented.

That Museum: Wright or Wrong?

Frank Lloyd Wright's unconventional structure has opened amid fiery debate. Is it a museum, or a monument to Mr. Wright?

'59

10,000 Flock to Wright Museum, But Only 6,039 Manage to Get In

Art Lovers, Tourists and Beatniks Jam Upper 5th Ave.—Some See Just the Cafeteria From the Outside

John Canaday, *New York Times* art critic, finds little to praise in the new museum, calling it "a war between architecture and painting in which both come out badly maimed." He complains that one is trapped in the space, unable to go back to favorite works, and he most objects to the building's form, "the sheer implacability of a spiral," for creating "the giddiness of the fun house in amusement parks where everything is built in a skewed perspective so that one tumbles and falls....The pictures seem to hang askew from one point, and to hang askew in the opposite direction seen from another." The *New York Mirror* decries the building's form: "The museum itself is one of Frank Lloyd Wright's most joyous monstrosities...On the outside it looks like a ball of mud...This imitation beehive does not fit any New York environment...Well, there it is, a building that should be put in a museum to show how mad the twentieth century is."

Despite the criticism, visitors throng the museum as it opens to the public.

'59

Letter to the Editor, *New York Times*, November 8, 1959

OCTOBER 26

William Lescaze, the architect best known for his Philadelphia Savings Fund Society building with George Howe, writes a letter to the *New York Times* to express his disappointment with the museum: "Frank Lloyd Wright strove for a museum-cathedral in concrete (not only for the main building but even for the minute administration building where surely nothing can really be administered) with tyrannical disregard of the objects of art to be shown, of the human beings who are to go to see them, of those who will eat in the cafeteria, and of those charged with the directing of the museum."

OCTOBER 22

The *New York Times* surveys a number of museum directors and architects about their reactions to the Solomon R. Guggenheim Museum.

Edward Durell Stone, architect of the Museum of Modern Art: "I personally think it's a wonderful museum. I have no reservations at all as to the building's ability to function as a museum. Why can't people relax and enjoy a fantastic structure instead of continually carping and criticizing?"

Philip Johnson, architect: "Mr. Wright's greatest building. New York's greatest building."

Rene d'Harnoncourt, director, MoMA: "It's something of burning interest. As a building the structure is absolutely superb, as a museum, it must be studied."

Dorothy Adlow, critic, the *Christian Science Monitor*: the museum "had reduced great pictures until they almost became postage stamps."

NOVEMBER

By contrast, *Architectural Engineering News* reports, "At last, Wright has vigorously freed the museum from its architectural enslavement and has restored the word 'museum' to its classical meaning—'a temple of the Muses.' He has provided a *living experience* in art and spatial form for even the most uninitiated."

'GENIUS VS. PUBLIC'

TO THE EDITOR:

The "fiery debate" over Frank Lloyd Wright's museum is again the eternal battle of the farsighted genius versus the nearsighted public.

As for the aesthetic individuals who find the rounded, sweeping building too offensive a contrast to the adjacent Fifth Avenue architecture, why have it moved only to Central Park? Why not to Philadelphia or Boston?

The objection that the powerful design inside distracts a viewer's absorption in the paintings is ridiculous. If a museum is to be a mediocrity in design, then please let's not have a genius such as Wright design one; or at least let us urge the genius to restrain his creative capacities. Is a music lover unable to listen to music in a beautiful concert hall, or a Catholic unable to pray in St. Patrick's Cathedral?

Very well then, let the viewer go to the Guggenheim Museum for the sole purpose of admiring the architecture. And woe unto him if he lets a painting distract him!

CAROL LaRUSSO.
Cleveland, Ohio.

NOVEMBER 8

The *New York Times* publishes a letter from 22-year-old Carol LaRusso in which she dismisses criticism of the museum building.

'59

BOTTOM Alan Dunn, cartoon commemorating the opening of the Solomon R. Guggenheim Museum, *New Yorker*, November 28, 1959. New Yorker Magazine, New York

TOP View of the Solomon R. Guggenheim Museum from Fifth Avenue looking southeast, New York, ca. 1959

NOVEMBER 15

A *New York Times* article features images of some of Wright's most daring projects, some built, others that went unrealized. Ada Louise Huxtable describes Wright as "a rebel against the straight-sided 'box'…[who] preferred rounded and angled forms."

NOVEMBER 28

The *New Yorker* runs four pages of cartoons by Alan Dunn that imagines museumgoers' responses to the building. The museum will continue to figure prominently in popular culture, with mentions in movies, appearances in comic books and advertisements, and commemoration on postage stamps.

In anticipation of the museum's completion, Wright prepared a statement to the press. In it, he describes how his design had been guided by organic architecture, the aesthetic philosophy that characterized his whole career, and with characteristic braggadocio—and humor— he predicts that the museum will court controversy. The Solomon R. Guggenheim Museum, he writes, had been created as "an inspiring place where great art could be seen to good advantage in human scale…. The architecture of this building will come close to achieving the ideal setting. It will be difficult to say where environment leaves off and exhibit begins."

FIG. 1 Scaffolding on the
museum in preparation for
exterior restoration, 2005

UPDATING WRIGHT'S MASTERPIECE: THE GUGGENHEIM RESTORATION, 2005–08

Angela Starita

IN DOZENS OF DRAWINGS, Frank Lloyd Wright depicted the main gallery of the Solomon R. Guggenheim Museum as a curved, sinuous form, as close to a living organism as a building could be. Yet when construction began thirteen years after the museum was conceived, his office prepared a startling set of working drawings that acknowledge the difficulty of realizing such a building. The main gallery is depicted not as round but as polygonal, straining towards a circle but never breaking free of straight lines. A small note on the drawing reads, "Walls shown facetted on 10' segments. May be continuous curve."

George N. Cohen and his Euclid Contracting Corporation did, in the end, deliver Wright's continuous curve. But the building has suffered damage in part because of the novelty of its form. The widening eddy of Wright's spiral, however generous an expression of human possibility, pushed the limits of late 1950s construction technology.

In the first forty-five years of its existence, the museum had undergone seven different restoration projects, in large part to tend to the many cracks that veined its exterior surface, most severely on the top level. By 2004, more cracks to the facade, as well as increased condensation at the windows, prompted the Solomon R. Guggenheim Foundation to gather a team of preservationists, architects, and engineers to comprehensively study the stresses on the building and remedy the problems. Organized by Paratus, a company that coordinates complex building projects, and generously supported by foundation trustee Peter B. Lewis, the team assessed the location and extent of damage to the museum's walls using state-of-the-art techniques

FIG. 2 A construction worker grinds
walls to remove form marks, ca. 1958

including metal detection, impulse radar, and impact echo, all nondestructive testing
methods that provide a picture of a building's inner structure.

In addition to monitoring the building as it now stood, the team needed to
understand the methods used by Euclid when constructing the building from 1956
to 1959. Gleaning that information depended on a far less technologically advanced
method: Angel Ayon of Wank Adams Slavin Associates (WASA), the team's architects,
spent more than a year poring over hundreds of working drawings, letters, construction logs, and photographs. It was painstaking work, but he found that the meticulous
records kept by Clerk of the Works William H. Short were invaluable for piecing
together how and in what order the building was built.

Ayon and his WASA colleagues learned that the first parts of the museum to be
built were the spiral ramp and the partition walls—called "web walls"—that punctuate the ramp every 30 degrees. They were made of poured concrete, a material Wright
had used on previous occasions to create flowing walls meant to convey unity between
man-made space and nature. This sense of fluid space is most simply articulated in
the interior of Wright's V. C. Morris Gift Shop (1948–49) in San Francisco.

The more complex part of the construction came with the addition of the walls
to the ramp structure. These were built by using a concrete known as gunite, more
frequently referred to as shotcrete, that is propelled from a high-powered hose onto
plywood forms that are later removed. Though gunite was often used as a surface

material, never before had it been used to create whole walls. To support the concrete, the walls were lined with wire mesh, steel T-bars that tie the walls to the web
partitions, and two bands of rebar—steel reinforcement for the concrete—that run
continuously through the spiral. While the cast-in-place portion of the construction
was well documented, there were no surviving records of how exactly the walls were
built, a serious challenge for the restoration team. To a large extent, the group had
to surrender their assumptions about building because of the exceptional nature of
the museum's form. "Structural engineers, we talk about beams and columns and
slabs, not ramps and web walls and gunite walls," says Nancy Hudson, an associate
at Robert Silman Associates, the structural engineers on the project. "This is unique
and required a separate terminology."

The group began comparing the construction record with their observations of
the present-day building. Ramps 3, 4, and 5 had suffered a few instances of corrosion
of the mesh and T-bars but were largely sound. On Ramp 6, where the walls are 16
feet high, twice the height of those of the lower ramps, the construction method first
appeared to be identical to that employed on the lower sections—T-bars to provide
vertical support and continuous rebar for horizontal, compressive strength. But while
inspecting Ramp 6, Hudson came across a piece of rebar unconnected to any other
piece of steel: "I thought, There's absolutely no reason that should be there." At that
finding, the Silman group, which had worked on other Wright buildings such as
Fallingwater (1934–37) and Wingspread (1937–39), began to make more tests of the
ramps and discovered what the noninvasive procedures couldn't tell them: though
the rebar had run throughout the lower levels, it was discontinuous on the top floor.
Instead, chords of steel were found every 10 feet, interrupted by the vertical T-bars.
With considerably less compressive strength than the rest of the building, the walls
of Ramp 6 were subject to far more movement in changing temperatures, which led
to cracks and water damage—not the kind of interaction of culture and nature that
Wright had envisioned. In all likelihood, the decision to change building methods
had resulted from unforeseen problems, perhaps due to Ramp 6's greater height,
that had had to be resolved with improvised, on-site solutions, a common occurrence
at any construction site, let alone one of such an unusual structure.

Hudson's discovery astonished the restorers. It also armed them with critical
information unavailable to earlier teams. Still, they struggled to find a way to fix the
considerable structural problems on Ramp 6, with the engineers and preservationists
taking very different positions. They all agreed that adding a continuous steel band
was out of the question, since that would have required breaking down original walls,
an untenable option given the building's landmark status. Silman Associates devised
a clever solution: the exterior of the building could be covered in a fiberglass coating

to tightly seal the surface, preventing water damage and giving the walls added support. Although the advantages of the method were considerable, the architects from WASA objected. A fiberglass coating, they argued, would create a notably smooth surface, a facade far more polished than the museum had ever had. For Hudson and her Silman colleagues, that effect was in keeping with Wright's vision of the building. Certainly, in countless letters and interviews, he described the museum in terms of its elegant and fluid curves. In fact, Ayon had discovered a letter from Wright to Cohen lambasting him for the form marks Euclid had left on the concrete. Wright demanded that the marks—imprints left behind by the wooden frames that hold the wet gunite—be ground down to leave a clean, uninterrupted surface. "I am sure your good conscience and pride in your work would tolerate nothing so derogatory to the work as a whole and consequently to your future reputation as a builder," Wright wrote, "not to mention mine as an architect."[1] For the structural engineers, the form marks represented how the building looked at the time of its opening but didn't reflect the architect's intention.

Nonetheless, WASA believed that the imperfections of the building's exterior had to be preserved because they illustrated how Wright's vision for the museum outstripped construction technology of the day. "You can stand on Fifth Avenue and

FIG. 4 Museum facade with paint
removed, 2005

see the original flaws," Ayon says, pointing out that, had Wright insisted on a completely smooth surface, he could have demanded that the concrete walls be ground
even further (fig. 2). To support their position, WASA noted that Wright had been pho-
tographed in January 1959 with a painting crew in the distance, evidence that he had
accepted that the museum's surface would not be absolutely smooth (fig. 3).

In the end, the team decided to add strips of carbon fiber to the interior walls
without applying the exterior fiberglass coating. First the interior walls were smoothed
and covered in an adhesive. Then the carbon-fiber fabric was saturated in adhesive
paste and rolled onto them like wallpaper. After adding an air barrier and a layer of
insulation, the walls were finished with a frame that was covered in plaster. Today
the walls are considerably more stable than before the restoration, but the exterior
maintains the orange-peel roughness of the building at its opening.

With that preservation question resolved, the team needed to wrestle with
another problem: how to keep the original window mullions of the Thannhauser
Galleries while avoiding condensation. William B. Rose & Associates, the group's
building-envelope specialists, studied the options. The restorers could leave in the
original frames, cover them in insulating cladding, and install new insulated glass
treated with low-emittance coating to minimize damaging light. Or the mullions
and the glass could be replaced. They chose the second option when it became clear

that, although the window frames themselves were in good condition, their appearance would have to be changed to support the new glass. The new mullions were manufactured to mimic the originals.

The question of the color of the museum, though not posing nearly the same level of complexity for the restorers, also required a good deal of historical research—and a Solomonic decision to settle a question that had been debated intensely well before the museum was ever completed. Wright believed that the building's exterior and interior should be painted in two different shades of ivory, believing white to be too jarring for viewing art. But James Johnson Sweeney, the museum's director from 1953 to 1960, objected: the ivory Wright had chosen for the interior wouldn't show the Guggenheim collection in its best light. He preferred white, which unlike Wright he considered to be a neutral color that wouldn't compete with the artwork.

For the recent restoration, all the paint was removed from the museum's surface, revealing ten to twelve layers that had been applied since 1959 (fig. 4). Pamela Jerome, WASA's director of preservation, describes the original color as a "creamy yellow," while the later shades are much lighter. Should the restorers choose Wright's color or instead select a hue closer to white, the color of the building when it was designated a landmark in 1990? Complicating matters further, the addition to the museum built by Gwathmey Siegel in 1992 is constructed of limestone, a material chosen in part because its beige color would fade into the background against the museum's white surface. If the team went back to Wright's color, the museum and the addition would match and the original building would not be highlighted, as Gwathmey Siegel had intended and surely Wright would have wanted.

In the end, the group reasoned that their job was not to preserve the building in a hermetically sealed time capsule from 1959. Instead, they felt an obligation to acknowledge the building's history and the alterations made to fit the museum's changing mission. They chose to paint the building a light buff color with a blue primer underneath (fig. 5). It may not be precisely what Wright would have selected, but it is in keeping with what was from the start the story of the building's creation: an ongoing negotiation between Wright's powerful conception of his temple for art and the evolving needs of the museum and the city.

Note
1   Frank Lloyd Wright to George N. Cohen, October 2, 1958, Solomon R. Guggenheim Museum Archives, New York.

FIG. 5 Solomon R. Guggenheim
Museum after restoration, seen from
Eighty-ninth Street, 2008

Sources for Entries in "Keeping Faith with an Idea: A Time Line of the Guggenheim Museum, 1943–59" (by page number)

146, July 14: Frank Lloyd Wright to Solomon R. Guggenheim, July 14, 1943. 146, July 26: Wright to Solomon R. Guggenheim, July 26, 1943. 152, April 5: Rebay to Wright, Apr. 5, 1944. 152, July 27: Solomon R. Guggenheim to Wright, July 28, 1944. 155, April: Wright to Rebay, Aug. 2, 1945. 156, July 9: "Museum Building to Rise as Spiral," *New York Times*, July 10, 1945. 157, August 11: Rebay to Wright, Aug. 11, 1945. 157, August 28: Wright to Solomon R. Guggenheim, Aug. 28, 1945. 158, July: Wright to Solomon R. Guggenheim, June 29, 1946. 161, March 6: Marshall E. Newton, "Atom Bomb Held Index of Failure," *New York Times*, Mar. 7, 1947. 161, September: Wright to Solomon R. Guggenheim, Sept. 11, 1947. 168, January 26: Wright quoted in Peter Blake, *Frank Lloyd Wright: Architecture and Space* (New York: Penguin Books, 1964), 55. 172, February 10: Talbot Hamlin, "Frank Lloyd Wright in Philadelphia," *The Nation*, Feb. 10, 1951. 173, Wright to Harry F. Guggenheim, Aug. 8, 1951. 174, April 22: Aline B. Louchheim, "Museum in Query," *New York Times*, Apr. 22, 1951. 175, March: Louchheim, "Museum Will File Plans for Building," *New York Times*, 1952. 176, Wright, "Concerning the Solomon R. Guggenheim Museum," Mar. 14, 1952, Solomon R. Guggenheim Museum Archives, New York. 176, April 3: Wright, *Letters to Architects* (Fresno: The Press at California State University, 1984), 152. 176, August: Louchheim, "New Ways of Building," *New York Times*, Aug. 31, 1952. 178 left, Sir Herbert Read quoted in Lewis Mumford, "A Phoenix Too Infrequent," *New Yorker*, Nov. 29, 1953. 178, January: Ernest Hemingway quoted in Troy Ainsworth, "Modernism Contested: Frank Lloyd Wright in Venice and the Masieri Memorial Debate" (Ph.D. diss., Texas Tech University, 2005). 179, February 14: Wright to Harry F. Guggenheim, Mar. 3, 1953. 182, May 27: Louchheim, "Wright Analyzes Architect's Need," *New York Times*, May 26, 1953. 184: "The Hanging Ramp: Frank Lloyd Wright Backs Down on Building Plans," *Oakland Tribune*, July 29, 1953. 185, July 28: Wright and Harris H. Murdock quoted in "Wright Retreats on Museum Plans," *New York Times*, July 29, 1953. 185, July 30: Murray Kempton, "Juvenile (Delinquent)," *New York Post*, July 30, 1953. 187 bottom: "Usonian House of '06 Awes Crowds at Wright's Exhibit," *Metropolitan Builder*, Nov. 1953; "Frank Lloyd Wright Builds in the Middle of Manhattan," *House & Home*, Nov. 1953, 118. 188 left: "Editorial: Mr. Wright's Architecture," *New York Times*, Sept. 5, 1953. 189, November 14: Wright quoted in Bernard Kalb, "The Great Uncompromiser: The Author," *Saturday Review of Literature*, Nov. 14, 1953, 15. 189, November 28: Lewis Mumford, "The Sky Line: A Phoenix Too Infrequent," *New Yorker*, Nov. 28, 1953. 190, January 12: Wright to Rebay, Dec. 22, 1953; Rebay to Wright, Jan. 12, 1954. 191, August: Wright, unreleased press release, ca. Aug. 1954. 192, August 8: Aline B. Saarinen, "Taliesin Week-end," *New York Times*, Aug. 8, 1954. 192, November 12: Wright, "In Reference to an Appeal to the Supreme Court of Wisconsin…" Nov. 18, 1954 (quoted in Wright to Robert Moses, Nov. 18, 1954). 194, May 21: Wright, "The Future of the City," *Saturday Review*, May 21, 1955, 10. 196, October: Harry F. Guggenheim to Moses, Oct. 5, 1955. 196, October 5: Wright to James Johnson Sweeney, Oct. 5, 1955. 197, December 15: Wright to Murdock, Dec. 15, 1955; Harry F. Guggenheim to Wright, Dec. 1955. 198, March 9: Wright to Sweeney, Mar. 9, 1956. 200, October 17: Wright quoted in Henry Brandon, "Beyond Modern Architecture," *The Sunday Times* (London), Nov. 3, 1957. 201, December 12: Sanka Knox, "21 Artists Assail Museum Interior," *New York Times*, Dec. 12, 1956. 204: Wright quoted in Aline B. Saarinen, "Tour with Mr. Wright," *New York Times Magazine*, Sept. 22, 1957, 22–23, 69–70. 205, Fall: Henry-Russell Hitchcock, "Architecture and the Architect," *New York Times Book Review*, Nov. 17, 1957. 208, Spring: Brendan Gill, *Many Masks: A Life of Frank Lloyd Wright* (New York: G. P. Putnam and Sons, 1987), 483. 209, May 8: Harry F. Guggenheim to Sweeney, May 8, 1958; Sweeney to Harry F. Guggenheim, May 10, 1958. 211: Herbert Mitgang, "Sidewalk Views of That Museum," *New York Times Magazine*, Oct. 12, 1958, 14. 216, October 21: "Text of Moses Remarks," *New York Times*, Oct. 22, 1959. 217, October 21: John Canaday, "Wright Vs. Painting," *New York Times*, Oct. 21, 1959. 218, October 22: Robert Alden, "Art Experts Laud Wright's Design," *New York Times*, Oct. 22, 1959. 218, November: JJC, "Editorial: The Solomon R. Guggenheim Museum," *Architectural Engineering News*, Nov. 1959, 34. 219, November 15: Ada Louise Huxtable, "Triple Legacy of Mr. Wright," *New York Times*, Nov. 15, 1959. 219, November 28: Alan Dunn, "The Guggenheim," *New Yorker*, Nov. 28, 1959. 219 right: Wright, "Frank Lloyd Wright Statement to the Press," n.d., Solomon R. Guggenheim Museum Archives, New York.